MOM

by Cathy Guisewite

**Andrews McMeel
Publishing**

Kansas City

MOM © 2001 by Cathy Guisewite. All rights reserved. Printed in the United States of America. No part of this book may be used or reproduced in any manner whatsoever without written permission except in the case of reprints in the context of reviews. For information, write Andrews McMeel Publishing, an Andrews McMeel Universal company, 4520 Main Street, Kansas City, Missouri 64111.

03 04 05 BAE 10 9 8 7 6 5 4 3 2

Library of Congress Catalog Card Number: 2001090638

ISBN: 0-7407-2060-0

Cathy® may be viewed on the Internet at:
www.uexpress.com

Cathy Guisewite encourages women to get yearly mammograms, as recommended by the American Cancer Society and its "Tell A Friend" program. For more information, got to www.cancer.org.

Contents

Introduction

I look across the table into my mother's beautiful eyes and see a thousand things.

I see that it's taking all her strength to keep from leaping up and helping the waitress clear the table.

I see how much she wants to run back into the restaurant's kitchen and wash the pans.

I see that she's worried about the busboy's tired arms, the cashier's tired feet, and that it's all she can do to not take the rest of her meal out to that "nice young man parking the cars."

Mom in a restaurant is like a single guy at a party.
Her eyes are always busy.
Who's here?
Who might need me?
Who has a spot she can't get out?
Who needs a dab more mashed potatoes?
Who has a loose shoelace?
Who can't read the menu?
Who needs a button fixed?
Who needs a tissue?
Who needs a shoulder?
Who needs help with the door?
Who needs directions to the rest room?
Who needs a compliment?
Who needs his faith restored?
Who needs a friend?
Who needs a husband or a wife?

Mom's radar extends so far beyond me. She's so many people's mom besides my own. A multispecies mom. She's takes in every stray animal. Drives injured birds to the vet. Carries bugs outside to be reunited with loved ones. Apologizes before squashing an ant.

She travels with as much as she can possibly carry of what everyone might need. Band-aids. Glue. Tape. Eye dropper. Paper clips. Sewing supplies. Ink remover. Travel iron. Nail polish. Pliers. Sunscreen. Thermometer. Juice box. Amphibian food.
Her purse is like a 15-pound rescue van.

Her mind is like a purse. She has everything in there. What to do if the child at the library gets the hiccups. Who to call if the park bench has a rough spot that might give a splinter. Where to find a map of Paris at midnight in Toledo. How to tell if a cantaloupe is ripe. What to say if a complete stranger looks a little bit sad. What to write on a note that will change someone's whole outlook on life.

She lives to help, to fix, to advise, to cheer, to uplift, to encourage, to feed, to humor, to heal. She's a friend, a therapist, a nurse, a guide, a saint.

Everyone, but everyone, loves my mom.

Me, she drives crazy.

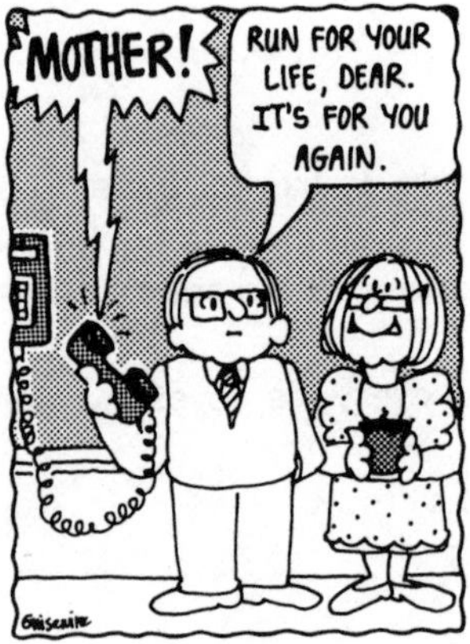
MOTHER!
RUN FOR YOUR LIFE, DEAR. IT'S FOR YOU AGAIN.

The Psychic

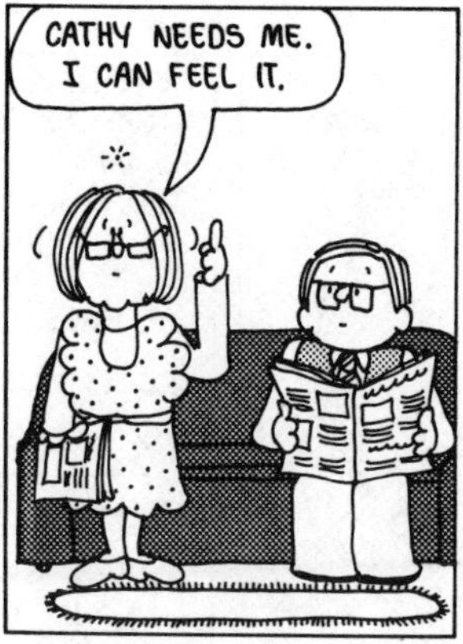
CATHY NEEDS ME. I CAN FEEL IT.

"She knows when you are sleeping
She knows when you're awake
She knows when you've been bad or good
So be good for goodness' sake."

Every daughter knows that the lines we sing about Santa Claus were originally written about Mother.

GRAB YOUR KEYS AND GET IN THE CAR, DEAR!
WHAT? WHAT HAPPENED?
FINANCIAL DISTRESS! CAREER TRAUMA! ROMANTIC FRUSTRATION! JELLY BEAN HANGOVER! HURRY! I FEEL IT! WE HAVE TO STOP HER!

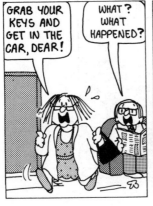

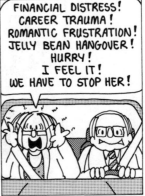

PUT DOWN THE PHONE, CATHY! THIS IS **NOT** THE TIME TO MAKE A HAIR APPOINTMENT!!
ALL MOTHERS HAVE A SIXTH SENSE. MOTHERS OF DAUGHTERS HAVE A SEVENTH SENSE.

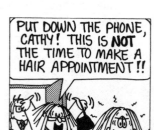

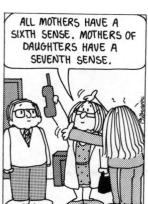

The very first wireless communication device, of course, was Mom. When I was an infant, she could hear the faintest peep from the opposite end of the house. Now that I'm an adult, she can hear the faintest peep from the opposite end of town or, for that matter, the country.

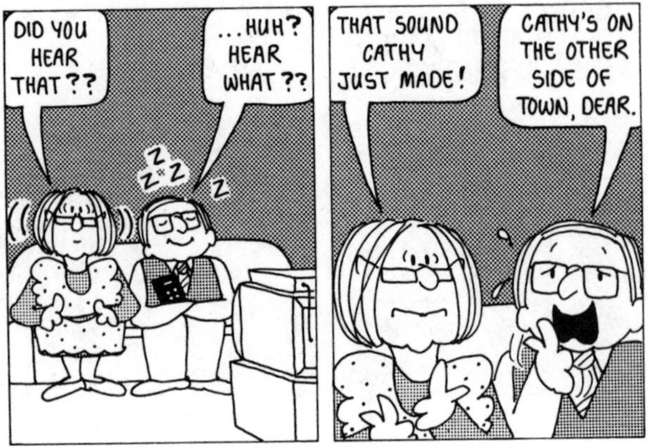
DID YOU HEAR THAT??
...HUH? HEAR WHAT??
THAT SOUND CATHY JUST MADE!
CATHY'S ON THE OTHER SIDE OF TOWN, DEAR.

GOOD HEAVENS! THERE SHE GOES AGAIN! I HAVEN'T HEARD HER MAKE THAT SOUND SINCE...UH, OH!...
WHAT SOUND?? WHAT SOUND??
DIAL DIAL DIAL
AACK! HE'S BACK, MOM!!
WHY YOU ALMOST NEVER SEE A MOTHER ASLEEP IN FRONT OF THE TV.

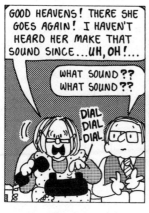

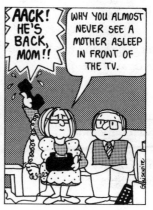

Without picking up the phone, Mom can sit in her living room and somehow tell what I had for breakfast 3,000 miles away.

She can detect a bad-hair day from my handwriting on a birthday card and feel a shopping blunder in the middle of the night.

She can sense my stress level by staring at the moon. She feels my carbohydrate intake in the air. She can predict exactly how unbalanced my next bank statement will be by looking west and squinting.

She knows if I'm happy, "really" happy, "sort of" happy, "trying to act happy" happy, or "completely miserable" happy.

On the phone, she's even more dangerous.

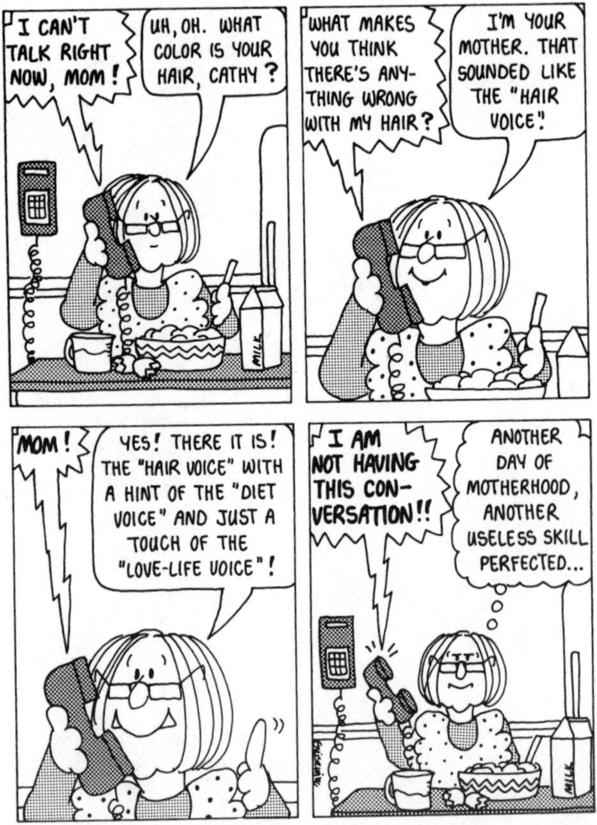
I CAN'T TALK RIGHT NOW, MOM!
UH, OH. WHAT COLOR IS YOUR HAIR, CATHY?
WHAT MAKES YOU THINK THERE'S ANY-THING WRONG WITH MY HAIR?
I'M YOUR MOTHER. THAT SOUNDED LIKE THE "HAIR VOICE."
MOM!
YES! THERE IT IS! THE "HAIR VOICE" WITH A HINT OF THE "DIET VOICE" AND JUST A TOUCH OF THE "LOVE-LIFE VOICE"!
I AM NOT HAVING THIS CON-VERSATION!!
ANOTHER DAY OF MOTHERHOOD, ANOTHER USELESS SKILL PERFECTED...
MILK
MILK

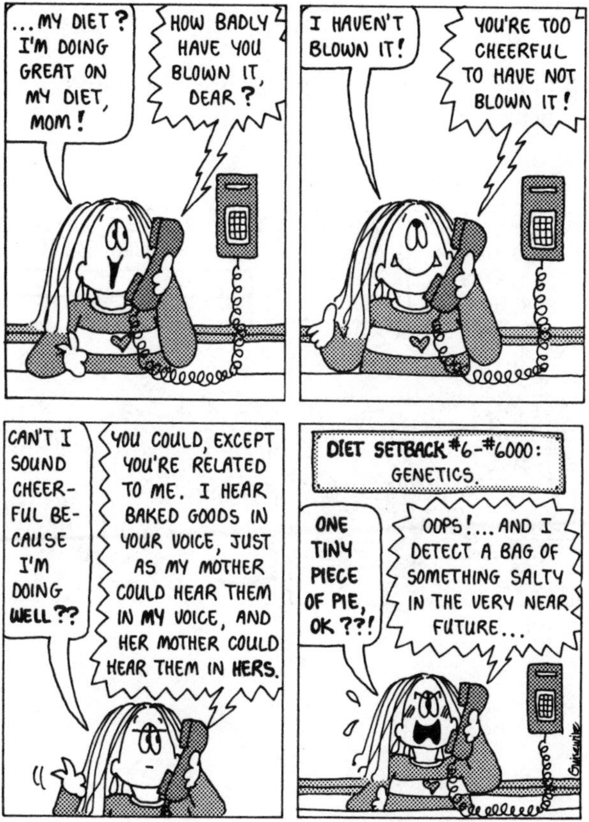
...MY DIET? I'M DOING GREAT ON MY DIET, MOM!
HOW BADLY HAVE YOU BLOWN IT, DEAR?
I HAVEN'T BLOWN IT!
YOU'RE TOO CHEERFUL TO HAVE NOT BLOWN IT!
CAN'T I SOUND CHEERFUL BECAUSE I'M DOING WELL??
YOU COULD, EXCEPT YOU'RE RELATED TO ME. I HEAR BAKED GOODS IN YOUR VOICE, JUST AS MY MOTHER COULD HEAR THEM IN MY VOICE, AND HER MOTHER COULD HEAR THEM IN HERS.
DIET SETBACK #6-#6000: GENETICS.
ONE TINY PIECE OF PIE, OK??!
OOPS!... AND I DETECT A BAG OF SOMETHING SALTY IN THE VERY NEAR FUTURE...
Guisewite

Mom's "gift" includes the good, old-fashioned approach:

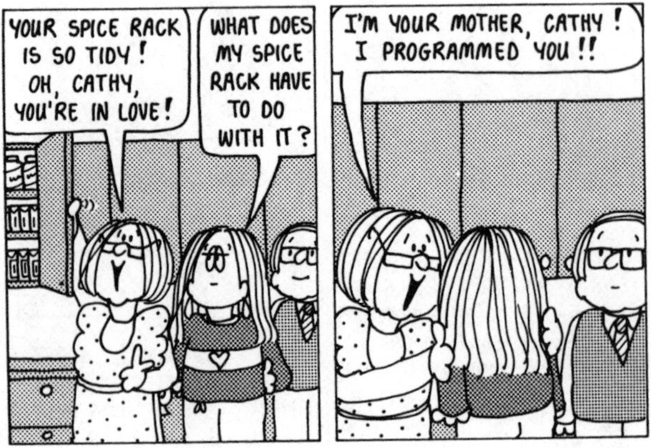
YOUR SPICE RACK IS SO TIDY! OH, CATHY, YOU'RE IN LOVE!
WHAT DOES MY SPICE RACK HAVE TO DO WITH IT?
I'M YOUR MOTHER, CATHY! I PROGRAMMED YOU!!

FROM THE TIME YOU WERE A BABY, I TAUGHT YOU TO TRANSFER YOUR EMOTIONS TO CUPBOARDS SO THAT WHEN YOU GREW UP I'D BE ABLE TO KNOW WHAT WAS GOING ON JUST BY OPENING A CLOSET DOOR!!

A TIDY SPICE RACK MEANS NEW LOVE IN YOUR HEART!!

TAKE HER HOME BEFORE SHE LOOKS IN MY UNDERWEAR DRAWER, DAD.

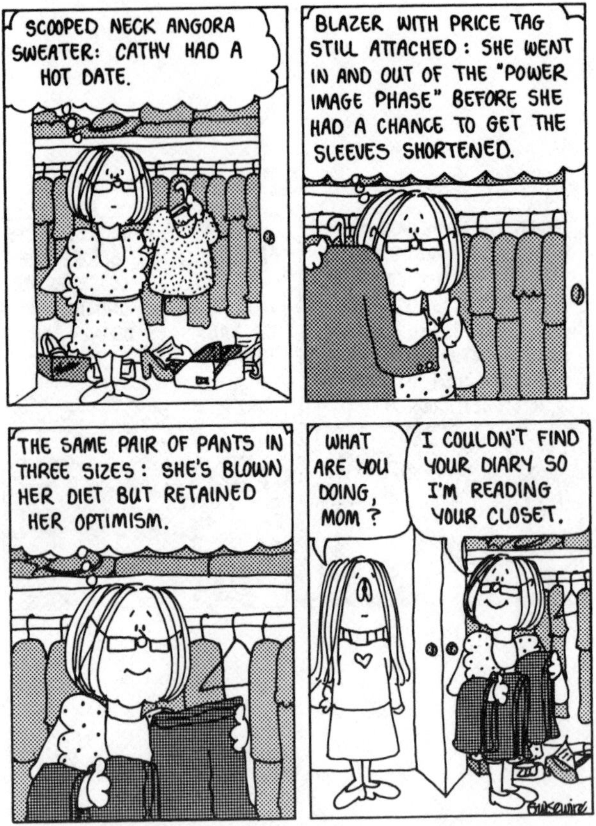
SCOOPED NECK ANGORA SWEATER: CATHY HAD A HOT DATE.
BLAZER WITH PRICE TAG STILL ATTACHED: SHE WENT IN AND OUT OF THE "POWER IMAGE PHASE" BEFORE SHE HAD A CHANCE TO GET THE SLEEVES SHORTENED.
THE SAME PAIR OF PANTS IN THREE SIZES: SHE'S BLOWN HER DIET BUT RETAINED HER OPTIMISM.
WHAT ARE YOU DOING, MOM?
I COULDN'T FIND YOUR DIARY SO I'M READING YOUR CLOSET.

Mom's "gift" has also evolved with time to include some modern technological advances:

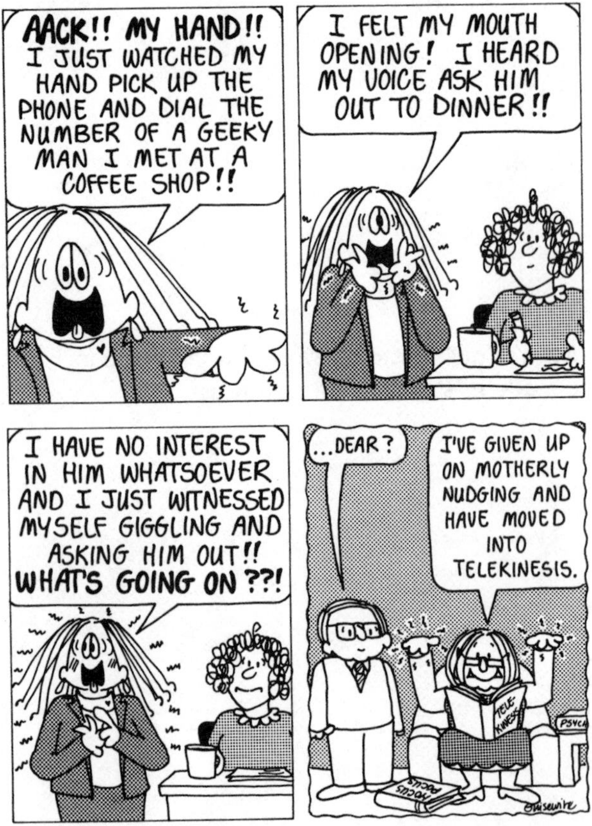
AACK!! MY HAND!! I JUST WATCHED MY HAND PICK UP THE PHONE AND DIAL THE NUMBER OF A GEEKY MAN I MET AT A COFFEE SHOP!!
I FELT MY MOUTH OPENING! I HEARD MY VOICE ASK HIM OUT TO DINNER!!
I HAVE NO INTEREST IN HIM WHATSOEVER AND I JUST WITNESSED MYSELF GIGGLING AND ASKING HIM OUT!! WHAT'S GOING ON??!
...DEAR?
I'VE GIVEN UP ON MOTHERLY NUDGING AND HAVE MOVED INTO TELEKINESIS.
TELE-KINESIS
PSYCH
HOCUS POCUS
Guisewite

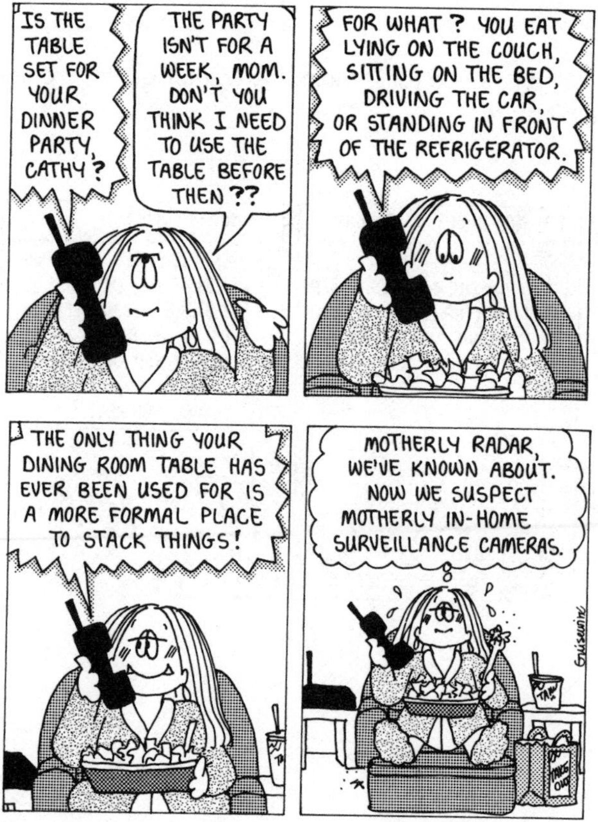
IS THE TABLE SET FOR YOUR DINNER PARTY, CATHY?
THE PARTY ISN'T FOR A WEEK, MOM. DON'T YOU THINK I NEED TO USE THE TABLE BEFORE THEN??
FOR WHAT? YOU EAT LYING ON THE COUCH, SITTING ON THE BED, DRIVING THE CAR, OR STANDING IN FRONT OF THE REFRIGERATOR.
THE ONLY THING YOUR DINING ROOM TABLE HAS EVER BEEN USED FOR IS A MORE FORMAL PLACE TO STACK THINGS!
MOTHERLY RADAR, WE'VE KNOWN ABOUT. NOW WE SUSPECT MOTHERLY IN-HOME SURVEILLANCE CAMERAS.
GUISEWITE

When all else fails, Mom, the creator of life, creates a little bit more.

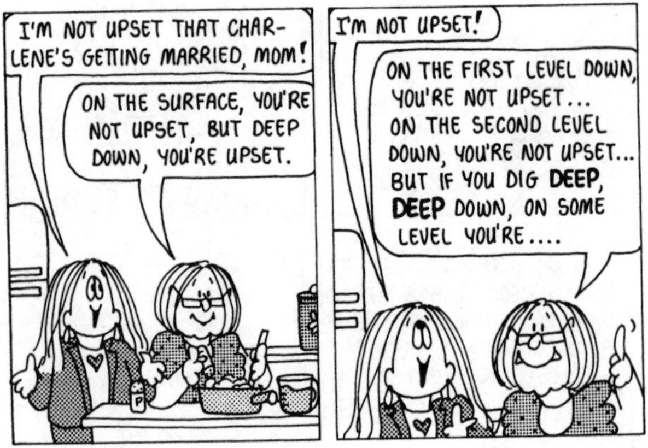
I'M NOT UPSET THAT CHARLENE'S GETTING MARRIED, MOM!
ON THE SURFACE, YOU'RE NOT UPSET, BUT DEEP DOWN, YOU'RE UPSET.
I'M NOT UPSET!
ON THE FIRST LEVEL DOWN, YOU'RE NOT UPSET... ON THE SECOND LEVEL DOWN, YOU'RE NOT UPSET... BUT IF YOU DIG DEEP, DEEP DOWN, ON SOME LEVEL YOU'RE....

AAUGH!
BINGO! LEVEL SIX! YOU'RE UPSET!
WHAT A MOTHER DOESN'T KNOW FOR SURE SHE CAN MAKE HAPPEN ANYWAY.
Guisewite

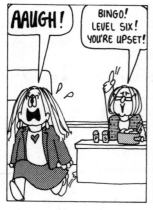

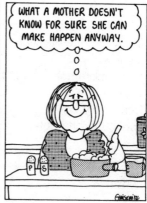

In my life, the question has gone from "How does Mom know?"

to the more horrifying: "How much more does Mom know that I don't know she knows?"

to the truly baffling: "How much more could there possibly be to find out?"

It turns out, quite a lot.

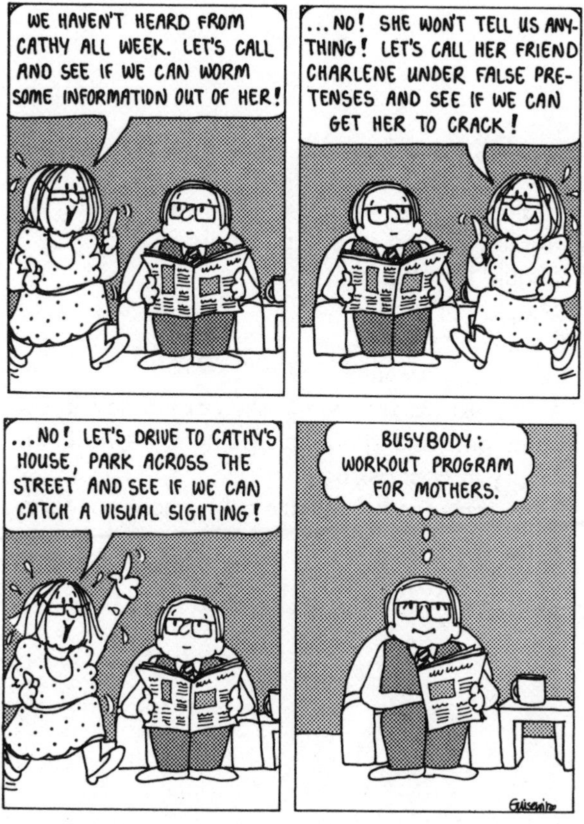
WE HAVEN'T HEARD FROM CATHY ALL WEEK. LET'S CALL AND SEE IF WE CAN WORM SOME INFORMATION OUT OF HER!
...NO! SHE WON'T TELL US ANYTHING! LET'S CALL HER FRIEND CHARLENE UNDER FALSE PRETENSES AND SEE IF WE CAN GET HER TO CRACK!
...NO! LET'S DRIVE TO CATHY'S HOUSE, PARK ACROSS THE STREET AND SEE IF WE CAN CATCH A VISUAL SIGHTING!
BUSYBODY: WORKOUT PROGRAM FOR MOTHERS.
Guisewite

In fairness, I know Mom wrestles with "prying" like she wrestles with the second piece of pie.

"Should I or shouldn't I?"

"Should I ask?"

"I shouldn't ask."

"But I really want to ask."

"Will I feel worse having asked or not having asked?"

"Is the post-asking remorse going to be worth the momentary thrill of asking?"

"How can I sneak in a little ask without appearing to be asking the whole thing?"

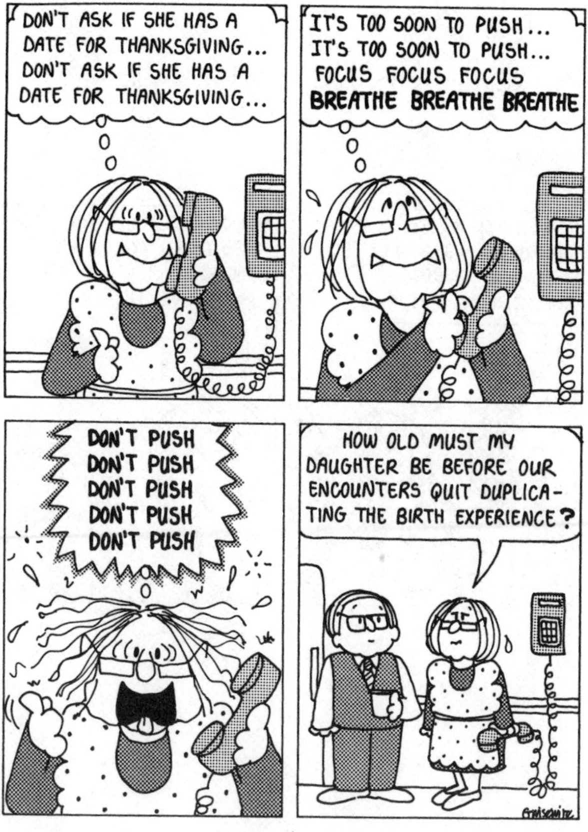
DON'T ASK IF SHE HAS A DATE FOR THANKSGIVING... DON'T ASK IF SHE HAS A DATE FOR THANKSGIVING...
IT'S TOO SOON TO PUSH... IT'S TOO SOON TO PUSH... FOCUS FOCUS FOCUS BREATHE BREATHE BREATHE
DON'T PUSH DON'T PUSH DON'T PUSH DON'T PUSH DON'T PUSH
HOW OLD MUST MY DAUGHTER BE BEFORE OUR ENCOUNTERS QUIT DUPLICA-TING THE BIRTH EXPERIENCE?
Guisewite

I've watched Mom steel herself with willpower.

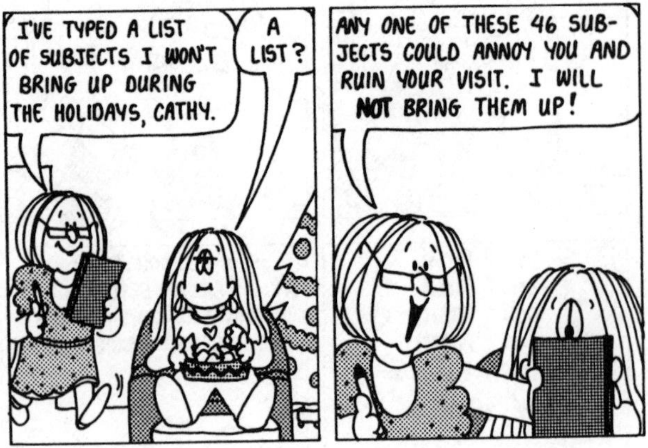
I'VE TYPED A LIST OF SUBJECTS I WON'T BRING UP DURING THE HOLIDAYS, CATHY.
A LIST?
ANY ONE OF THESE 46 SUBJECTS COULD ANNOY YOU AND RUIN YOUR VISIT. I WILL NOT BRING THEM UP!

MOTHER, DO YOU THINK I'M SO IMMATURE YOU HAVE TO HAVE A LIST OF TOPICS TO AVOID?! I CAN'T BELIEVE IT!!
#47: DO NOT MENTION THE LIST.
Guisewite

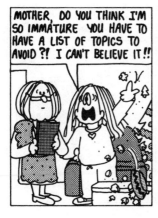

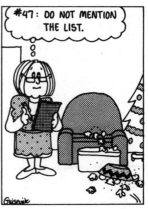

I've watched Mom dive head-first into the "informational dessert platter."

I COULD SLOWLY PRY FOR DETAILS ON CATHY'S CLASS REUNION, CAUSING MANY SMALL CONFRONTATIONS...
OR I COULD GET IT ALL OVER WITH IN ONE SURPRISE BLITZ.
knock

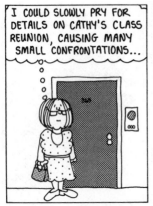

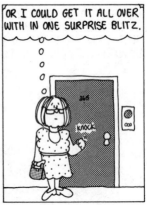

HOW WAS THE REUNION? ANY HOT PROSPECTS? ANY LEADS? ANY LOOKERS? ANY LIVE ONES? STILL SPEAKING TO IRVING? ANYONE NEW?
AACK! AACK! NO! NO! YES! YES! NO! AACK!
THE "RIPPING OFF THE BAND-AID" SCHOOL OF MOTHERHOOD.

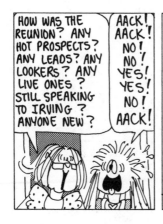

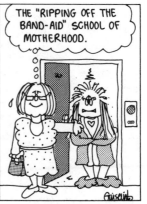

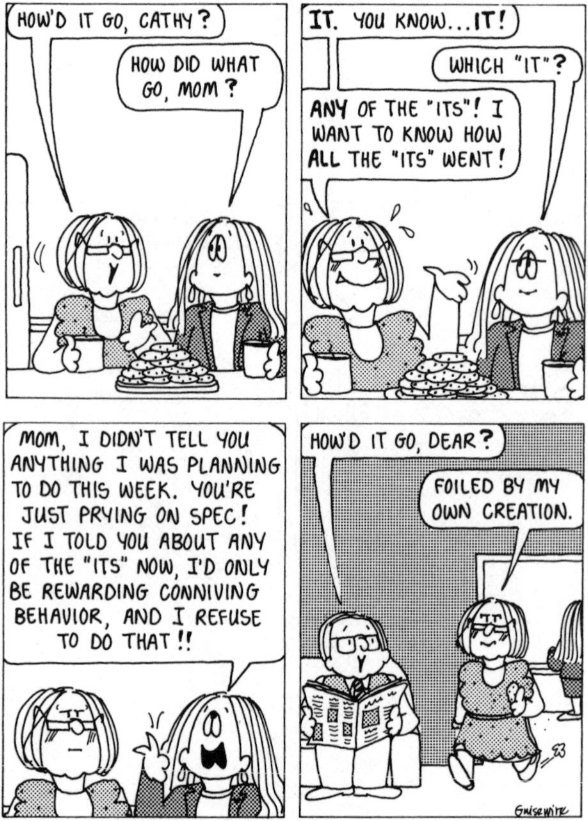
HOW'D IT GO, CATHY?
HOW DID WHAT GO, MOM?
IT. YOU KNOW... IT!
WHICH "IT"?
ANY OF THE "ITS"! I WANT TO KNOW HOW ALL THE "ITS" WENT!
MOM, I DIDN'T TELL YOU ANYTHING I WAS PLANNING TO DO THIS WEEK. YOU'RE JUST PRYING ON SPEC! IF I TOLD YOU ABOUT ANY OF THE "ITS" NOW, I'D ONLY BE REWARDING CONNIVING BEHAVIOR, AND I REFUSE TO DO THAT!!
HOW'D IT GO, DEAR?
FOILED BY MY OWN CREATION.
Guisewite

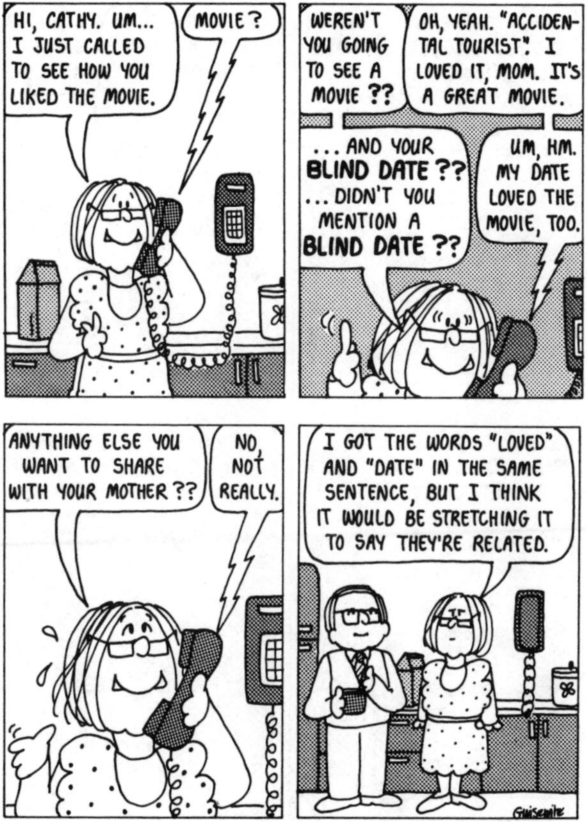
HI, CATHY. UM... I JUST CALLED TO SEE HOW YOU LIKED THE MOVIE.
MOVIE?
WEREN'T YOU GOING TO SEE A MOVIE??
OH, YEAH. "ACCIDENTAL TOURIST". I LOVED IT, MOM. IT'S A GREAT MOVIE.
... AND YOUR BLIND DATE?? ... DIDN'T YOU MENTION A BLIND DATE??
UM, HM. MY DATE LOVED THE MOVIE, TOO.
ANYTHING ELSE YOU WANT TO SHARE WITH YOUR MOTHER??
NO, NOT REALLY.
I GOT THE WORDS "LOVED" AND "DATE" IN THE SAME SENTENCE, BUT I THINK IT WOULD BE STRETCHING IT TO SAY THEY'RE RELATED.
Guisewite

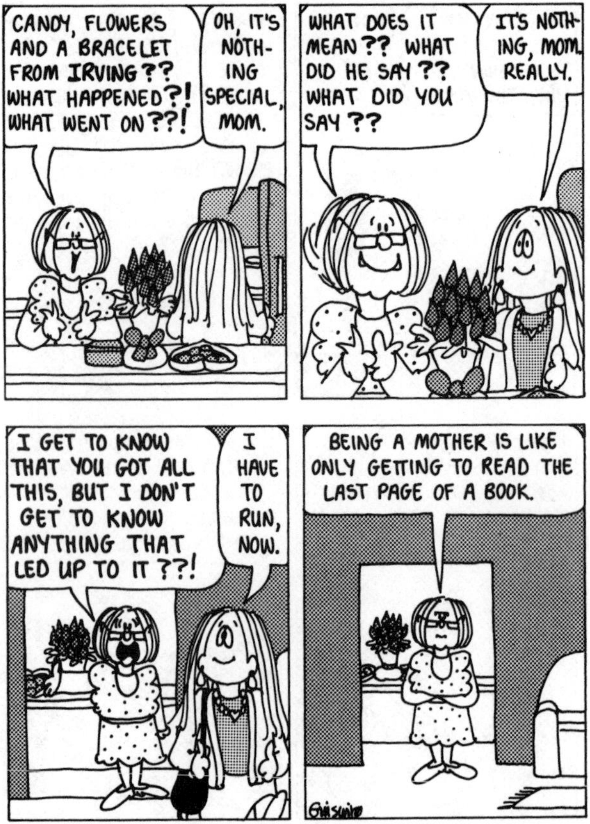
CANDY, FLOWERS AND A BRACELET FROM IRVING?? WHAT HAPPENED?! WHAT WENT ON??!
OH, IT'S NOTH-ING SPECIAL, MOM.
WHAT DOES IT MEAN?? WHAT DID HE SAY?? WHAT DID YOU SAY??
IT'S NOTH-ING, MOM. REALLY.
I GET TO KNOW THAT YOU GOT ALL THIS, BUT I DON'T GET TO KNOW ANYTHING THAT LED UP TO IT??!
I HAVE TO RUN, NOW.
BEING A MOTHER IS LIKE ONLY GETTING TO READ THE LAST PAGE OF A BOOK.
Guisewite

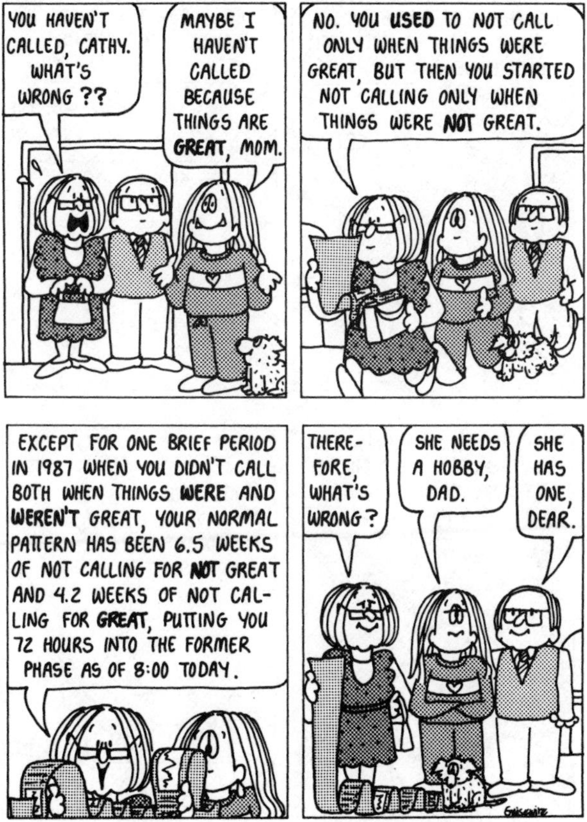
YOU HAVEN'T CALLED, CATHY. WHAT'S WRONG ??
MAYBE I HAVEN'T CALLED BECAUSE THINGS ARE GREAT, MOM.
NO. YOU USED TO NOT CALL ONLY WHEN THINGS WERE GREAT, BUT THEN YOU STARTED NOT CALLING ONLY WHEN THINGS WERE NOT GREAT.
EXCEPT FOR ONE BRIEF PERIOD IN 1987 WHEN YOU DIDN'T CALL BOTH WHEN THINGS WERE AND WEREN'T GREAT, YOUR NORMAL PATTERN HAS BEEN 6.5 WEEKS OF NOT CALLING FOR NOT GREAT AND 4.2 WEEKS OF NOT CAL-LING FOR GREAT, PUTTING YOU 72 HOURS INTO THE FORMER PHASE AS OF 8:00 TODAY.
THERE-FORE, WHAT'S WRONG?
SHE NEEDS A HOBBY, DAD.
SHE HAS ONE, DEAR.

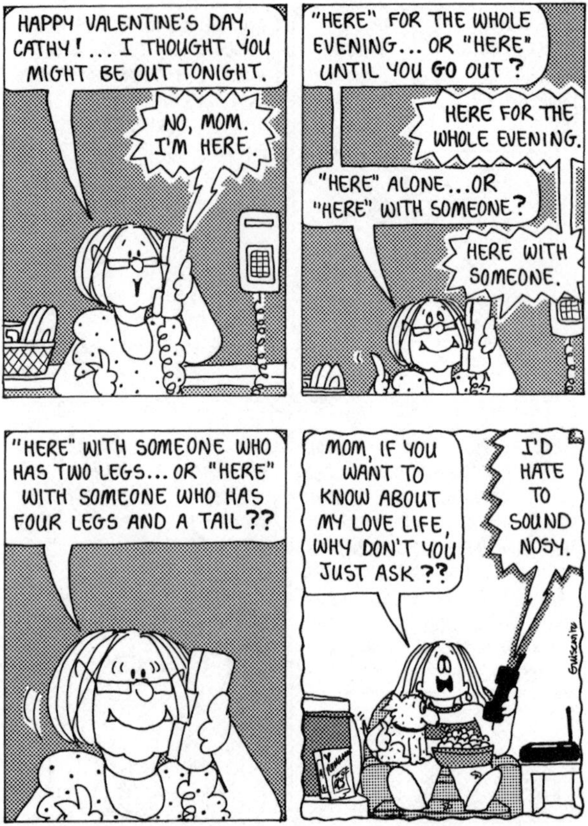

HAPPY VALENTINE'S DAY, CATHY! ... I THOUGHT YOU MIGHT BE OUT TONIGHT.
NO, MOM. I'M HERE.
"HERE" FOR THE WHOLE EVENING... OR "HERE" UNTIL YOU GO OUT?
HERE FOR THE WHOLE EVENING.
"HERE" ALONE...OR "HERE" WITH SOMEONE?
HERE WITH SOMEONE.
"HERE" WITH SOMEONE WHO HAS TWO LEGS... OR "HERE" WITH SOMEONE WHO HAS FOUR LEGS AND A TAIL??
MOM, IF YOU WANT TO KNOW ABOUT MY LOVE LIFE, WHY DON'T YOU JUST ASK??
I'D HATE TO SOUND NOSY.

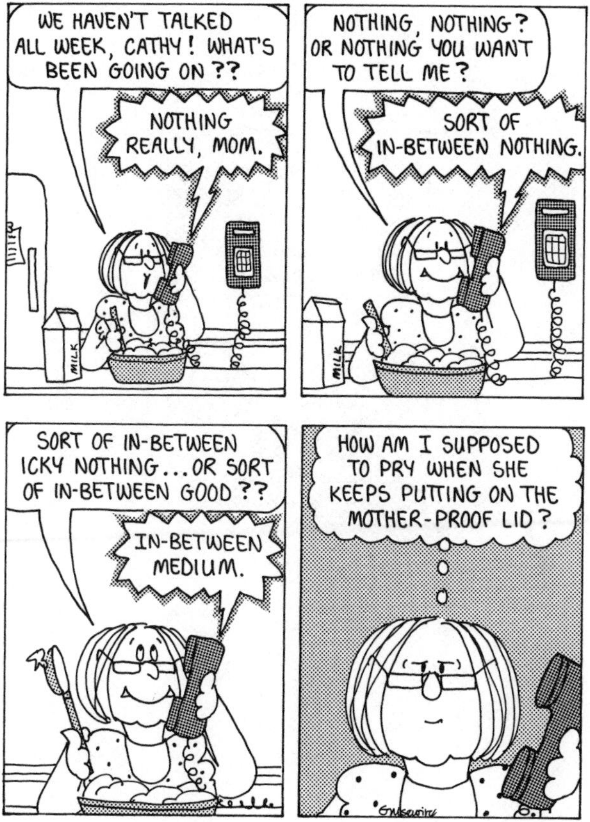
WE HAVEN'T TALKED ALL WEEK, CATHY! WHAT'S BEEN GOING ON??
NOTHING REALLY, MOM.
NOTHING, NOTHING? OR NOTHING YOU WANT TO TELL ME?
SORT OF IN-BETWEEN NOTHING.
MILK
SORT OF IN-BETWEEN ICKY NOTHING...OR SORT OF IN-BETWEEN GOOD??
IN-BETWEEN MEDIUM.
HOW AM I SUPPOSED TO PRY WHEN SHE KEEPS PUTTING ON THE MOTHER-PROOF LID?

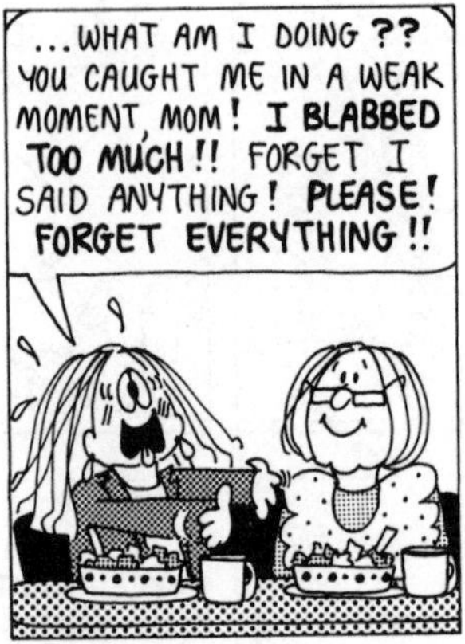
...WHAT AM I DOING?? YOU CAUGHT ME IN A WEAK MOMENT, MOM! I BLABBED TOO MUCH!! FORGET I SAID ANYTHING! PLEASE! FORGET EVERYTHING!!

The Clipper

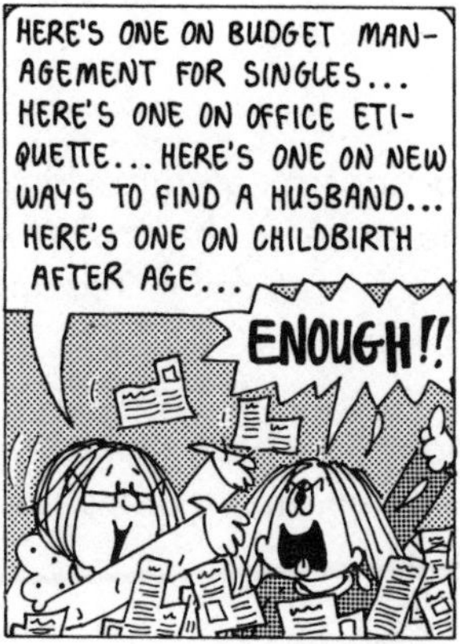
HERE'S ONE ON BUDGET MAN-AGEMENT FOR SINGLES... HERE'S ONE ON OFFICE ETI-QUETTE... HERE'S ONE ON NEW WAYS TO FIND A HUSBAND... HERE'S ONE ON CHILDBIRTH AFTER AGE...
ENOUGH!!

My mother can't read the newspaper without a pair of scissors clutched in one hand.

Actually, Mom doesn't even read the paper so much as she studies the paper so she can cut it up and send it to people. She doesn't even call it "reading" the paper, like most people. She says she's going to "go through" the paper, a way more accurate description of the two-hour-to-two-week-long project each daily newspaper is.

When Mom is "finished with the paper," there isn't much left.

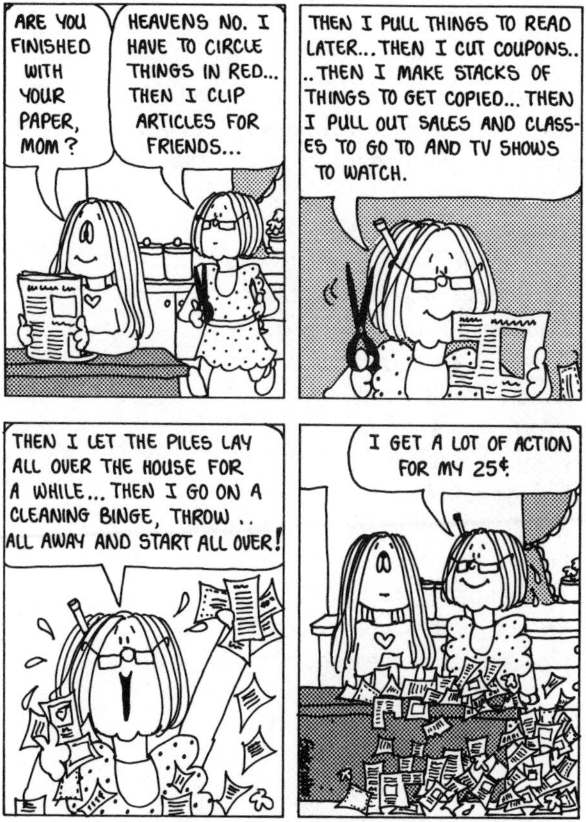
ARE YOU FINISHED WITH YOUR PAPER, MOM?
HEAVENS NO. I HAVE TO CIRCLE THINGS IN RED... THEN I CLIP ARTICLES FOR FRIENDS...
THEN I PULL THINGS TO READ LATER... THEN I CUT COUPONS.. ..THEN I MAKE STACKS OF THINGS TO GET COPIED... THEN I PULL OUT SALES AND CLASS-ES TO GO TO AND TV SHOWS TO WATCH.
THEN I LET THE PILES LAY ALL OVER THE HOUSE FOR A WHILE... THEN I GO ON A CLEANING BINGE, THROW .. ALL AWAY AND START ALL OVER!
I GET A LOT OF ACTION FOR MY 25¢.

Years and years before computers, Mom was a one-woman information superhighway, the original interactive medium . . . a kitchen table-based data distribution center.

Recipes for the McNabbs.
Investment ideas for the Holecs.
Household hints for Aunt Dorothy.
Coupons for the Johnstons.
Jokes for the Brownes.
Theater news for the Turoffs.
Worthy causes for the Michels.
Family fun for the Churches.
Fishing news for the Recers.
Reading festivals for the Knoxes.
Editorials for the Kilpatricks.
Travel tips for the Hermans.
Politics for the Schlossbergs.
Gardening for the Segals.

And for my two sisters and me:
Dating tips.
Disease tips.
Dry-cleaning tips.
Driving tips.
Packing tips.
Savings tips.
Cleaning tips.
Safety tips.
Pet tips.
Cooking tips.
Posture tips.
Organizing tips.
Etiquette tips.
Entertaining tips.
Laundry tips.
Business tips.
Shopping tips.
Exercise tips.
Vitamin tips.
Efficiency tips.
Emergency tips.
Sewing tips.
Wrapping tips.
Shoe tips.

My sisters and I have always marked life transitions by the new category of clippings Mom has graduated us into.

The day we quit getting the "How to Get a Man to Commit" articles and started getting the "How to Unclog a Backed-Up Drain" articles . . .

The day we quit getting the "How to Get Red Wine Stains Out of White Carpet" articles and started getting the "How to Get Strained-Pea Stains Out of White Onesies" articles . . .

The day we quit getting the "Wrinkle Prevention" articles and started getting the "Wrinkle Concealing" articles.

My clipping folder from Mom is a little diary of stages I've been through, crises I've survived, relationships I've recovered from, and disasters I've avoided, all with a little help from Mom and her scissors.

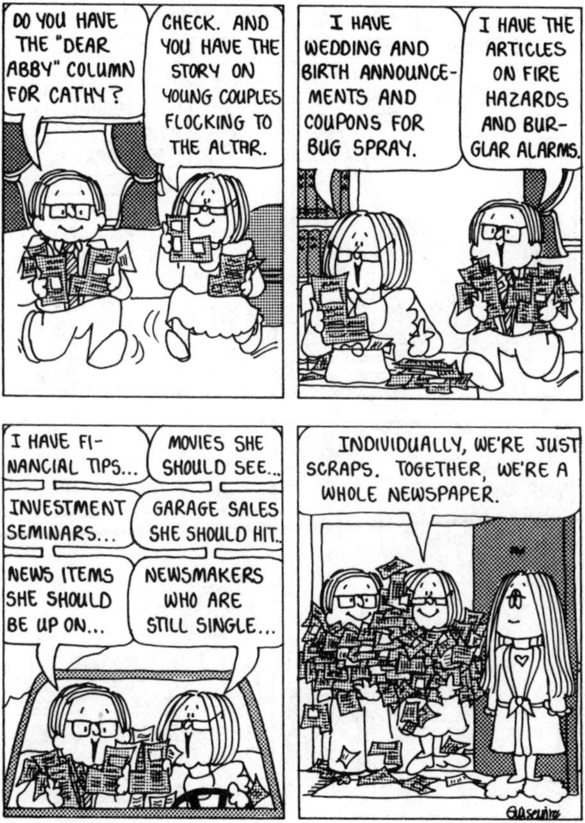
DO YOU HAVE THE "DEAR ABBY" COLUMN FOR CATHY?
CHECK. AND YOU HAVE THE STORY ON YOUNG COUPLES FLOCKING TO THE ALTAR.
I HAVE WEDDING AND BIRTH ANNOUNCEMENTS AND COUPONS FOR BUG SPRAY.
I HAVE THE ARTICLES ON FIRE HAZARDS AND BURGLAR ALARMS.
I HAVE FINANCIAL TIPS...
MOVIES SHE SHOULD SEE...
INVESTMENT SEMINARS...
GARAGE SALES SHE SHOULD HIT...
NEWS ITEMS SHE SHOULD BE UP ON...
NEWSMAKERS WHO ARE STILL SINGLE...
INDIVIDUALLY, WE'RE JUST SCRAPS. TOGETHER, WE'RE A WHOLE NEWSPAPER.

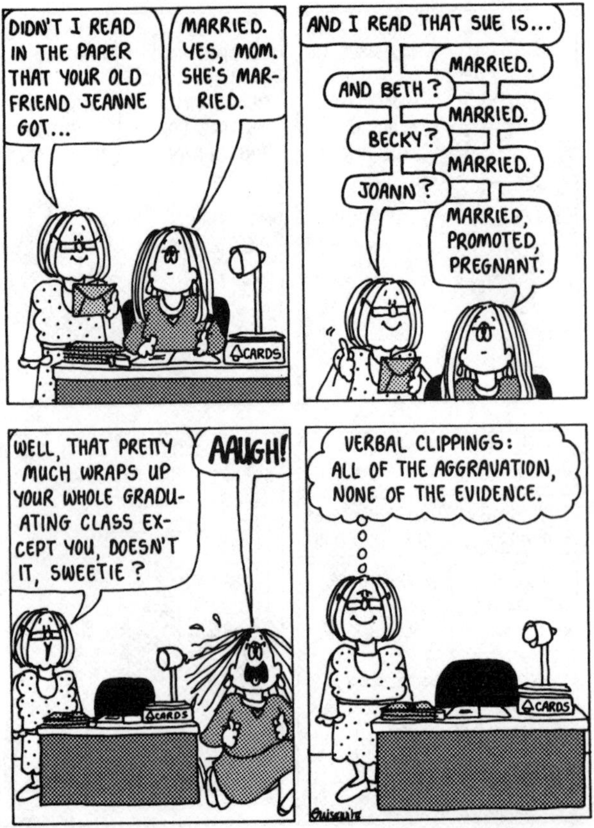
DIDN'T I READ IN THE PAPER THAT YOUR OLD FRIEND JEANNE GOT...
MARRIED. YES, MOM. SHE'S MAR-RIED.
AND I READ THAT SUE IS...
MARRIED.
AND BETH?
MARRIED.
BECKY?
MARRIED.
JOANN?
MARRIED, PROMOTED, PREGNANT.
CARDS
WELL, THAT PRETTY MUCH WRAPS UP YOUR WHOLE GRADU-ATING CLASS EX-CEPT YOU, DOESN'T IT, SWEETIE?
AAUGH!
VERBAL CLIPPINGS: ALL OF THE AGGRAVATION, NONE OF THE EVIDENCE.
Guisewite

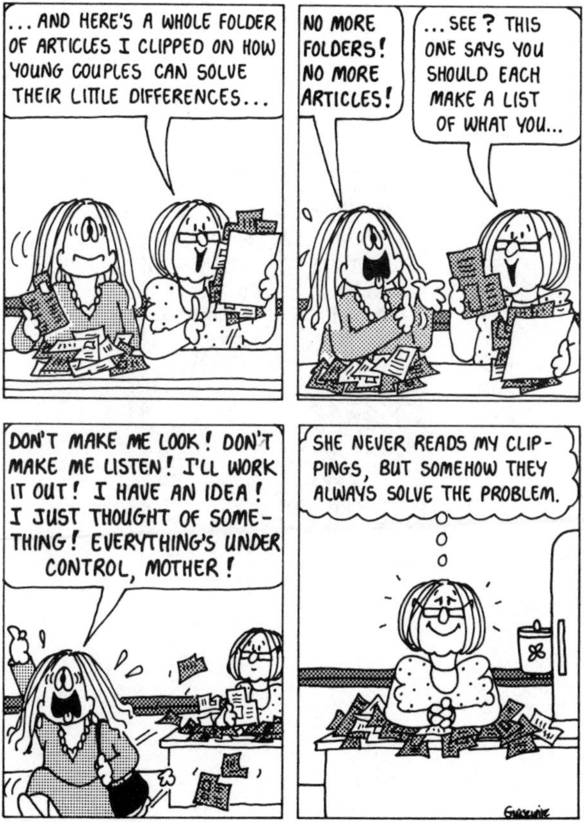
...AND HERE'S A WHOLE FOLDER OF ARTICLES I CLIPPED ON HOW YOUNG COUPLES CAN SOLVE THEIR LITTLE DIFFERENCES...
NO MORE FOLDERS! NO MORE ARTICLES!
...SEE? THIS ONE SAYS YOU SHOULD EACH MAKE A LIST OF WHAT YOU...
DON'T MAKE ME LOOK! DON'T MAKE ME LISTEN! I'LL WORK IT OUT! I HAVE AN IDEA! I JUST THOUGHT OF SOMETHING! EVERYTHING'S UNDER CONTROL, MOTHER!
SHE NEVER READS MY CLIPPINGS, BUT SOMEHOW THEY ALWAYS SOLVE THE PROBLEM.
GUISEWITE

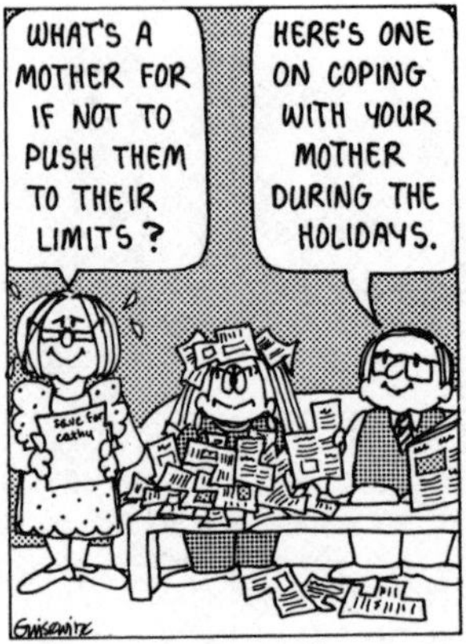
WHAT'S A MOTHER FOR IF NOT TO PUSH THEM TO THEIR LIMITS?
HERE'S ONE ON COPING WITH YOUR MOTHER DURING THE HOLIDAYS.
Save for Cathy
Guisewite

The Genius

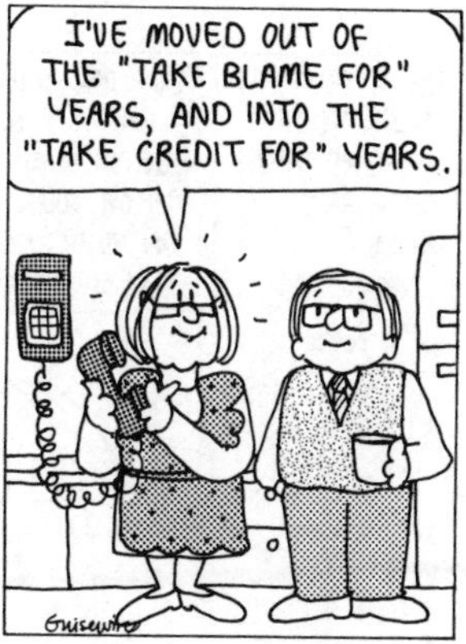
I'VE MOVED OUT OF THE "TAKE BLAME FOR" YEARS, AND INTO THE "TAKE CREDIT FOR" YEARS.

Fearing that I just throw out all the clippings she sends, Mom has had no choice but to deliver advice in person.

CAREFUL WITH THOSE SUIT-CASES! YOU'LL BREAK YOUR BACK! CAREFUL WHERE YOU WALK! YOU'LL SLIP AND CRACK YOUR SKULL!
PUT ON YOUR HAT! YOU'LL CATCH PNEUMONIA! BUTTON YOUR COAT! YOU'LL CATCH YOUR DEATH! PUT ON YOUR GLOVES! YOUR FINGERS WILL FALL OFF!

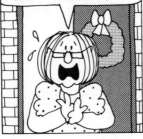

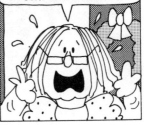

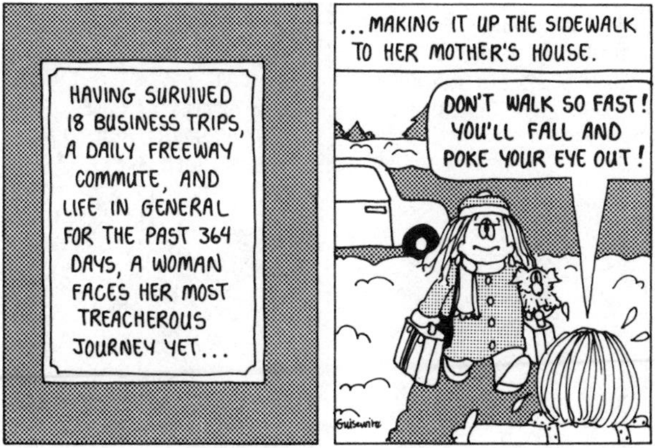
HAVING SURVIVED 18 BUSINESS TRIPS, A DAILY FREEWAY COMMUTE, AND LIFE IN GENERAL FOR THE PAST 364 DAYS, A WOMAN FACES HER MOST TREACHEROUS JOURNEY YET...
...MAKING IT UP THE SIDEWALK TO HER MOTHER'S HOUSE.
DON'T WALK SO FAST! YOU'LL FALL AND POKE YOUR EYE OUT!
Guisewite

It's the essence of our relationship—a 50-year-long dance of hanging on and letting go.

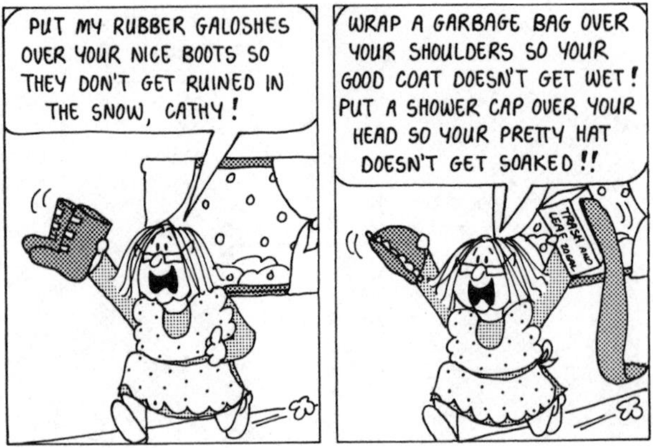
PUT MY RUBBER GALOSHES OVER YOUR NICE BOOTS SO THEY DON'T GET RUINED IN THE SNOW, CATHY!
WRAP A GARBAGE BAG OVER YOUR SHOULDERS SO YOUR GOOD COAT DOESN'T GET WET! PUT A SHOWER CAP OVER YOUR HEAD SO YOUR PRETTY HAT DOESN'T GET SOAKED!!
TRASH AND LEAF

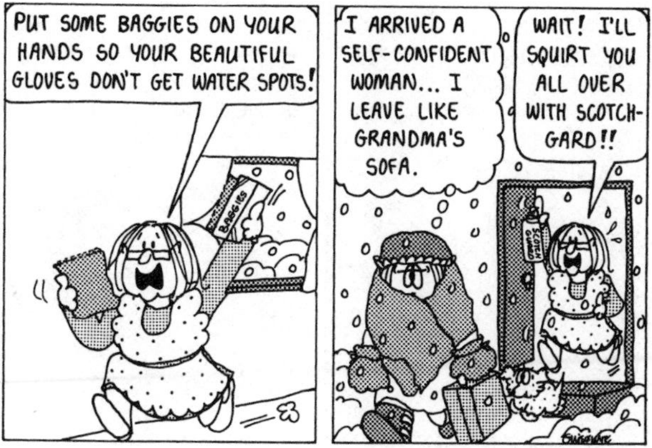
PUT SOME BAGGIES ON YOUR HANDS SO YOUR BEAUTIFUL GLOVES DON'T GET WATER SPOTS!
BAGGIES
I ARRIVED A SELF-CONFIDENT WOMAN... I LEAVE LIKE GRANDMA'S SOFA.
WAIT! I'LL SQUIRT YOU ALL OVER WITH SCOTCH-GARD!!

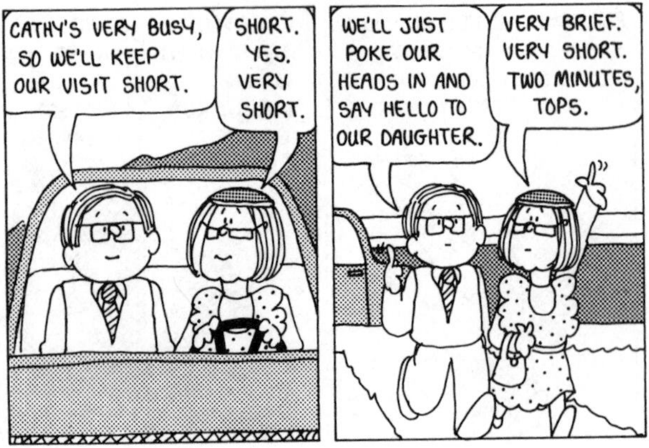
CATHY'S VERY BUSY, SO WE'LL KEEP OUR VISIT SHORT.
SHORT. YES. VERY VERY SHORT.
WE'LL JUST POKE OUR HEADS IN AND SAY HELLO TO OUR DAUGHTER.
VERY BRIEF. VERY SHORT. TWO MINUTES, TOPS.

HI CATHY.
EAT MORE FRUIT. SAVE YOUR MONEY. ADD BLEACH TO YOUR WASH. DO UNTO OTHERS. HOLD YOUR HEAD HIGH AND KEEP ALL OF YOUR BUTTONS BUTTONED.
I BLOSSOM UNDER PRESSURE.

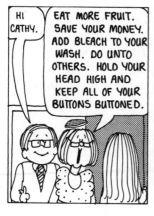

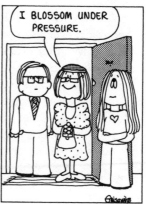

I beg Mom for advice, then snap at her for giving her opinion.

I call Mom from 3,000 miles away to ask her what to do, then reject every suggestion.

I turn to Mom for every crisis, then get annoyed at her for butting in on my life.

I pooh-pooh Mom's suggestions, then make the same suggestions to other people.

Mom's silly speeches become my brilliant lectures. Mom's ridiculous ideas become my strokes of genius. Mom's Rules to Live By are my Rules to Live By, unless Mother is within earshot, in which case I deny the whole thing.

I fire up the Mom Machine, then move on without warning.

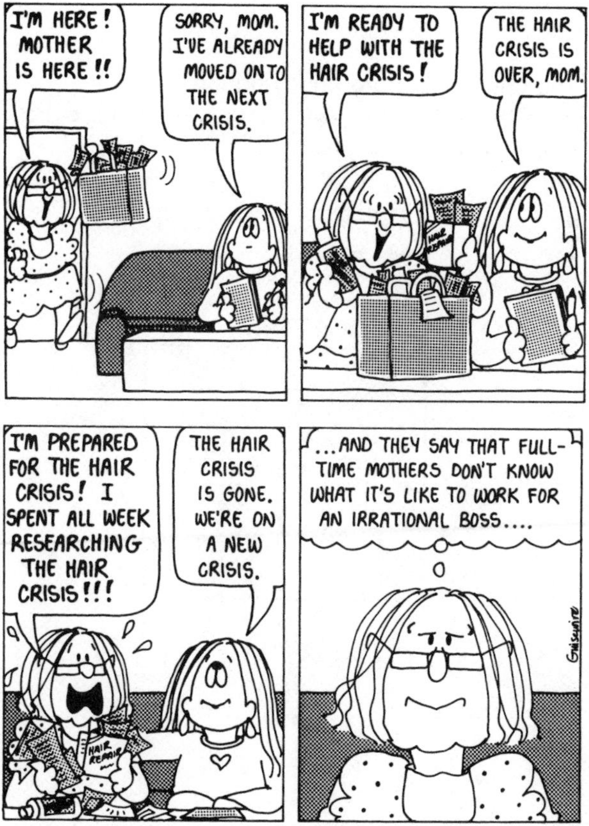
I'M HERE! MOTHER IS HERE!!
SORRY, MOM. I'VE ALREADY MOVED ON TO THE NEXT CRISIS.
I'M READY TO HELP WITH THE HAIR CRISIS!
THE HAIR CRISIS IS OVER, MOM.
HAIR REPAIR
I'M PREPARED FOR THE HAIR CRISIS! I SPENT ALL WEEK RESEARCHING THE HAIR CRISIS!!!
THE HAIR CRISIS IS GONE. WE'RE ON A NEW CRISIS.
HAIR REPAIR
...AND THEY SAY THAT FULL-TIME MOTHERS DON'T KNOW WHAT IT'S LIKE TO WORK FOR AN IRRATIONAL BOSS....
Guisewite

The only thing more annoying than receiving the advice is the fact that in every case, without exception, Mom is right.

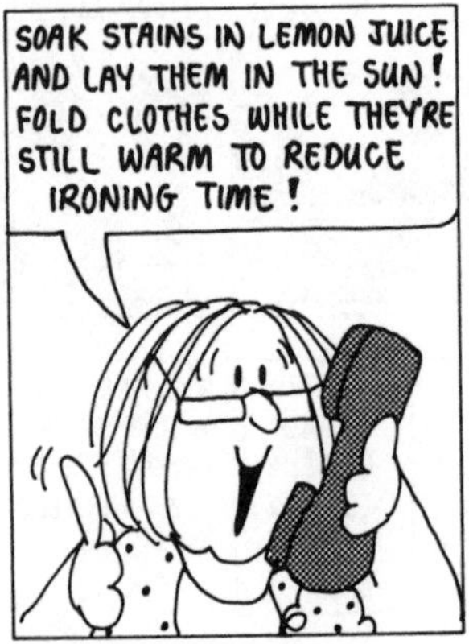
SOAK STAINS IN LEMON JUICE AND LAY THEM IN THE SUN! FOLD CLOTHES WHILE THEY'RE STILL WARM TO REDUCE IRONING TIME!

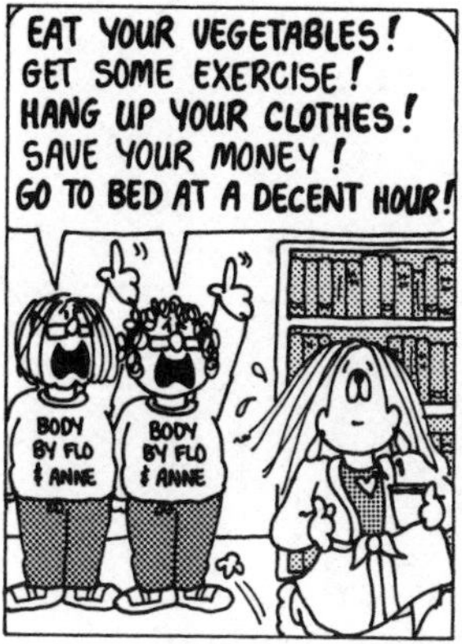
EAT YOUR VEGETABLES! GET SOME EXERCISE! HANG UP YOUR CLOTHES! SAVE YOUR MONEY! GO TO BED AT A DECENT HOUR!
BODY BY FLO & ANNE
BODY BY FLO & ANNE

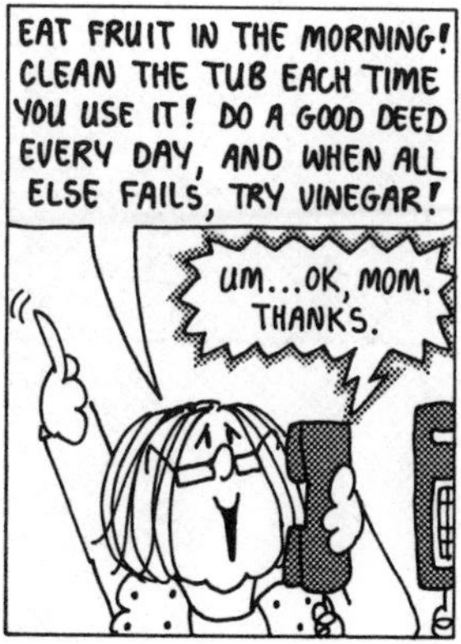
EAT FRUIT IN THE MORNING! CLEAN THE TUB EACH TIME YOU USE IT! DO A GOOD DEED EVERY DAY, AND WHEN ALL ELSE FAILS, TRY VINEGAR!
UM...OK, MOM. THANKS.

HOW CAN I EVER SAVE MONEY, MOM ?!
BUY IN BULK! USE GENERIC BRANDS! CLIP COUPONS! SHOP DISCOUNT STORES! GO TO THE LIBRARY! TURN OFF LIGHTS! WALK MORE, DRIVE LESS! REUSE! REFURBISH! REDEEM!
OOPS.

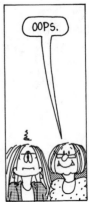

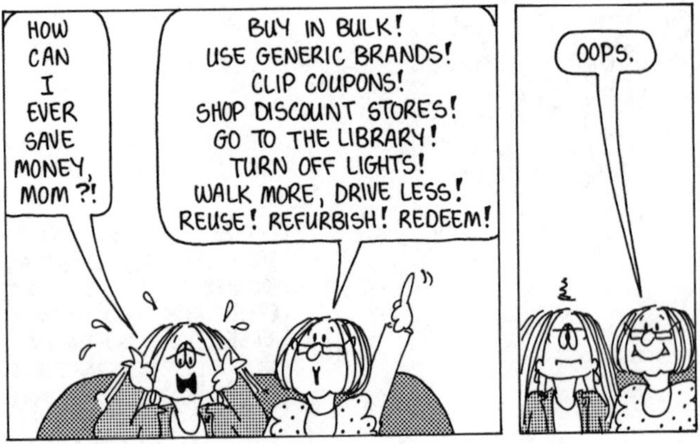

POOR BABY! IT'S JUST IMPOSSIBLE, ISN'T IT??
HARDWARE GLITCH. SHE CLICKED ON THE "SYMPATHY SITE", AND THE "ADVICE PAGE" POPPED UP AGAIN.
TISSUE
Guisewite

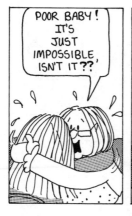

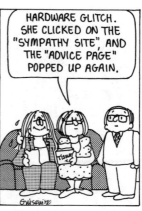

Mom tries to restrain herself . . .

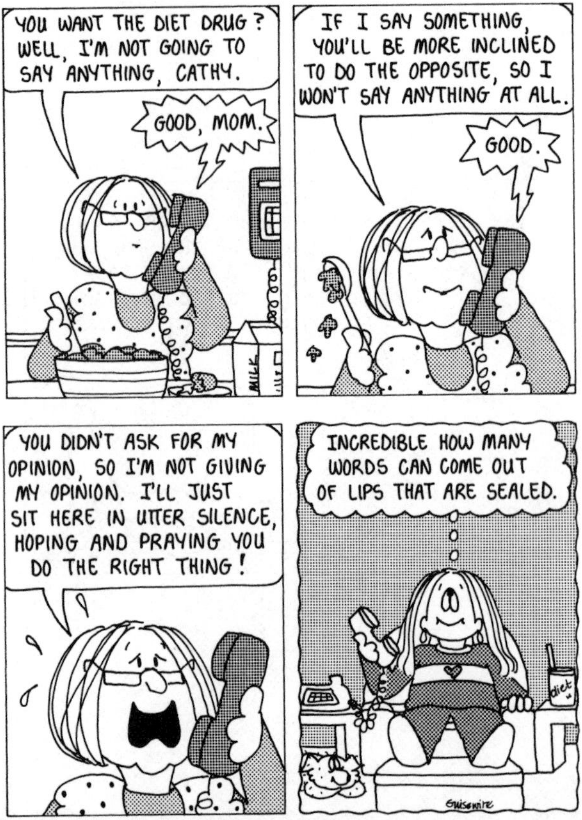
YOU WANT THE DIET DRUG? WELL, I'M NOT GOING TO SAY ANYTHING, CATHY.
GOOD, MOM.
IF I SAY SOMETHING, YOU'LL BE MORE INCLINED TO DO THE OPPOSITE, SO I WON'T SAY ANYTHING AT ALL.
GOOD.
YOU DIDN'T ASK FOR MY OPINION, SO I'M NOT GIVING MY OPINION. I'LL JUST SIT HERE IN UTTER SILENCE, HOPING AND PRAYING YOU DO THE RIGHT THING!
INCREDIBLE HOW MANY WORDS CAN COME OUT OF LIPS THAT ARE SEALED.
MILK
diet
Guisewite

Mom can't resist.

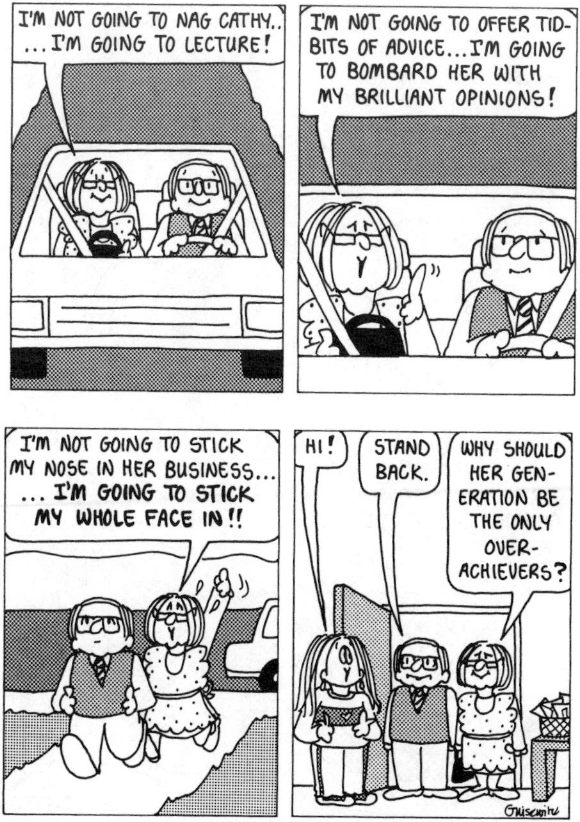

I'M NOT GOING TO NAG CATHY.. ...I'M GOING TO LECTURE!
I'M NOT GOING TO OFFER TID-BITS OF ADVICE...I'M GOING TO BOMBARD HER WITH MY BRILLIANT OPINIONS!
I'M NOT GOING TO STICK MY NOSE IN HER BUSINESS... ...I'M GOING TO STICK MY WHOLE FACE IN!!
HI!
STAND BACK.
WHY SHOULD HER GEN-ERATION BE THE ONLY OVER-ACHIEVERS?
Guisewite

Mom tries to stay out of it . . .

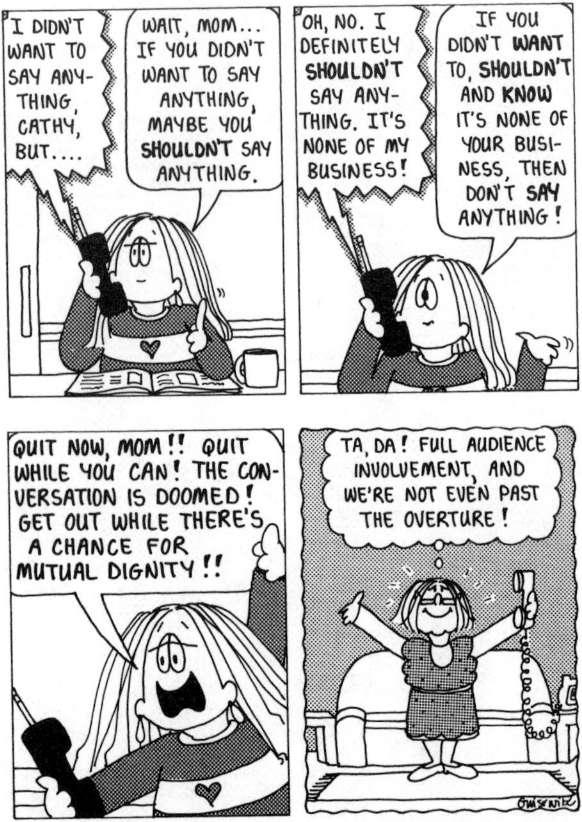
I DIDN'T WANT TO SAY ANYTHING, CATHY, BUT....
WAIT, MOM... IF YOU DIDN'T WANT TO SAY ANYTHING, MAYBE YOU SHOULDN'T SAY ANYTHING.
OH, NO. I DEFINITELY SHOULDN'T SAY ANYTHING. IT'S NONE OF MY BUSINESS!
IF YOU DIDN'T WANT TO, SHOULDN'T AND KNOW IT'S NONE OF YOUR BUSINESS, THEN DON'T SAY ANYTHING!
QUIT NOW, MOM!! QUIT WHILE YOU CAN! THE CONVERSATION IS DOOMED! GET OUT WHILE THERE'S A CHANCE FOR MUTUAL DIGNITY!!
TA, DA! FULL AUDIENCE INVOLVEMENT, AND WE'RE NOT EVEN PAST THE OVERTURE!

Mom finds a more creative way in the door.

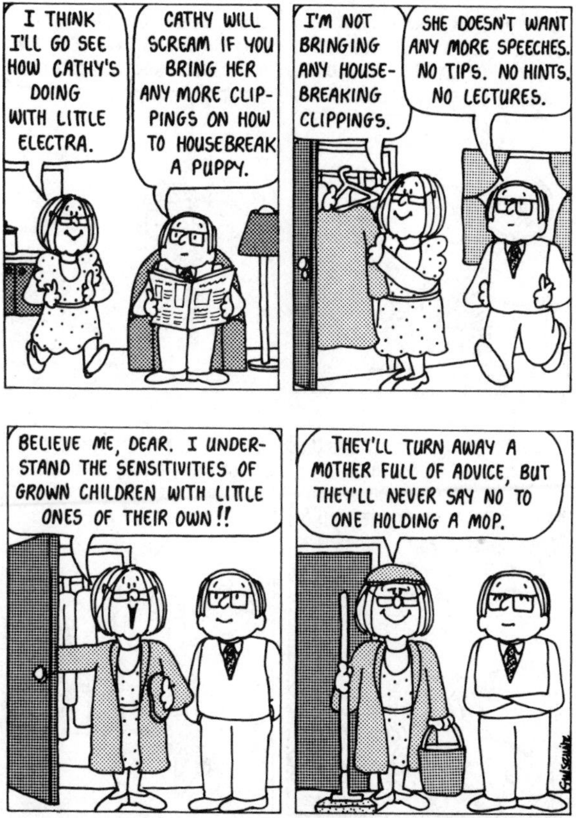
I THINK I'LL GO SEE HOW CATHY'S DOING WITH LITTLE ELECTRA.
CATHY WILL SCREAM IF YOU BRING HER ANY MORE CLIPPINGS ON HOW TO HOUSEBREAK A PUPPY.
I'M NOT BRINGING ANY HOUSE-BREAKING CLIPPINGS.
SHE DOESN'T WANT ANY MORE SPEECHES. NO TIPS. NO HINTS. NO LECTURES.
BELIEVE ME, DEAR. I UNDERSTAND THE SENSITIVITIES OF GROWN CHILDREN WITH LITTLE ONES OF THEIR OWN!!
THEY'LL TURN AWAY A MOTHER FULL OF ADVICE, BUT THEY'LL NEVER SAY NO TO ONE HOLDING A MOP.

Mom holds back . . .

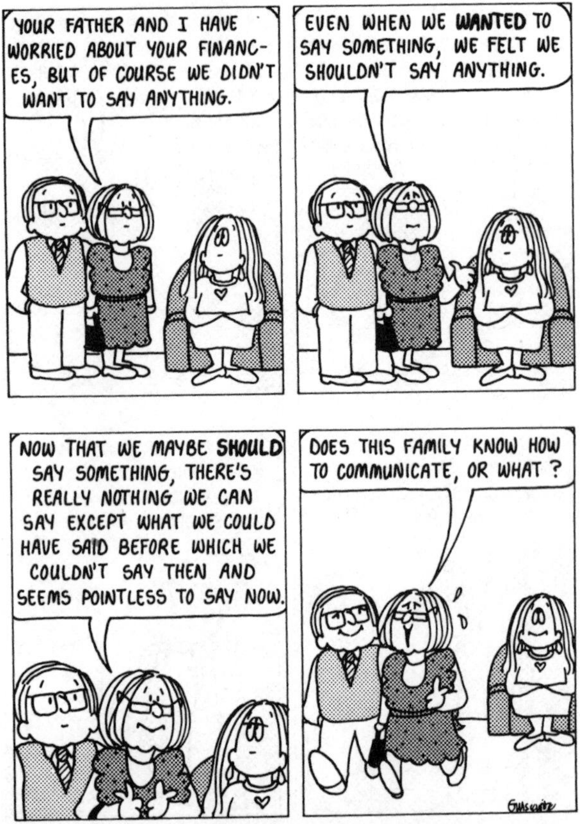
YOUR FATHER AND I HAVE WORRIED ABOUT YOUR FINANCES, BUT OF COURSE WE DIDN'T WANT TO SAY ANYTHING.
EVEN WHEN WE **WANTED** TO SAY SOMETHING, WE FELT WE SHOULDN'T SAY ANYTHING.
NOW THAT WE MAYBE **SHOULD** SAY SOMETHING, THERE'S REALLY NOTHING WE CAN SAY EXCEPT WHAT WE COULD HAVE SAID BEFORE WHICH WE COULDN'T SAY THEN AND SEEMS POINTLESS TO SAY NOW.
DOES THIS FAMILY KNOW HOW TO COMMUNICATE, OR WHAT ?
Guisewite

Mom lets go.

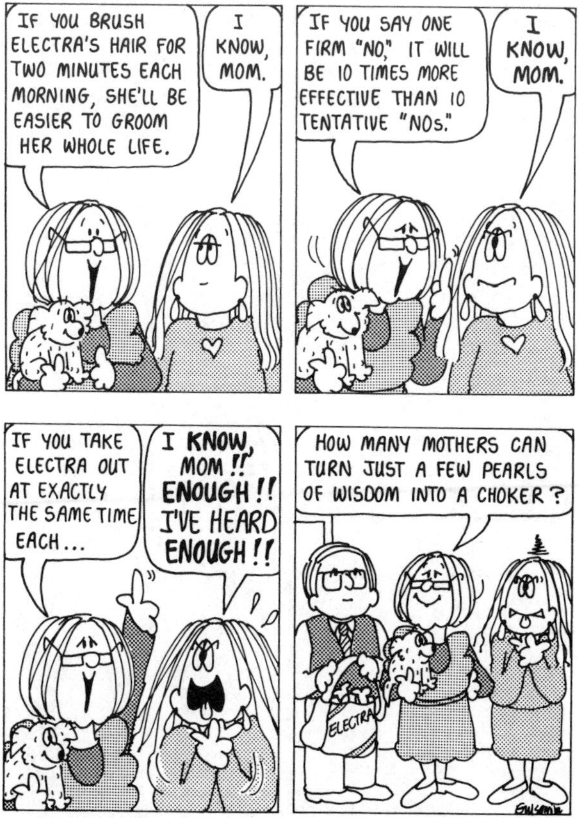
IF YOU BRUSH ELECTRA'S HAIR FOR TWO MINUTES EACH MORNING, SHE'LL BE EASIER TO GROOM HER WHOLE LIFE.
I KNOW, MOM.
IF YOU SAY ONE FIRM "NO," IT WILL BE 10 TIMES MORE EFFECTIVE THAN 10 TENTATIVE "NOs."
I KNOW, MOM.
IF YOU TAKE ELECTRA OUT AT EXACTLY THE SAME TIME EACH...
I KNOW, MOM!! ENOUGH!! I'VE HEARD ENOUGH!!
HOW MANY MOTHERS CAN TURN JUST A FEW PEARLS OF WISDOM INTO A CHOKER?
ELECTRA

Mom backs off . . .

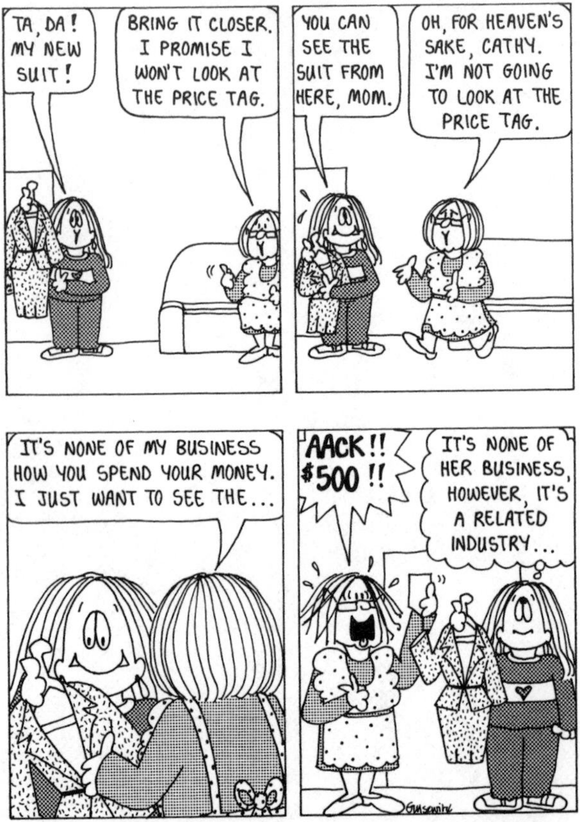

TA, DA! MY NEW SUIT!
BRING IT CLOSER. I PROMISE I WON'T LOOK AT THE PRICE TAG.
YOU CAN SEE THE SUIT FROM HERE, MOM.
OH, FOR HEAVEN'S SAKE, CATHY. I'M NOT GOING TO LOOK AT THE PRICE TAG.
IT'S NONE OF MY BUSINESS HOW YOU SPEND YOUR MONEY. I JUST WANT TO SEE THE...
AACK!! $500!!
IT'S NONE OF HER BUSINESS, HOWEVER, IT'S A RELATED INDUSTRY...

Mom jumps back in.

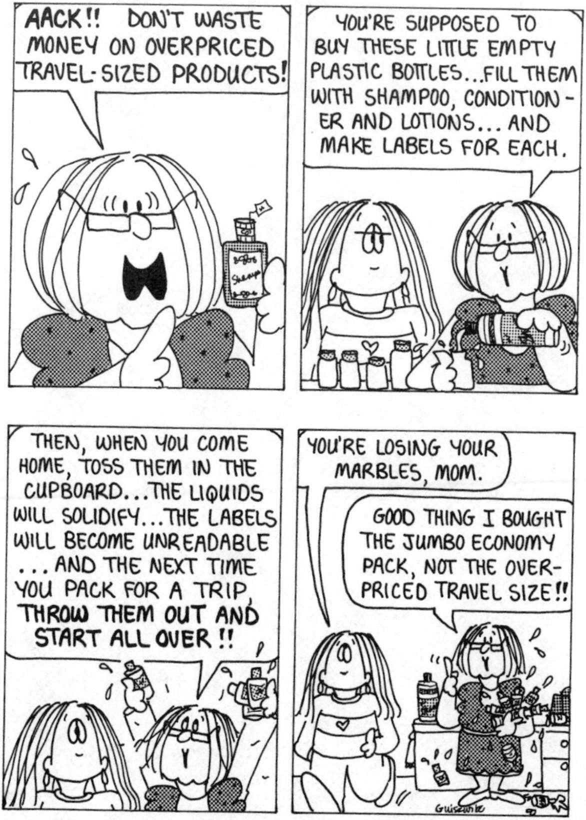

AACK!! DON'T WASTE MONEY ON OVERPRICED TRAVEL-SIZED PRODUCTS!
YOU'RE SUPPOSED TO BUY THESE LITTLE EMPTY PLASTIC BOTTLES...FILL THEM WITH SHAMPOO, CONDITIONER AND LOTIONS... AND MAKE LABELS FOR EACH.
THEN, WHEN YOU COME HOME, TOSS THEM IN THE CUPBOARD...THE LIQUIDS WILL SOLIDIFY...THE LABELS WILL BECOME UNREADABLE ...AND THE NEXT TIME YOU PACK FOR A TRIP, THROW THEM OUT AND START ALL OVER!!
YOU'RE LOSING YOUR MARBLES, MOM.
GOOD THING I BOUGHT THE JUMBO ECONOMY PACK, NOT THE OVER-PRICED TRAVEL SIZE!!
Guisewite

Mom rehearses eloquence . . .

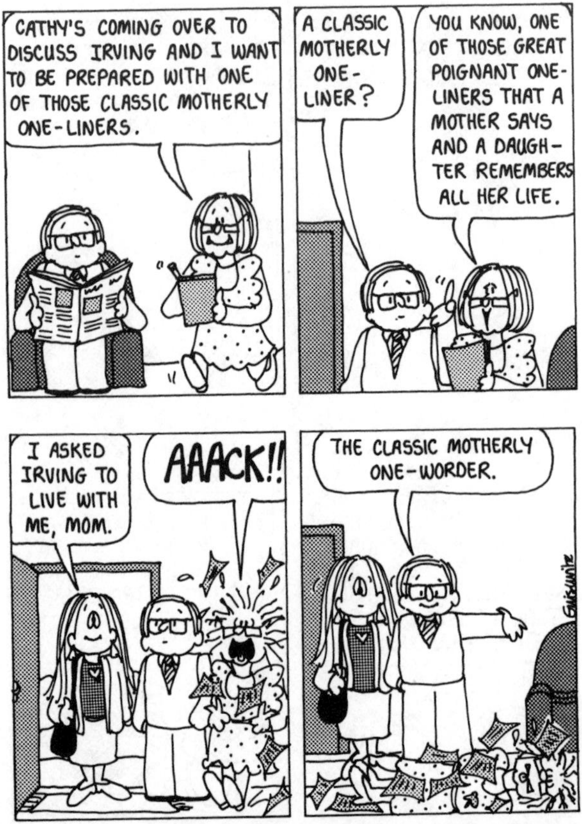
CATHY'S COMING OVER TO DISCUSS IRVING AND I WANT TO BE PREPARED WITH ONE OF THOSE CLASSIC MOTHERLY ONE-LINERS.
A CLASSIC MOTHERLY ONE-LINER?
YOU KNOW, ONE OF THOSE GREAT POIGNANT ONE-LINERS THAT A MOTHER SAYS AND A DAUGHTER REMEMBERS ALL HER LIFE.
I ASKED IRVING TO LIVE WITH ME, MOM.
AAACK!!
THE CLASSIC MOTHERLY ONE-WORDER.
Guisewite

Mom blurts the truth.

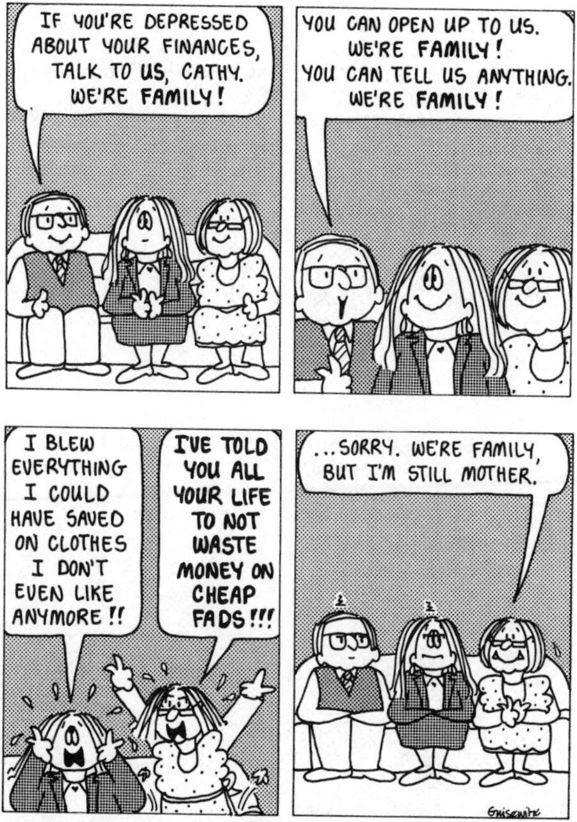
IF YOU'RE DEPRESSED ABOUT YOUR FINANCES, TALK TO US, CATHY. WE'RE FAMILY!
YOU CAN OPEN UP TO US. WE'RE FAMILY! YOU CAN TELL US ANYTHING. WE'RE FAMILY!
I BLEW EVERYTHING I COULD HAVE SAVED ON CLOTHES I DON'T EVEN LIKE ANYMORE!!
I'VE TOLD YOU ALL YOUR LIFE TO NOT WASTE MONEY ON CHEAP FADS!!!
...SORRY. WE'RE FAMILY, BUT I'M STILL MOTHER.
Guisewite

Mom squelches the urge . . .

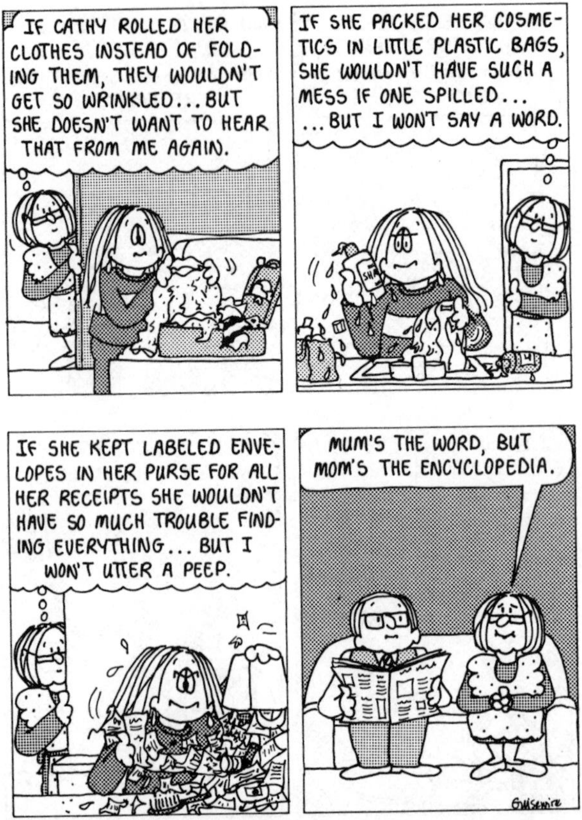
IF CATHY ROLLED HER CLOTHES INSTEAD OF FOLDING THEM, THEY WOULDN'T GET SO WRINKLED... BUT SHE DOESN'T WANT TO HEAR THAT FROM ME AGAIN.
IF SHE PACKED HER COSMETICS IN LITTLE PLASTIC BAGS, SHE WOULDN'T HAVE SUCH A MESS IF ONE SPILLED... ...BUT I WON'T SAY A WORD.
IF SHE KEPT LABELED ENVELOPES IN HER PURSE FOR ALL HER RECEIPTS SHE WOULDN'T HAVE SO MUCH TROUBLE FINDING EVERYTHING... BUT I WON'T UTTER A PEEP.
MUM'S THE WORD, BUT MOM'S THE ENCYCLOPEDIA.
Guisewite

Mom makes the audience beg for more.

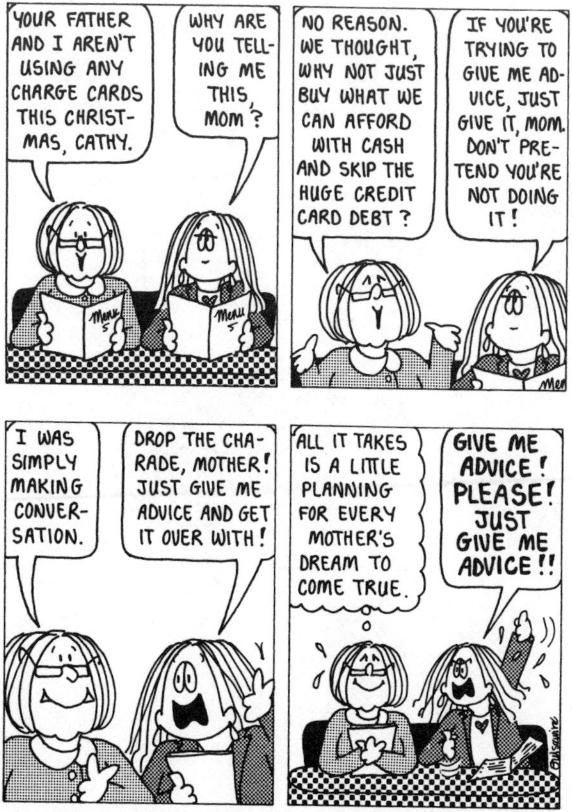

YOUR FATHER AND I AREN'T USING ANY CHARGE CARDS THIS CHRISTMAS, CATHY.
WHY ARE YOU TELLING ME THIS, MOM?
Menu
Menu
NO REASON. WE THOUGHT, WHY NOT JUST BUY WHAT WE CAN AFFORD WITH CASH AND SKIP THE HUGE CREDIT CARD DEBT?
IF YOU'RE TRYING TO GIVE ME ADVICE, JUST GIVE IT, MOM. DON'T PRETEND YOU'RE NOT DOING IT!
I WAS SIMPLY MAKING CONVERSATION.
DROP THE CHARADE, MOTHER! JUST GIVE ME ADVICE AND GET IT OVER WITH!
ALL IT TAKES IS A LITTLE PLANNING FOR EVERY MOTHER'S DREAM TO COME TRUE.
GIVE ME ADVICE! PLEASE! JUST GIVE ME ADVICE!!
Guisewite

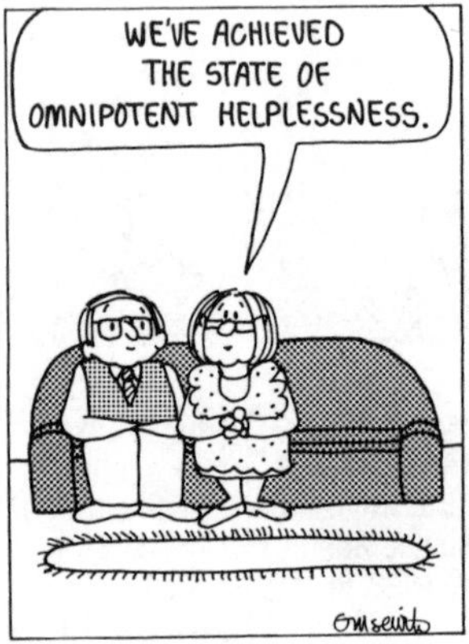
WE'VE ACHIEVED THE STATE OF OMNIPOTENT HELPLESSNESS.

The Dreamer

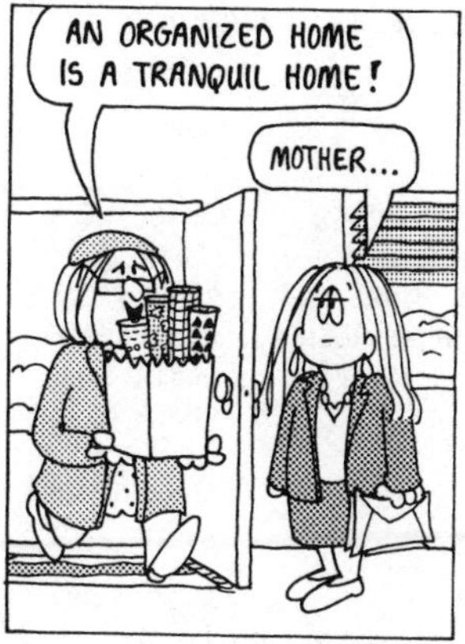
AN ORGANIZED HOME IS A TRANQUIL HOME!
MOTHER...

On December 2, 1949, concerned that she wouldn't be able to find a second photo album that exactly matched the one she'd started for my one-month-old sister, Mom put aside the picture project until she could contact the manufacturer.

This attention to detail, the drive for perfection, the ability to visualize what could be, the willingness to sacrifice small bits of progress for the Grand Life Program, are all part of the reason that December 2, 1949, was the last day a photo actually made it into an album in our family.

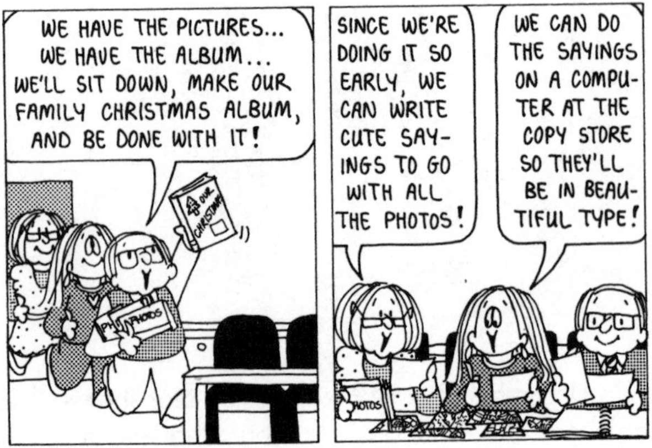

WE HAVE THE PICTURES... WE HAVE THE ALBUM... WE'LL SIT DOWN, MAKE OUR FAMILY CHRISTMAS ALBUM, AND BE DONE WITH IT!
OUR CHRISTMAS
PHOTOS
SINCE WE'RE DOING IT SO EARLY, WE CAN WRITE CUTE SAYINGS TO GO WITH ALL THE PHOTOS!
WE CAN DO THE SAYINGS ON A COMPUTER AT THE COPY STORE SO THEY'LL BE IN BEAUTIFUL TYPE!

WE'LL MAKE A "SPECIAL THOUGHTS" PAGE WHERE WE EACH COMPOSE A LITTLE ESSAY ON WHAT THIS CHRISTMAS MEANT TO US!
AND BLOWUPS! WE'LL GET BLOWUPS OF THE BEST SHOTS!
WE'LL START TOMORROW WHEN WE'RE NICE AND FRESH.
IT'S AMAZING HOW LITTLE WE CAN DO WHEN WE PUT OUR HEADS TOGETHER.

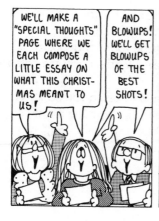

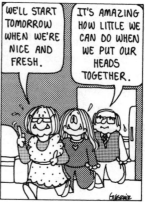

While some families sit and look through "Summer Vacation, 1990" and "Christmas, 1978" books, we stand in Mom and Dad's storage room and look at 43 giant boxes of photos that never made it past the category of "Miscellaneous."

Boxes which, through years of being raided for "a baby picture for my yearbook," "a montage for my collage project," a "cute shot of Dad with our dog," are, in truth, way beyond "miscellaneous."

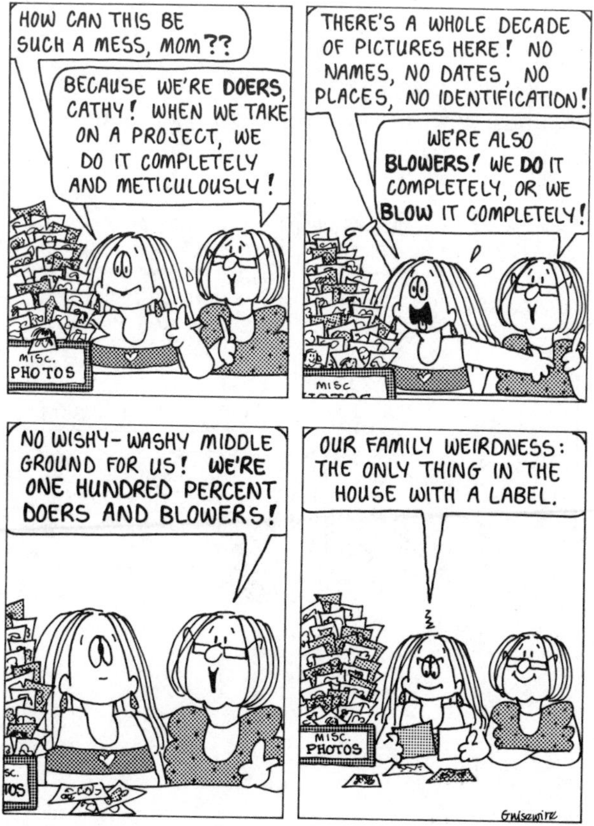
HOW CAN THIS BE SUCH A MESS, MOM??
BECAUSE WE'RE **DOERS**, CATHY! WHEN WE TAKE ON A PROJECT, WE DO IT COMPLETELY AND METICULOUSLY!
MISC. PHOTOS
THERE'S A WHOLE DECADE OF PICTURES HERE! NO NAMES, NO DATES, NO PLACES, NO IDENTIFICATION!
WE'RE ALSO **BLOWERS**! WE **DO** IT COMPLETELY, OR WE **BLOW** IT COMPLETELY!
MISC
NO WISHY-WASHY MIDDLE GROUND FOR US! **WE'RE** ONE HUNDRED PERCENT DOERS AND BLOWERS!
OUR FAMILY WEIRDNESS: THE ONLY THING IN THE HOUSE WITH A LABEL.
MISC. PHOTOS
Guisewite

With her unlabeled, unsorted, unalbumed boxes, Mom has, in fact, given us the perfect picture of our family.

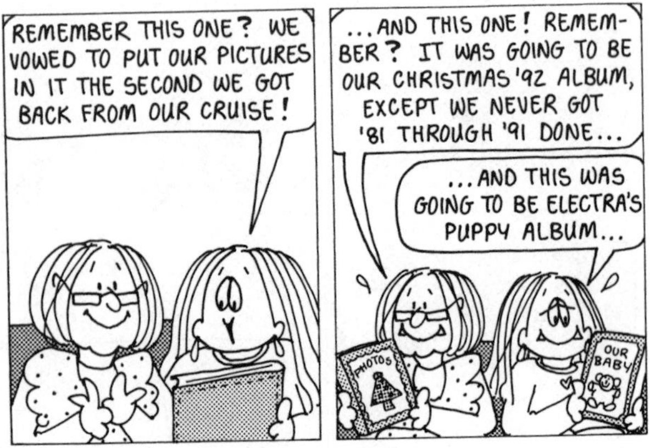
REMEMBER THIS ONE? WE VOWED TO PUT OUR PICTURES IN IT THE SECOND WE GOT BACK FROM OUR CRUISE!
...AND THIS ONE! REMEMBER? IT WAS GOING TO BE OUR CHRISTMAS '92 ALBUM, EXCEPT WE NEVER GOT '81 THROUGH '91 DONE...
...AND THIS WAS GOING TO BE ELECTRA'S PUPPY ALBUM...
PHOTOS
OUR BABY

WE GOT THIS ONE FOR YOUR GRADUATION PICTURES!..
...FOR YOUR ANNIVERSARY!
...FOR OUR YOSEMITE TRIP!
...FOR MY 21ST BIRTHDAY!
PHOTOS
SOME PEOPLE CRY OVER OLD PHOTOGRAPHS. WE CRY OVER BLANK PHOTO ALBUMS.
MISC PHOTOS
MISC PHOTO
Guisewite

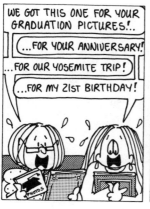

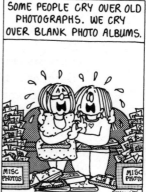

Mom's boxes are a classic family portrait:
    Decades of big dreams.
    Astounding optimism.
    Impeccable plans.

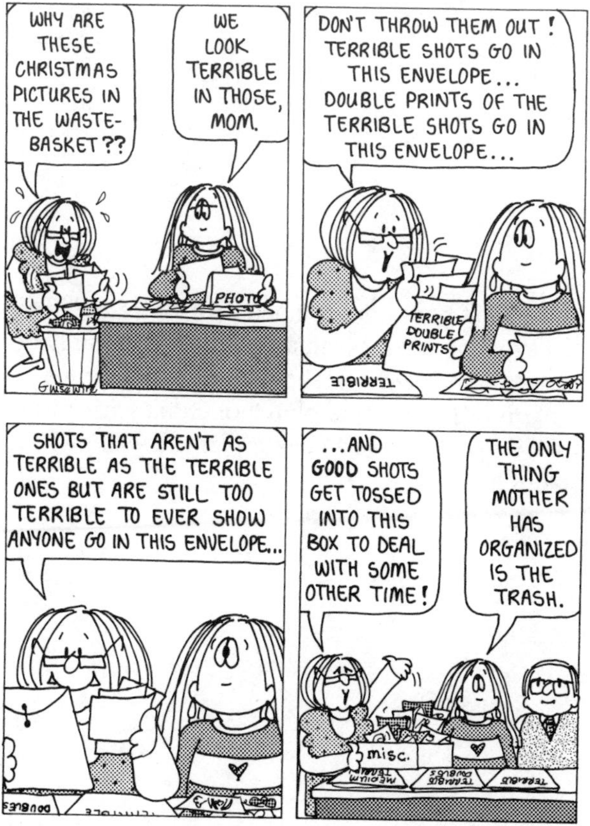
WHY ARE THESE CHRISTMAS PICTURES IN THE WASTE-BASKET??
WE LOOK TERRIBLE IN THOSE, MOM.
PHOTO
DON'T THROW THEM OUT! TERRIBLE SHOTS GO IN THIS ENVELOPE... DOUBLE PRINTS OF THE TERRIBLE SHOTS GO IN THIS ENVELOPE...
TERRIBLE DOUBLE PRINTS
SHOTS THAT AREN'T AS TERRIBLE AS THE TERRIBLE ONES BUT ARE STILL TOO TERRIBLE TO EVER SHOW ANYONE GO IN THIS ENVELOPE...
...AND GOOD SHOTS GET TOSSED INTO THIS BOX TO DEAL WITH SOME OTHER TIME!
THE ONLY THING MOTHER HAS ORGANIZED IS THE TRASH.
misc.

Mom's boxes are a monument to her ability to believe that, after a lifetime of training me in her system, things will somehow be different for me—that an organizational plan that didn't work for her for 50 years will start working for me with my next roll of film.

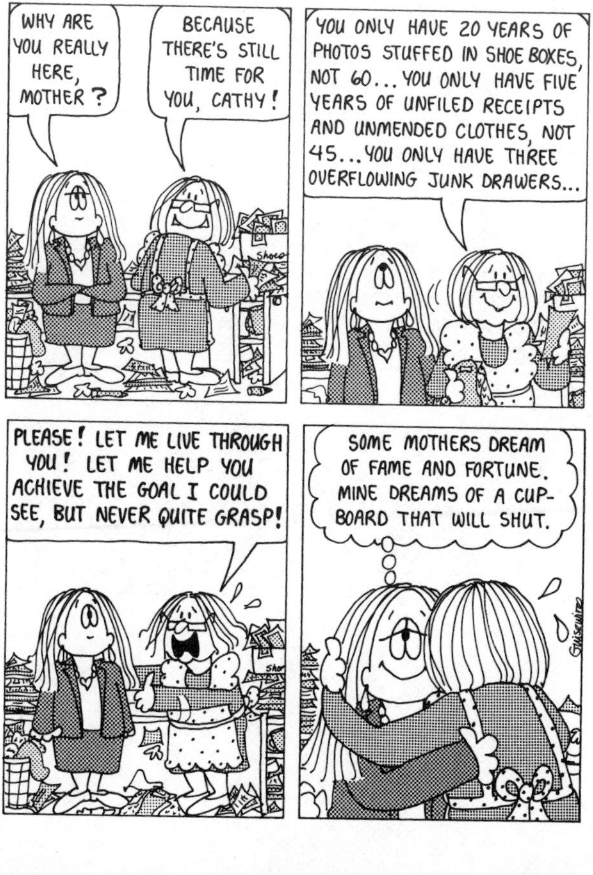
WHY ARE YOU REALLY HERE, MOTHER?
BECAUSE THERE'S STILL TIME FOR YOU, CATHY!
YOU ONLY HAVE 20 YEARS OF PHOTOS STUFFED IN SHOE BOXES, NOT 60... YOU ONLY HAVE FIVE YEARS OF UNFILED RECEIPTS AND UNMENDED CLOTHES, NOT 45... YOU ONLY HAVE THREE OVERFLOWING JUNK DRAWERS...
PLEASE! LET ME LIVE THROUGH YOU! LET ME HELP YOU ACHIEVE THE GOAL I COULD SEE, BUT NEVER QUITE GRASP!
SOME MOTHERS DREAM OF FAME AND FORTUNE. MINE DREAMS OF A CUPBOARD THAT WILL SHUT.

Photos are only the beginning.

Nothing bonds my mother and me like all the things we haven't organized.

I KEEP WAITING FOR A TIME WHEN I'LL GET MY HOUSE COMPLETELY ORGANIZED... AND THEN I SEE THAT **YOU'RE** STILL WAITING FOR THAT SAME TIME, MOM.
to read
I KEEP THINKING I'LL TURN INTO A DIFFERENT PERSON... AND THEN I SEE THAT **YOU** STILL THINK **YOU'RE** GOING TO TURN INTO A DIFFERENT PERSON!
to mend

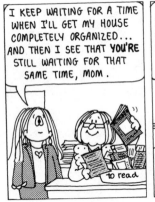

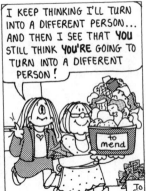

I LOOK AT YOU AND SEE THAT IT'S HOPELESS, MOM! I LOOK AT YOU AND AM FILLED WITH A PASSION TO FIND MY OWN ENTIRELY NEW SYSTEM!
to read
to mend
to file
IS THERE ANYTHING MORE THANKLESS THAN REALIZING WHAT AN INSPIRATION YOU ARE?
to read
to mend
to file
Guisewite

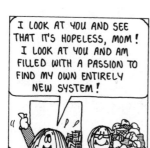

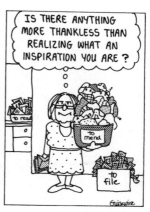

The bathroom cupboard of rejected beauty products
that we can't stand to get rid of . . .

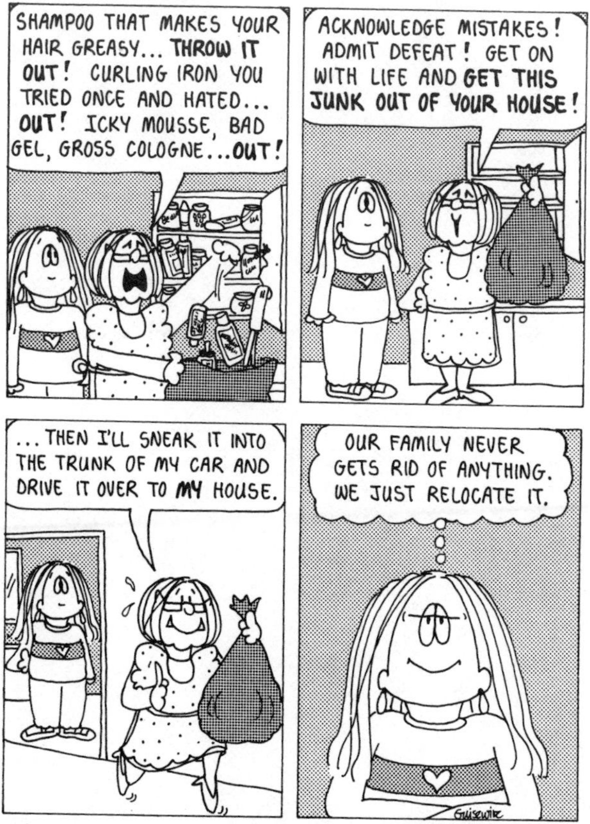

SHAMPOO THAT MAKES YOUR HAIR GREASY... **THROW IT OUT!** CURLING IRON YOU TRIED ONCE AND HATED... **OUT!** ICKY MOUSSE, BAD GEL, GROSS COLOGNE... **OUT!**
ACKNOWLEDGE MISTAKES! ADMIT DEFEAT! GET ON WITH LIFE AND **GET THIS JUNK OUT OF YOUR HOUSE!**
...THEN I'LL SNEAK IT INTO THE TRUNK OF MY CAR AND DRIVE IT OVER TO **MY** HOUSE.
OUR FAMILY NEVER GETS RID OF ANYTHING. WE JUST RELOCATE IT.
Guisewite

The kitchen counter full of good intentions . . .

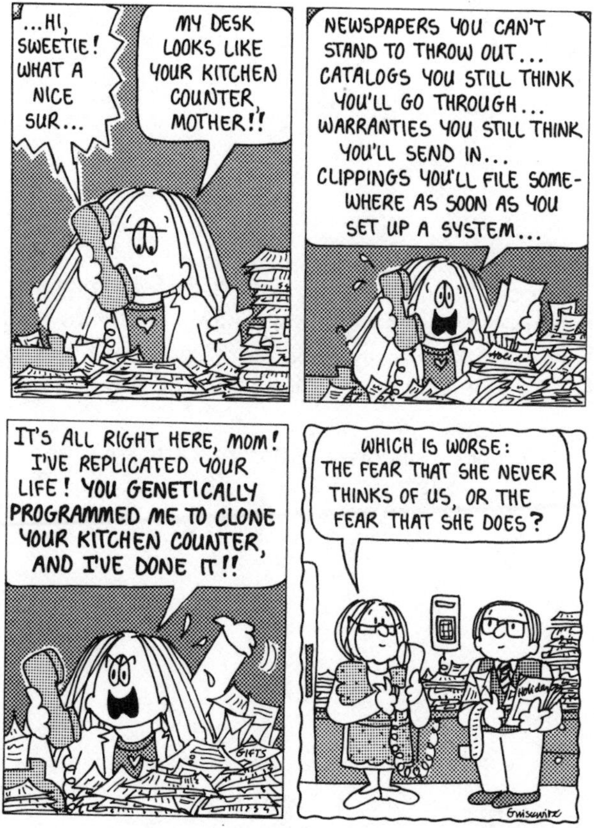
...HI, SWEETIE! WHAT A NICE SUR...
MY DESK LOOKS LIKE YOUR KITCHEN COUNTER, MOTHER!!
NEWSPAPERS YOU CAN'T STAND TO THROW OUT... CATALOGS YOU STILL THINK YOU'LL GO THROUGH... WARRANTIES YOU STILL THINK YOU'LL SEND IN... CLIPPINGS YOU'LL FILE SOMEWHERE AS SOON AS YOU SET UP A SYSTEM...
IT'S ALL RIGHT HERE, MOM! I'VE REPLICATED YOUR LIFE! YOU GENETICALLY PROGRAMMED ME TO CLONE YOUR KITCHEN COUNTER, AND I'VE DONE IT!!
GIFTS
WHICH IS WORSE: THE FEAR THAT SHE NEVER THINKS OF US, OR THE FEAR THAT SHE DOES?
Guisewite

Food that came in gift baskets that we can't eat because "it will go right to our hips," can't throw out because "it's perfectly good food," and can't give away because "it would be insulting because it was a gift."

Owner's manuals, registration certificates and warranty cards . . .

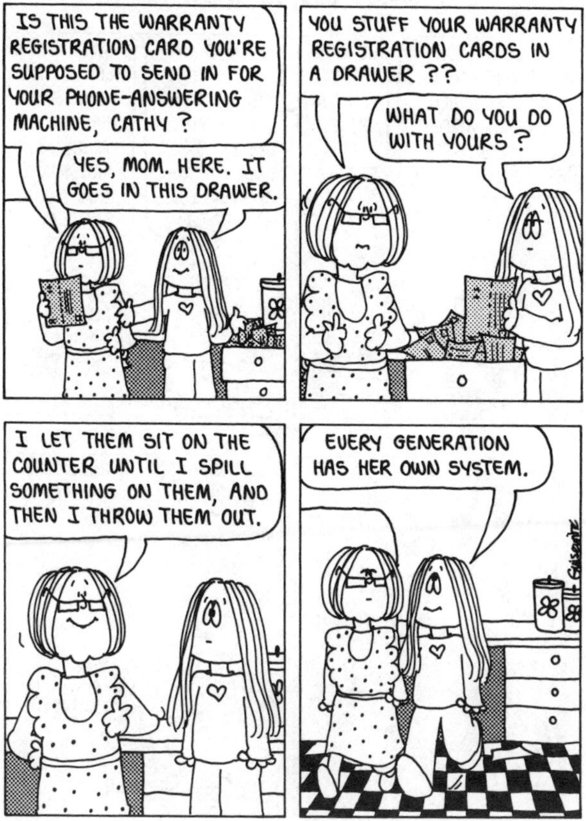
IS THIS THE WARRANTY REGISTRATION CARD YOU'RE SUPPOSED TO SEND IN FOR YOUR PHONE-ANSWERING MACHINE, CATHY ?
YES, MOM. HERE. IT GOES IN THIS DRAWER.
YOU STUFF YOUR WARRANTY REGISTRATION CARDS IN A DRAWER ??
WHAT DO YOU DO WITH YOURS ?
I LET THEM SIT ON THE COUNTER UNTIL I SPILL SOMETHING ON THEM, AND THEN I THROW THEM OUT.
EVERY GENERATION HAS HER OWN SYSTEM.
Guisewite

Mom's Coupon System:

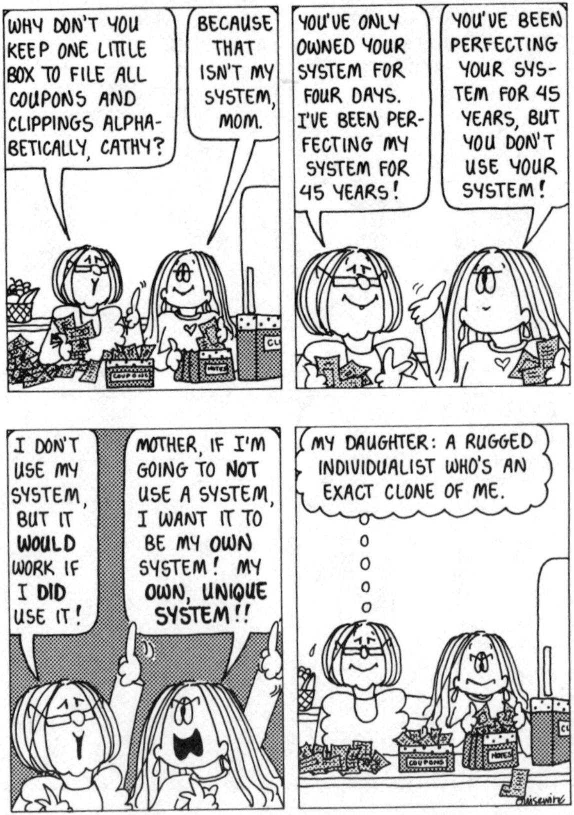
WHY DON'T YOU KEEP ONE LITTLE BOX TO FILE ALL COUPONS AND CLIPPINGS ALPHABETICALLY, CATHY?
BECAUSE THAT ISN'T MY SYSTEM, MOM.
YOU'VE ONLY OWNED YOUR SYSTEM FOR FOUR DAYS. I'VE BEEN PERFECTING MY SYSTEM FOR 45 YEARS!
YOU'VE BEEN PERFECTING YOUR SYSTEM FOR 45 YEARS, BUT YOU DON'T USE YOUR SYSTEM!
I DON'T USE MY SYSTEM, BUT IT **WOULD** WORK IF I **DID** USE IT!
MOTHER, IF I'M GOING TO **NOT** USE A SYSTEM, I WANT IT TO BE MY **OWN** SYSTEM! MY **OWN, UNIQUE SYSTEM!!**
MY DAUGHTER: A RUGGED INDIVIDUALIST WHO'S AN EXACT CLONE OF ME.
COUPONS
NOTES
Guisewite

Mom's Catalog System:

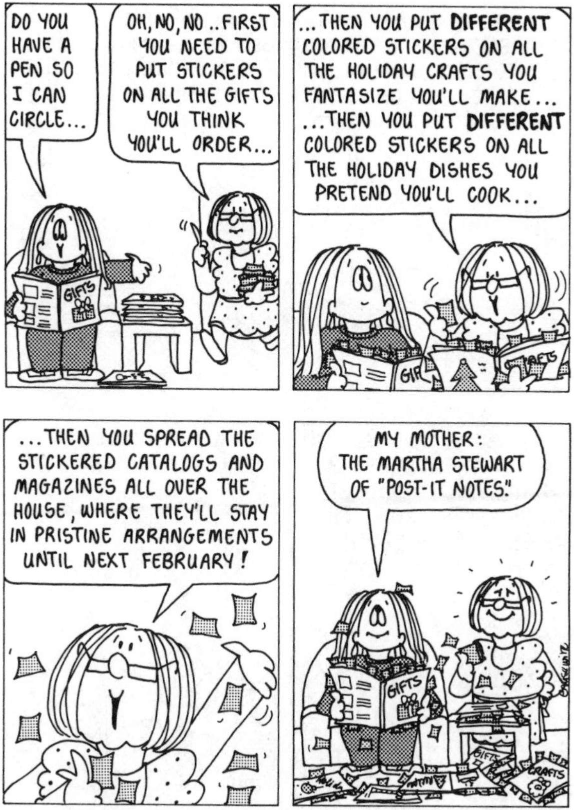

DO YOU HAVE A PEN SO I CAN CIRCLE...
OH, NO, NO .. FIRST YOU NEED TO PUT STICKERS ON ALL THE GIFTS YOU THINK YOU'LL ORDER...
GIFTS
...THEN YOU PUT **DIFFERENT** COLORED STICKERS ON ALL THE HOLIDAY CRAFTS YOU FANTASIZE YOU'LL MAKE... ...THEN YOU PUT **DIFFERENT** COLORED STICKERS ON ALL THE HOLIDAY DISHES YOU PRETEND YOU'LL COOK...
CRAFTS
...THEN YOU SPREAD THE STICKERED CATALOGS AND MAGAZINES ALL OVER THE HOUSE, WHERE THEY'LL STAY IN PRISTINE ARRANGEMENTS UNTIL NEXT FEBRUARY!
MY MOTHER: THE MARTHA STEWART OF "POST-IT NOTES."
GIFTS
CRAFTS

Mom's Christmas Card System:

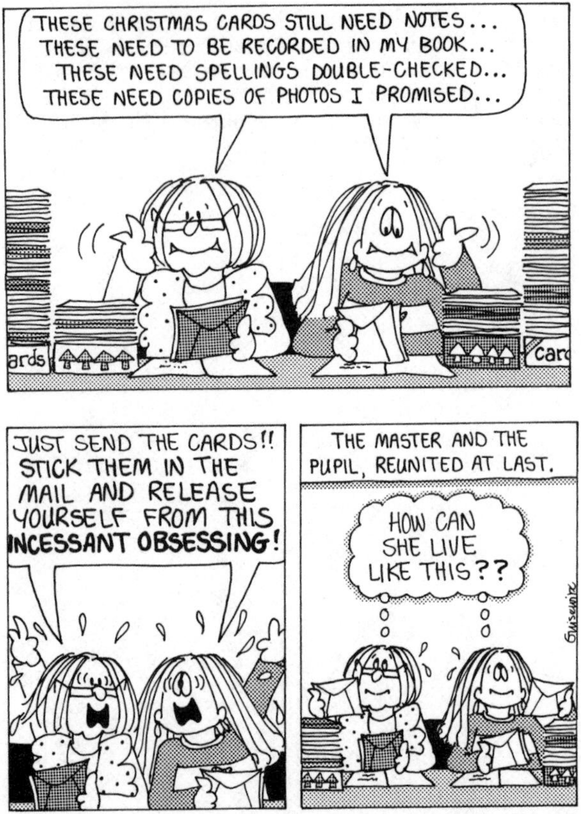
THESE CHRISTMAS CARDS STILL NEED NOTES... THESE NEED TO BE RECORDED IN MY BOOK... THESE NEED SPELLINGS DOUBLE-CHECKED... THESE NEED COPIES OF PHOTOS I PROMISED...
JUST SEND THE CARDS!! STICK THEM IN THE MAIL AND RELEASE YOURSELF FROM THIS INCESSANT OBSESSING!
THE MASTER AND THE PUPIL, REUNITED AT LAST.
HOW CAN SHE LIVE LIKE THIS??

Mom's Holiday Savings System:

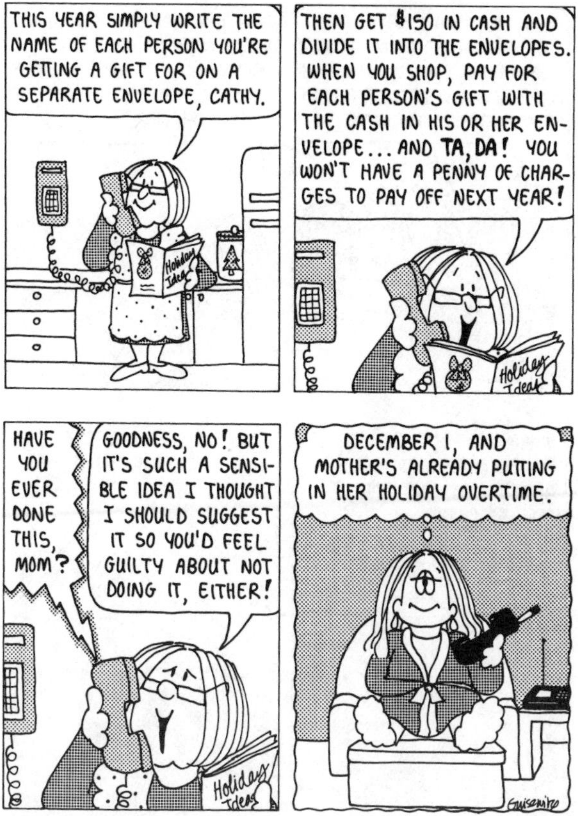
THIS YEAR SIMPLY WRITE THE NAME OF EACH PERSON YOU'RE GETTING A GIFT FOR ON A SEPARATE ENVELOPE, CATHY.
Holiday Ideas
THEN GET $150 IN CASH AND DIVIDE IT INTO THE ENVELOPES. WHEN YOU SHOP, PAY FOR EACH PERSON'S GIFT WITH THE CASH IN HIS OR HER ENVELOPE... AND TA, DA! YOU WON'T HAVE A PENNY OF CHARGES TO PAY OFF NEXT YEAR!
Holiday Ideas
HAVE YOU EVER DONE THIS, MOM?
GOODNESS, NO! BUT IT'S SUCH A SENSIBLE IDEA I THOUGHT I SHOULD SUGGEST IT SO YOU'D FEEL GUILTY ABOUT NOT DOING IT, EITHER!
Holiday Ideas
DECEMBER 1, AND MOTHER'S ALREADY PUTTING IN HER HOLIDAY OVERTIME.
Guisewite

Mom's Receipt System:

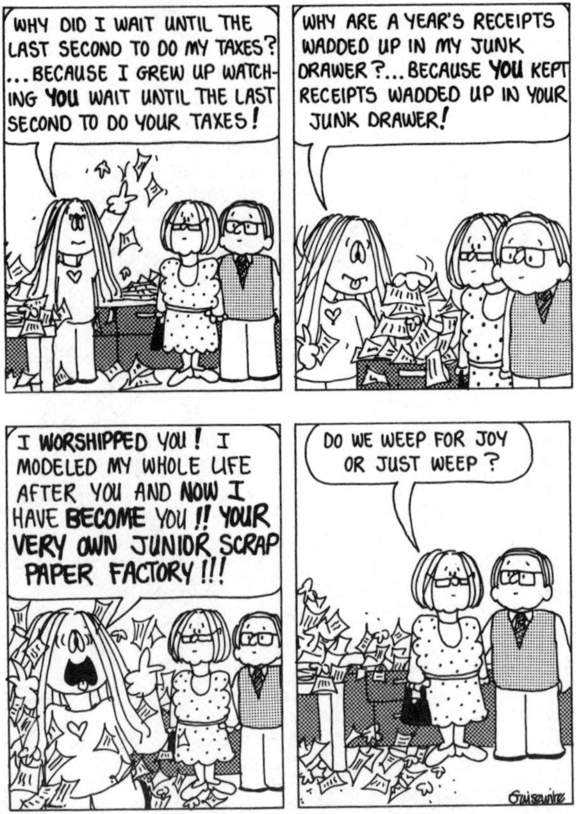

WHY DID I WAIT UNTIL THE LAST SECOND TO DO MY TAXES? ...BECAUSE I GREW UP WATCHING **YOU** WAIT UNTIL THE LAST SECOND TO DO YOUR TAXES!
WHY ARE A YEAR'S RECEIPTS WADDED UP IN MY JUNK DRAWER?... BECAUSE **YOU** KEPT RECEIPTS WADDED UP IN YOUR JUNK DRAWER!
I **WORSHIPPED** YOU! I MODELED MY WHOLE LIFE AFTER YOU AND **NOW** I HAVE **BECOME** YOU!! **YOUR VERY OWN JUNIOR SCRAP PAPER FACTORY!!!**
DO WE WEEP FOR JOY OR JUST WEEP?
Guisewite

Mom's Packing System:

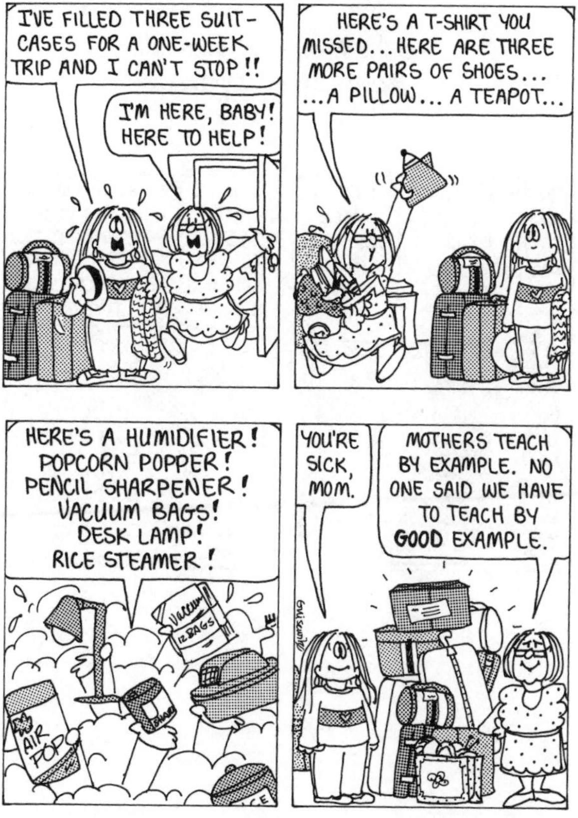
I'VE FILLED THREE SUIT-CASES FOR A ONE-WEEK TRIP AND I CAN'T STOP!!
I'M HERE, BABY! HERE TO HELP!
HERE'S A T-SHIRT YOU MISSED... HERE ARE THREE MORE PAIRS OF SHOES... ...A PILLOW... A TEAPOT...
HERE'S A HUMIDIFIER! POPCORN POPPER! PENCIL SHARPENER! VACUUM BAGS! DESK LAMP! RICE STEAMER!
VACUUM
12 BAGS
AIR POP
YOU'RE SICK, MOM.
MOTHERS TEACH BY EXAMPLE. NO ONE SAID WE HAVE TO TEACH BY GOOD EXAMPLE.

And the Mother of them all:

Mom's Closet System

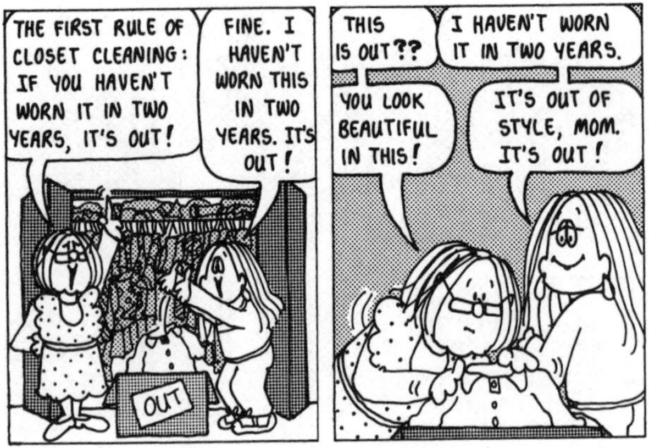
THE FIRST RULE OF CLOSET CLEANING: IF YOU HAVEN'T WORN IT IN TWO YEARS, IT'S OUT!
FINE. I HAVEN'T WORN THIS IN TWO YEARS. IT'S OUT!
OUT
THIS IS OUT??
I HAVEN'T WORN IT IN TWO YEARS.
YOU LOOK BEAUTIFUL IN THIS!
IT'S OUT OF STYLE, MOM. IT'S OUT!

WE COULD UPDATE IT WITH A NEW BELT...DYE IT A NEW COLOR...THIS IS THE DRESS YOU WORE ON MY BIRTHDAY IN 1983! YOU CAN'T THROW THIS SPECIAL DRESS OUT!!

THE SECOND RULE OF CLOSET CLEANING: DON'T DO IT WITH YOUR MOTHER.

Suits that are waiting for the skirts to be altered, pants that are waiting for the thighs to be altered.

Closets full of clothes that we never wear, don't like, and can't fit into.

Shrines to little phases, grand fantasies, and really, really good sales.

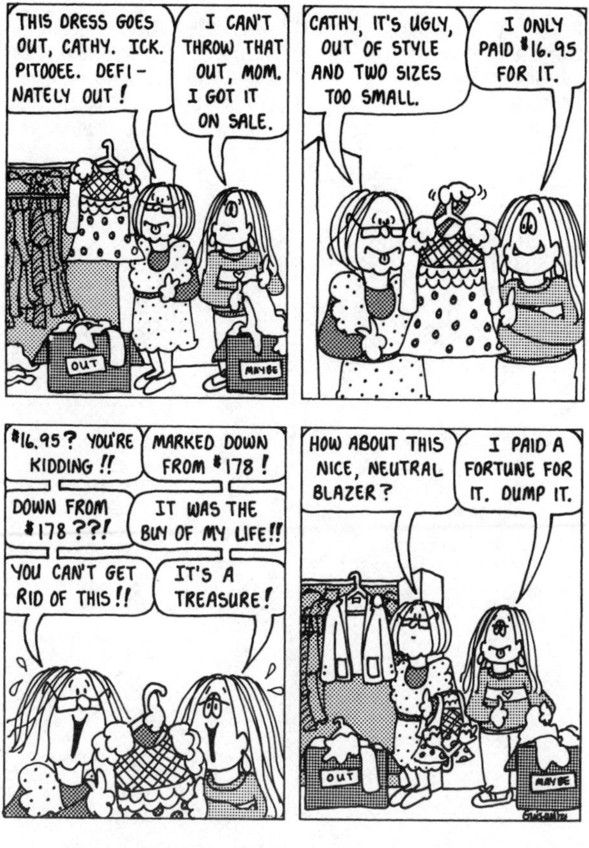
THIS DRESS GOES OUT, CATHY. ICK. PITOOEE. DEFI-NATELY OUT!
I CAN'T THROW THAT OUT, MOM. I GOT IT ON SALE.
CATHY, IT'S UGLY, OUT OF STYLE AND TWO SIZES TOO SMALL.
I ONLY PAID $16.95 FOR IT.
$16.95? YOU'RE KIDDING!!
MARKED DOWN FROM $178!
DOWN FROM $178??!
IT WAS THE BUY OF MY LIFE!!
YOU CAN'T GET RID OF THIS!!
IT'S A TREASURE!
HOW ABOUT THIS NICE, NEUTRAL BLAZER?
I PAID A FORTUNE FOR IT. DUMP IT.
OUT
MAYBE

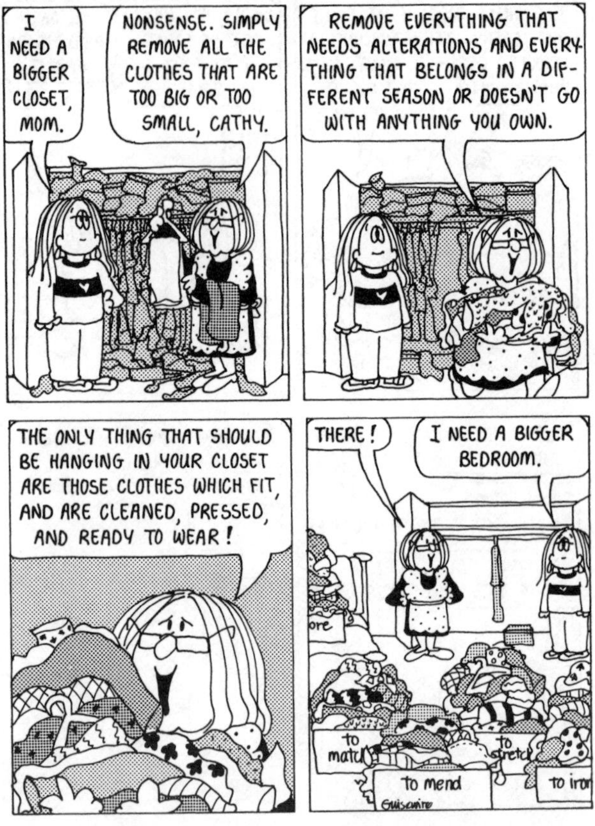
I NEED A BIGGER CLOSET, MOM.
NONSENSE. SIMPLY REMOVE ALL THE CLOTHES THAT ARE TOO BIG OR TOO SMALL, CATHY.
REMOVE EVERYTHING THAT NEEDS ALTERATIONS AND EVERYTHING THAT BELONGS IN A DIFFERENT SEASON OR DOESN'T GO WITH ANYTHING YOU OWN.
THE ONLY THING THAT SHOULD BE HANGING IN YOUR CLOSET ARE THOSE CLOTHES WHICH FIT, AND ARE CLEANED, PRESSED, AND READY TO WEAR!
THERE!
I NEED A BIGGER BEDROOM.
to match
to stretch
to mend
to iron
Guisewite

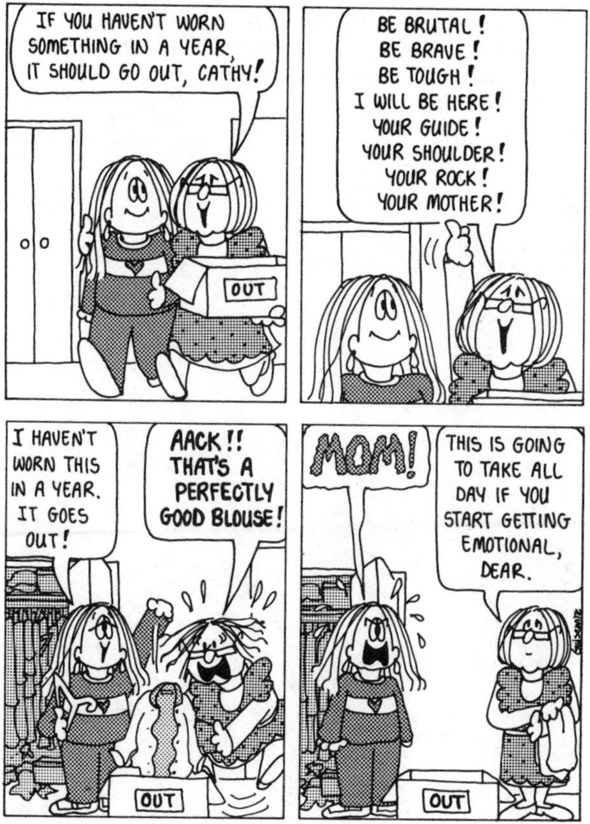
IF YOU HAVEN'T WORN SOMETHING IN A YEAR, IT SHOULD GO OUT, CATHY!
OUT
BE BRUTAL! BE BRAVE! BE TOUGH! I WILL BE HERE! YOUR GUIDE! YOUR SHOULDER! YOUR ROCK! YOUR MOTHER!
I HAVEN'T WORN THIS IN A YEAR. IT GOES OUT!
AACK!! THAT'S A PERFECTLY GOOD BLOUSE!
OUT
MOM!
THIS IS GOING TO TAKE ALL DAY IF YOU START GETTING EMOTIONAL, DEAR.
OUT

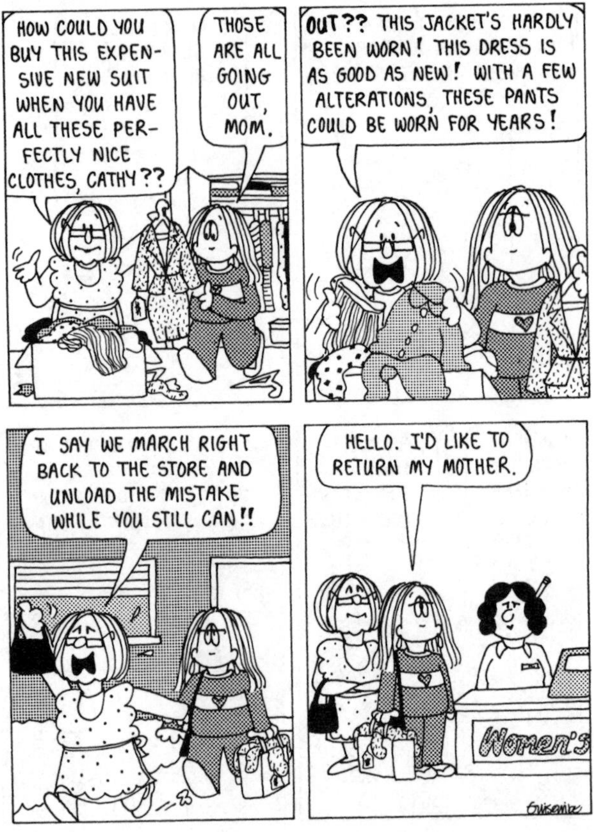
HOW COULD YOU BUY THIS EXPENSIVE NEW SUIT WHEN YOU HAVE ALL THESE PERFECTLY NICE CLOTHES, CATHY??
THOSE ARE ALL GOING OUT, MOM.
OUT?? THIS JACKET'S HARDLY BEEN WORN! THIS DRESS IS AS GOOD AS NEW! WITH A FEW ALTERATIONS, THESE PANTS COULD BE WORN FOR YEARS!
I SAY WE MARCH RIGHT BACK TO THE STORE AND UNLOAD THE MISTAKE WHILE YOU STILL CAN!!
HELLO. I'D LIKE TO RETURN MY MOTHER.
Women's
Guisewite

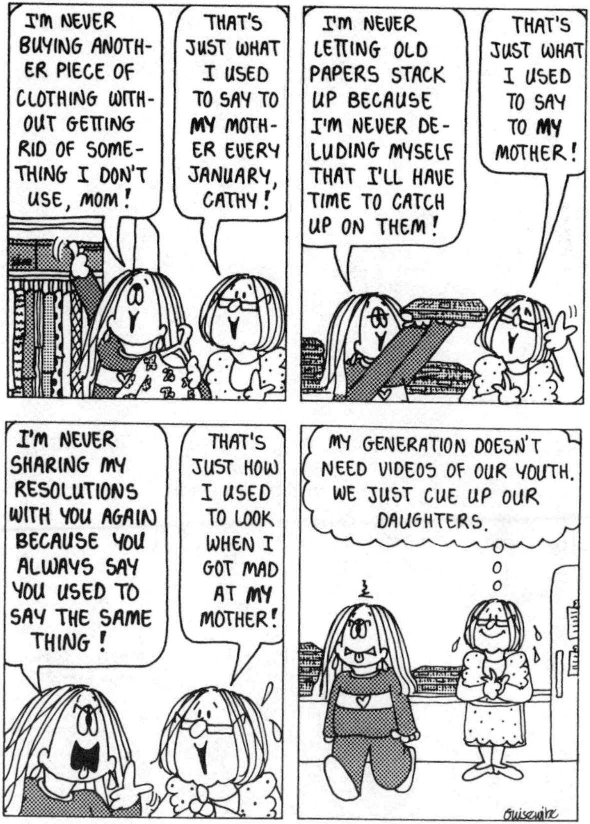
I'M NEVER BUYING ANOTHER PIECE OF CLOTHING WITHOUT GETTING RID OF SOMETHING I DON'T USE, MOM!
THAT'S JUST WHAT I USED TO SAY TO MY MOTHER EVERY JANUARY, CATHY!
I'M NEVER LETTING OLD PAPERS STACK UP BECAUSE I'M NEVER DELUDING MYSELF THAT I'LL HAVE TIME TO CATCH UP ON THEM!
THAT'S JUST WHAT I USED TO SAY TO MY MOTHER!
I'M NEVER SHARING MY RESOLUTIONS WITH YOU AGAIN BECAUSE YOU ALWAYS SAY YOU USED TO SAY THE SAME THING!
THAT'S JUST HOW I USED TO LOOK WHEN I GOT MAD AT MY MOTHER!
MY GENERATION DOESN'T NEED VIDEOS OF OUR YOUTH. WE JUST CUE UP OUR DAUGHTERS.
Guisewite

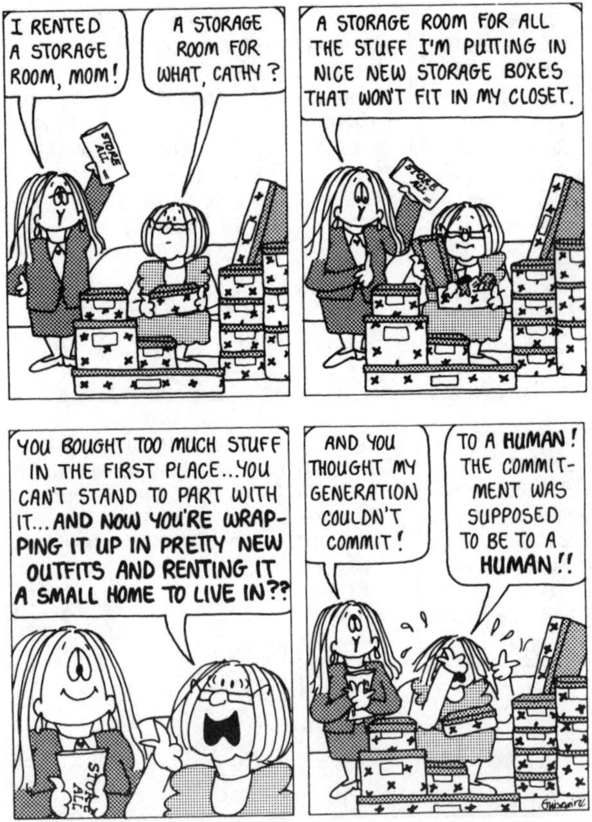
I RENTED A STORAGE ROOM, MOM!
A STORAGE ROOM FOR WHAT, CATHY?
STORE ALL
A STORAGE ROOM FOR ALL THE STUFF I'M PUTTING IN NICE NEW STORAGE BOXES THAT WON'T FIT IN MY CLOSET.
STORE ALL
YOU BOUGHT TOO MUCH STUFF IN THE FIRST PLACE...YOU CAN'T STAND TO PART WITH IT...AND NOW YOU'RE WRAPPING IT UP IN PRETTY NEW OUTFITS AND RENTING IT A SMALL HOME TO LIVE IN??
STORE ALL
AND YOU THOUGHT MY GENERATION COULDN'T COMMIT!
TO A HUMAN! THE COMMITMENT WAS SUPPOSED TO BE TO A HUMAN!!

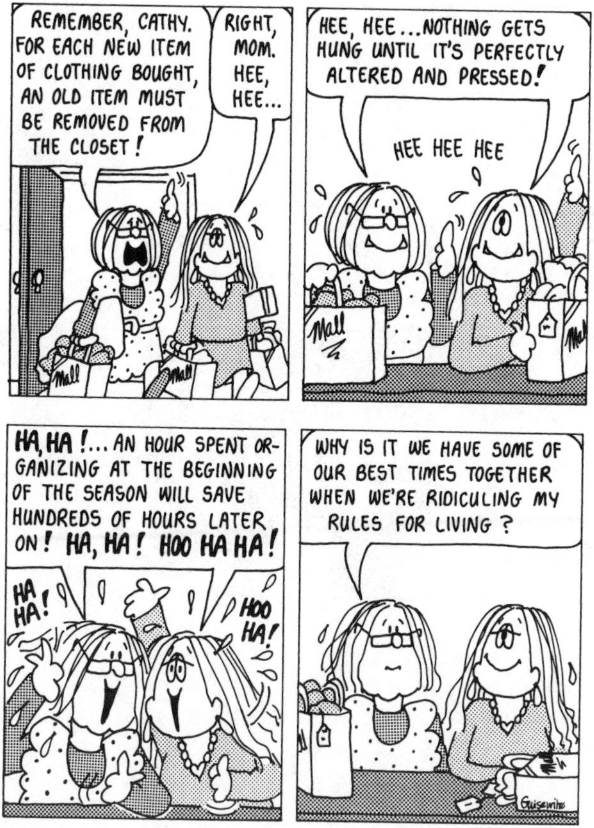
REMEMBER, CATHY. FOR EACH NEW ITEM OF CLOTHING BOUGHT, AN OLD ITEM MUST BE REMOVED FROM THE CLOSET!
RIGHT, MOM. HEE, HEE...
HEE, HEE...NOTHING GETS HUNG UNTIL IT'S PERFECTLY ALTERED AND PRESSED!
HEE HEE HEE
Mall
HA, HA!... AN HOUR SPENT ORGANIZING AT THE BEGINNING OF THE SEASON WILL SAVE HUNDREDS OF HOURS LATER ON! HA, HA! HOO HA HA!
HA HA!
HOO HA!
WHY IS IT WE HAVE SOME OF OUR BEST TIMES TOGETHER WHEN WE'RE RIDICULING MY RULES FOR LIVING?
Guisewite

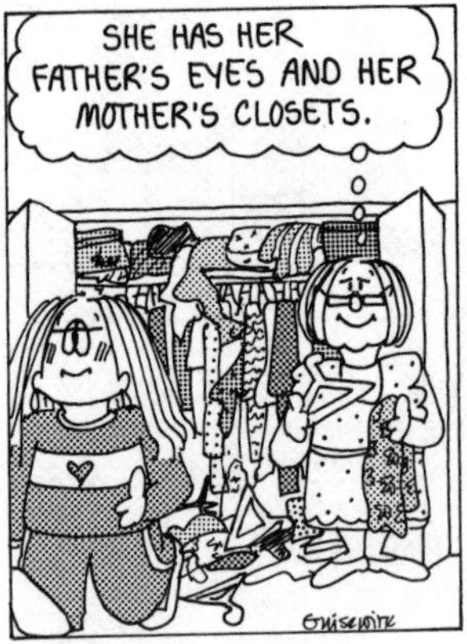
SHE HAS HER FATHER'S EYES AND HER MOTHER'S CLOSETS.
Guisewite

The Body Double

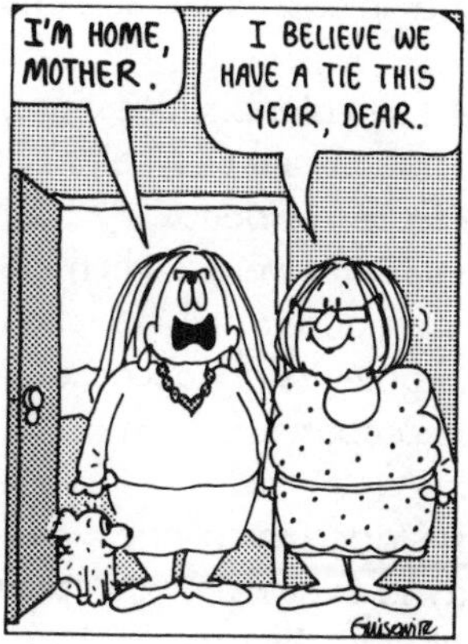
I'M HOME, MOTHER.
I BELIEVE WE HAVE A TIE THIS YEAR, DEAR.

In a last, grand gasp of belligerence, I still want to eat the exact opposite of whatever Mom tells me to.

Mom suggests a "nice salad." I order a grilled ham and cheese sandwich.

Mom suggests a "nice cup of soup." I order fried chicken and fries.

Mom offers a "nice fruit plate." I heat up a plate of lasagna.

I ignore her low-calorie suggestions, reject her healthy dishes, stuff myself with self-righteousness, and then blame her for every ounce.

Lots of people gain weight when they go home for the holidays because of all the fattening food their mothers cook. I gain weight because of all the steamed vegetables mine prepares.

For me, this started in college, where I discovered the quickest way to express my independence was to eat all the things Mom told me not to.

By the end of college, I had "matured" 45 pounds, from a dependent size 5 to a really, really independent size 14. The important thing being, of course, that I had shown Mom what I could accomplish on my own.

Many years have passed, we've both grown and changed, and Mom and I can now sit down at a table together and behave quite differently:

Mom suggests pie à la mode. I order a small glass of mineral water.

Mom orders a chicken salad-stuffed croissant. I ask for clear broth.

Mom dives into the holiday turkey and stuffing. I announce that I'm a vegetarian, peel a carrot, and roll my eyes.

This is "sacrificial weight gain" for Mom. Now, when she sees I've put on too much "defiance weight," she simply reverses her dinner order.

Because she knows I feel obliged to do the opposite of what she says and/or does, she will force me into a low-cal meal when she thinks I need it by having a great big spaghetti and meatball platter for herself.

This is just one of the ways that Mom—by maternal remote control—is still governing every bite of food I eat and which size jeans I fit into on any given week.

I'M SURE YOUR STOMACH WANTS MORE PIE, BUT WHAT IS YOUR BRAIN TELLING YOU, CATHY?
MY BRAIN WANTS THE PIE, TOO.
WHAT IS YOUR COMMON SENSE TELLING YOU?
MY COMMON SENSE WANTS THE PIE.
WHAT IS YOUR HEART TELLING YOU?
MY HEART WANTS PIE.

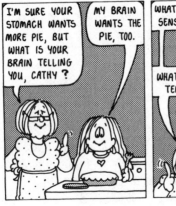

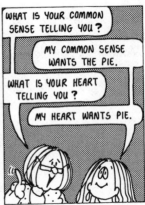

FINE. EAT THE PIE! YOU'RE A GROWN WOMAN! YOU KNOW WHAT YOU'RE DOING! EAT THE WHOLE PIE!
MOTHER MADE ME EAT A PIE.
Guisewite

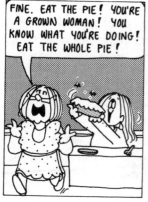

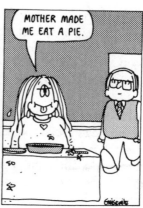

It's amazing that anyone in our house ever gained weight since all the fattening food was always frozen solid.

Anytime anything good came through the door—cookies, cake, pie, strudel, coffee cake, candy, turnovers, sweet rolls—Mom would whip out the Reynolds Wrap, mummify the goodies, and bury them in the freezer so "we wouldn't be tempted."

Because of Mom, I not only learned to eat doughnuts that were frozen solid, but to prefer them that way. Most people ask to have their cinnamon rolls warmed up a little to remind them of the warm, cozy feeling of being in Mom's kitchen. I ask the waitress to pop mine in the freezer for a few minutes.

Because of Mom, I still sometimes have one-woman dinner parties featuring a Sara Lee cake that was lovingly "bought for company" and then frozen like a 4,000 calorie rock.

Food fills so many functions in our family, so few having anything to do with actual hunger.

Food as Truce:

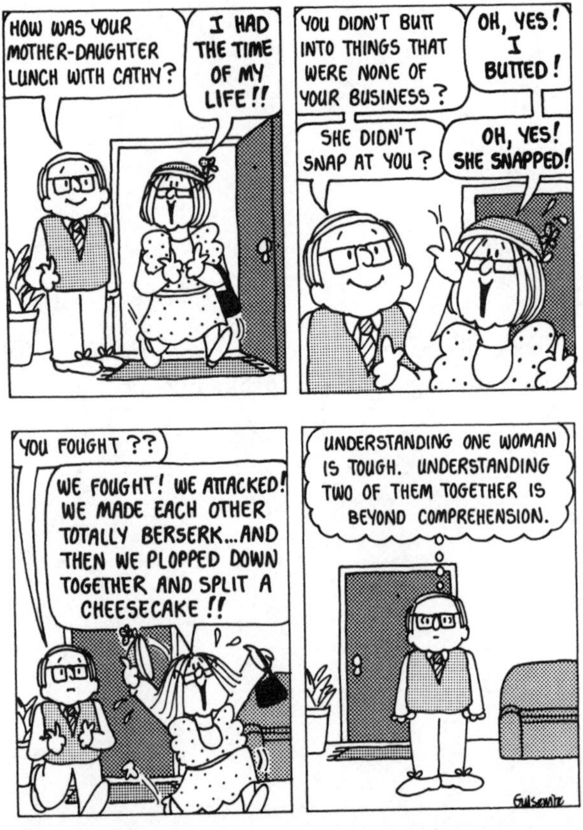
HOW WAS YOUR MOTHER-DAUGHTER LUNCH WITH CATHY?
I HAD THE TIME OF MY LIFE!!
YOU DIDN'T BUTT INTO THINGS THAT WERE NONE OF YOUR BUSINESS?
OH, YES! I BUTTED!
SHE DIDN'T SNAP AT YOU?
OH, YES! SHE SNAPPED!
YOU FOUGHT??
WE FOUGHT! WE ATTACKED! WE MADE EACH OTHER TOTALLY BERSERK...AND THEN WE PLOPPED DOWN TOGETHER AND SPLIT A CHEESECAKE!!
UNDERSTANDING ONE WOMAN IS TOUGH. UNDERSTANDING TWO OF THEM TOGETHER IS BEYOND COMPREHENSION.
GUISEWITE

Food as Memory Maker:

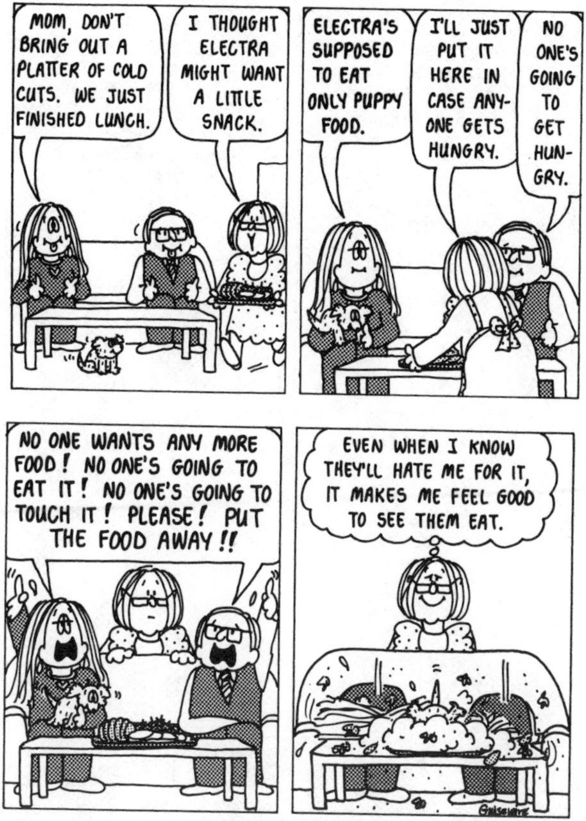
MOM, DON'T BRING OUT A PLATTER OF COLD CUTS. WE JUST FINISHED LUNCH.
I THOUGHT ELECTRA MIGHT WANT A LITTLE SNACK.
ELECTRA'S SUPPOSED TO EAT ONLY PUPPY FOOD.
I'LL JUST PUT IT HERE IN CASE ANY-ONE GETS HUNGRY.
NO ONE'S GOING TO GET HUN-GRY.
NO ONE WANTS ANY MORE FOOD! NO ONE'S GOING TO EAT IT! NO ONE'S GOING TO TOUCH IT! PLEASE! PUT THE FOOD AWAY!!
EVEN WHEN I KNOW THEY'LL HATE ME FOR IT, IT MAKES ME FEEL GOOD TO SEE THEM EAT.

Food as Motivator:

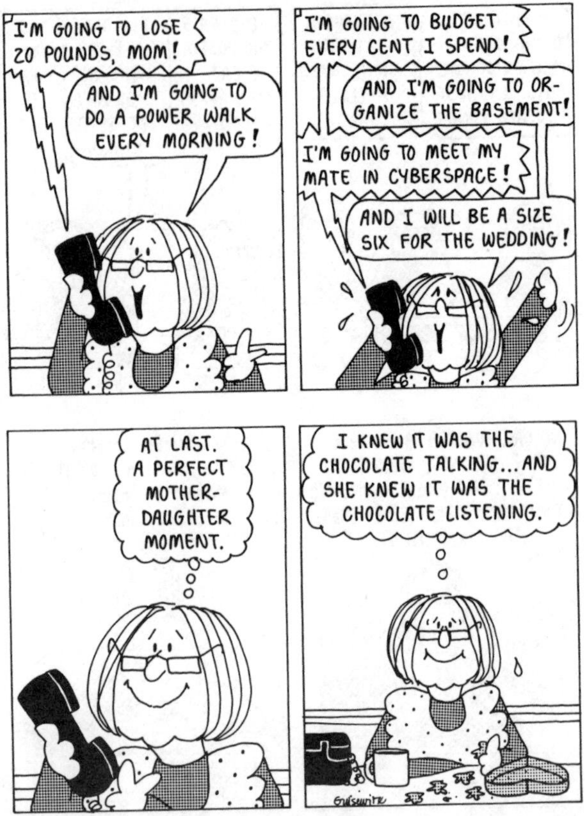
I'M GOING TO LOSE 20 POUNDS, MOM!
AND I'M GOING TO DO A POWER WALK EVERY MORNING!
I'M GOING TO BUDGET EVERY CENT I SPEND!
AND I'M GOING TO ORGANIZE THE BASEMENT!
I'M GOING TO MEET MY MATE IN CYBERSPACE!
AND I WILL BE A SIZE SIX FOR THE WEDDING!
AT LAST. A PERFECT MOTHER-DAUGHTER MOMENT.
I KNEW IT WAS THE CHOCOLATE TALKING... AND SHE KNEW IT WAS THE CHOCOLATE LISTENING.
Guisewite

Food as Backseat Driver:

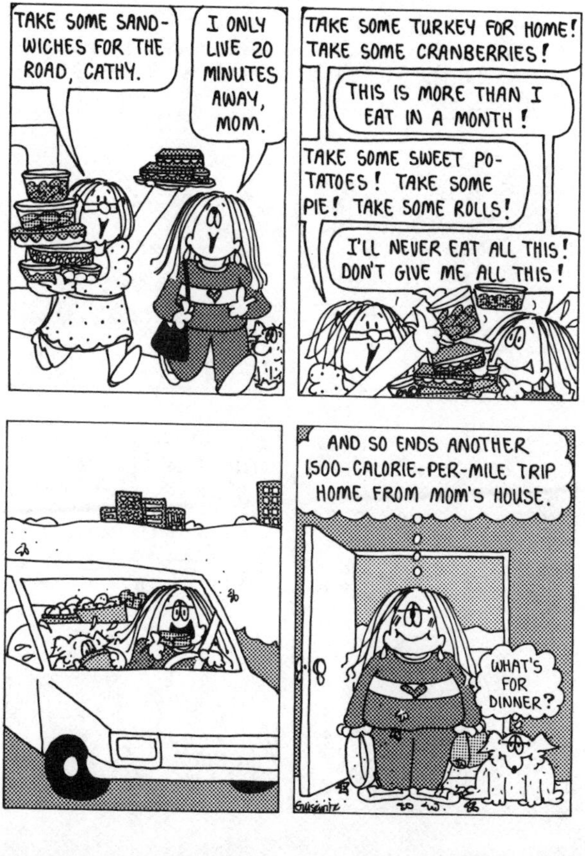
TAKE SOME SAND-WICHES FOR THE ROAD, CATHY.
I ONLY LIVE 20 MINUTES AWAY, MOM.
TAKE SOME TURKEY FOR HOME! TAKE SOME CRANBERRIES!
THIS IS MORE THAN I EAT IN A MONTH!
TAKE SOME SWEET PO-TATOES! TAKE SOME PIE! TAKE SOME ROLLS!
I'LL NEVER EAT ALL THIS! DON'T GIVE ME ALL THIS!
AND SO ENDS ANOTHER 1,500-CALORIE-PER-MILE TRIP HOME FROM MOM'S HOUSE.
WHAT'S FOR DINNER?

Food as Higher Education:

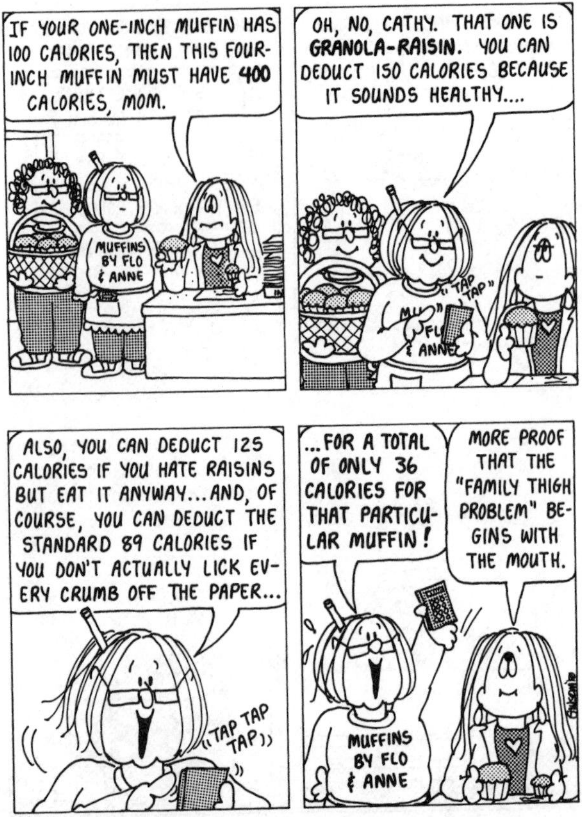
IF YOUR ONE-INCH MUFFIN HAS 100 CALORIES, THEN THIS FOUR-INCH MUFFIN MUST HAVE 400 CALORIES, MOM.
MUFFINS BY FLO & ANNE
OH, NO, CATHY. THAT ONE IS GRANOLA-RAISIN. YOU CAN DEDUCT 150 CALORIES BECAUSE IT SOUNDS HEALTHY....
"TAP TAP"
ALSO, YOU CAN DEDUCT 125 CALORIES IF YOU HATE RAISINS BUT EAT IT ANYWAY... AND, OF COURSE, YOU CAN DEDUCT THE STANDARD 89 CALORIES IF YOU DON'T ACTUALLY LICK EVERY CRUMB OFF THE PAPER...
"TAP TAP TAP"
...FOR A TOTAL OF ONLY 36 CALORIES FOR THAT PARTICULAR MUFFIN!
MORE PROOF THAT THE "FAMILY THIGH PROBLEM" BEGINS WITH THE MOUTH.
MUFFINS BY FLO & ANNE

Food as Therapist:

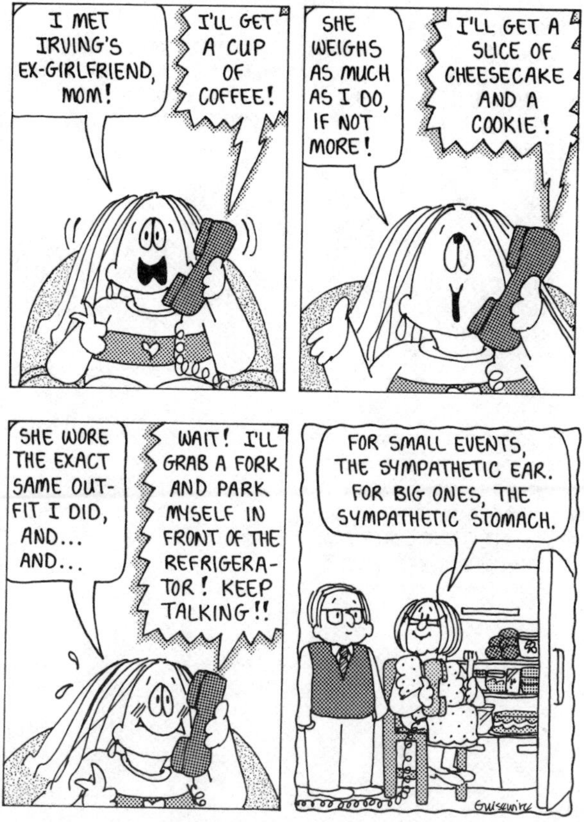
I MET IRVING'S EX-GIRLFRIEND, MOM!
I'LL GET A CUP OF COFFEE!
SHE WEIGHS AS MUCH AS I DO, IF NOT MORE!
I'LL GET A SLICE OF CHEESECAKE AND A COOKIE!
SHE WORE THE EXACT SAME OUT-FIT I DID, AND... AND...
WAIT! I'LL GRAB A FORK AND PARK MYSELF IN FRONT OF THE REFRIGERA-TOR! KEEP TALKING!!
FOR SMALL EVENTS, THE SYMPATHETIC EAR. FOR BIG ONES, THE SYMPATHETIC STOMACH.
Guisewite

Food as Entertainment:

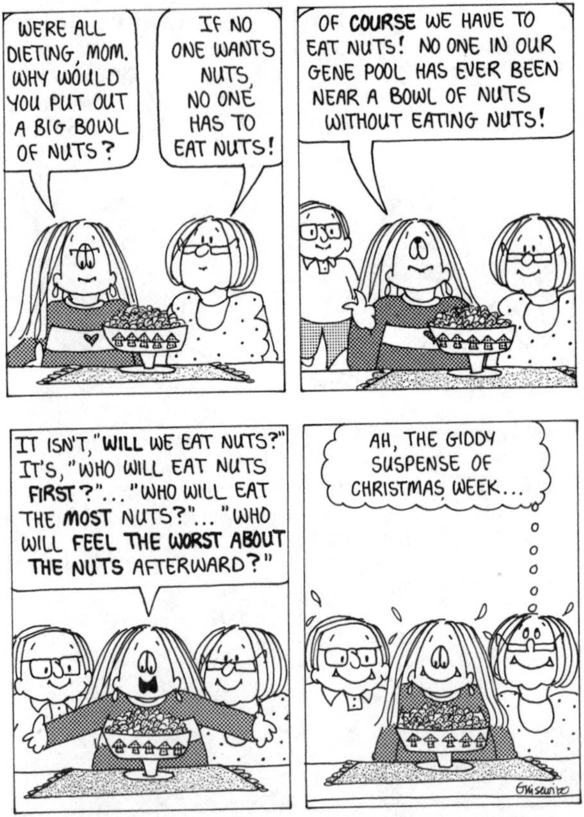
WE'RE ALL DIETING, MOM. WHY WOULD YOU PUT OUT A BIG BOWL OF NUTS?
IF NO ONE WANTS NUTS, NO ONE HAS TO EAT NUTS!
OF COURSE WE HAVE TO EAT NUTS! NO ONE IN OUR GENE POOL HAS EVER BEEN NEAR A BOWL OF NUTS WITHOUT EATING NUTS!
IT ISN'T, "WILL WE EAT NUTS?" IT'S, "WHO WILL EAT NUTS FIRST?"... "WHO WILL EAT THE MOST NUTS?"... "WHO WILL FEEL THE WORST ABOUT THE NUTS AFTERWARD?"
AH, THE GIDDY SUSPENSE OF CHRISTMAS WEEK...
Guisewite

Food as Day Planner:

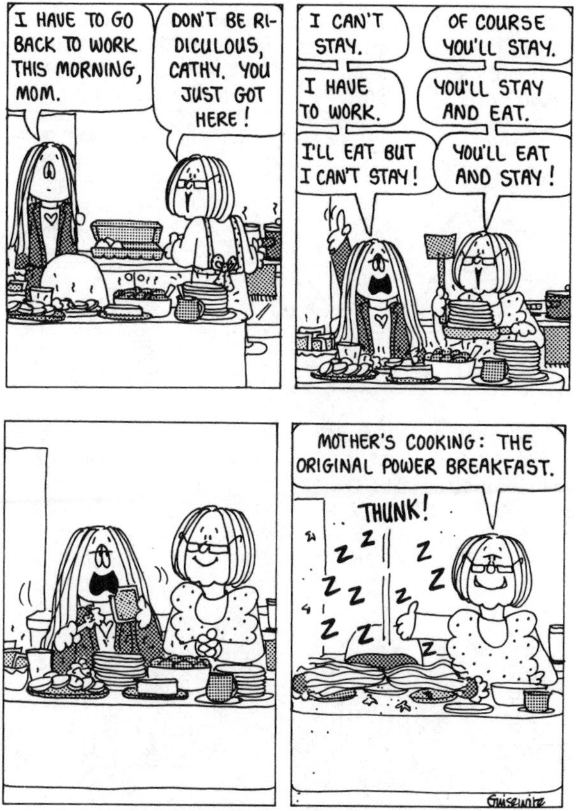
I HAVE TO GO BACK TO WORK THIS MORNING, MOM.
DON'T BE RIDICULOUS, CATHY. YOU JUST GOT HERE!
I CAN'T STAY.
OF COURSE YOU'LL STAY.
I HAVE TO WORK.
YOU'LL STAY AND EAT.
I'LL EAT BUT I CAN'T STAY!
YOU'LL EAT AND STAY!
MOTHER'S COOKING: THE ORIGINAL POWER BREAKFAST.
THUNK!
Guisewite

Food as Guilt:

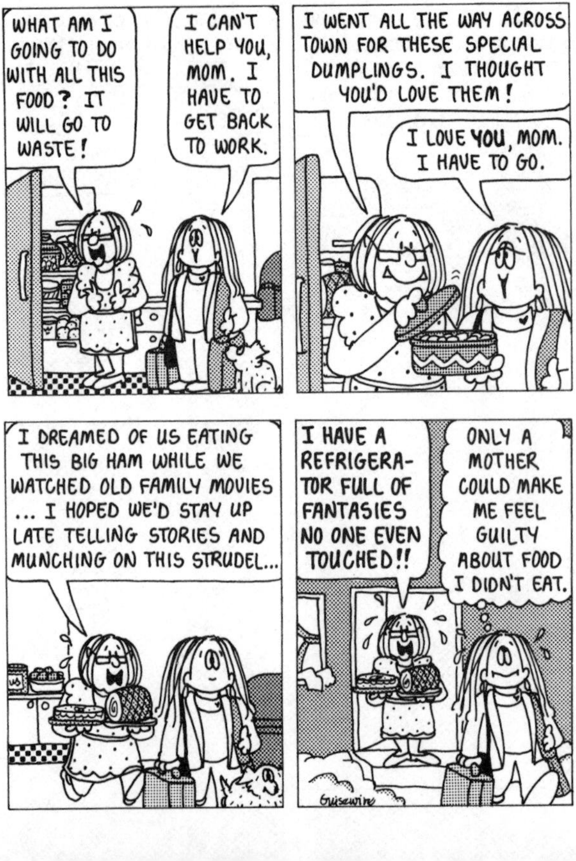
WHAT AM I GOING TO DO WITH ALL THIS FOOD? IT WILL GO TO WASTE!
I CAN'T HELP YOU, MOM. I HAVE TO GET BACK TO WORK.
I WENT ALL THE WAY ACROSS TOWN FOR THESE SPECIAL DUMPLINGS. I THOUGHT YOU'D LOVE THEM!
I LOVE **YOU**, MOM. I HAVE TO GO.
I DREAMED OF US EATING THIS BIG HAM WHILE WE WATCHED OLD FAMILY MOVIES ... I HOPED WE'D STAY UP LATE TELLING STORIES AND MUNCHING ON THIS STRUDEL...
I HAVE A REFRIGERATOR FULL OF FANTASIES NO ONE EVEN TOUCHED!!
ONLY A MOTHER COULD MAKE ME FEEL GUILTY ABOUT FOOD I DIDN'T EAT.
Guisewite

Food as Travel Companion:

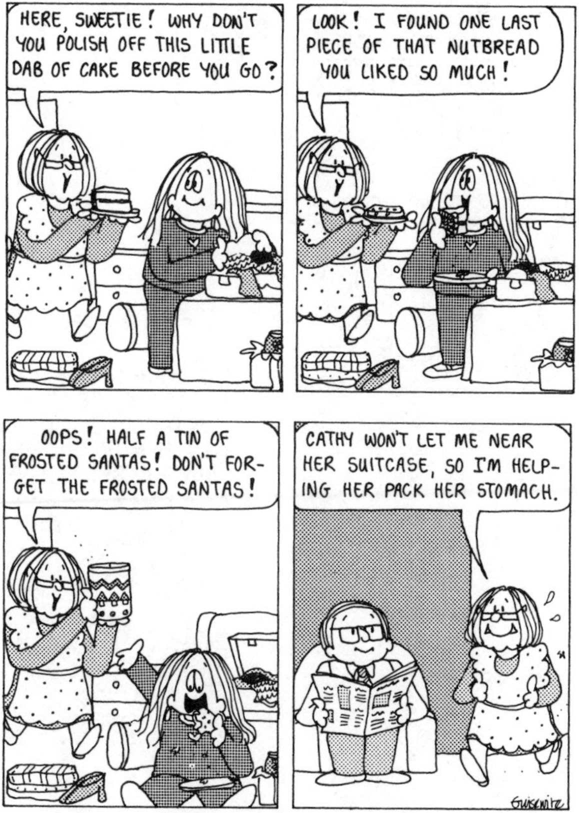
HERE, SWEETIE! WHY DON'T YOU POLISH OFF THIS LITTLE DAB OF CAKE BEFORE YOU GO?
LOOK! I FOUND ONE LAST PIECE OF THAT NUTBREAD YOU LIKED SO MUCH!
OOPS! HALF A TIN OF FROSTED SANTAS! DON'T FOR-GET THE FROSTED SANTAS!
CATHY WON'T LET ME NEAR HER SUITCASE, SO I'M HELP-ING HER PACK HER STOMACH.
Guisewite

Food as Late-Night Workout:

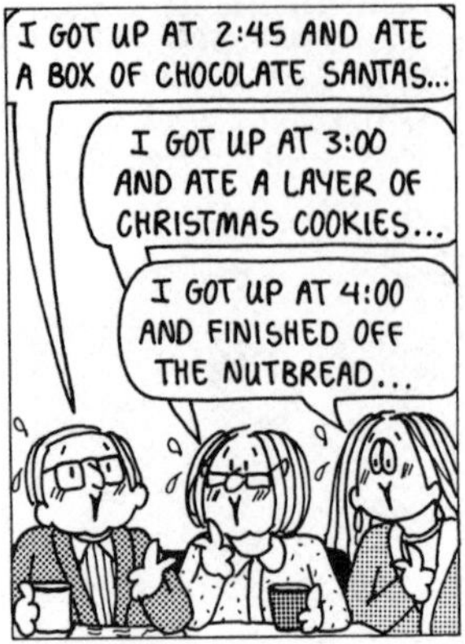

I GOT UP AT 2:45 AND ATE A BOX OF CHOCOLATE SANTAS...
I GOT UP AT 3:00 AND ATE A LAYER OF CHRISTMAS COOKIES...
I GOT UP AT 4:00 AND FINISHED OFF THE NUTBREAD...

Food as Sacrifice:

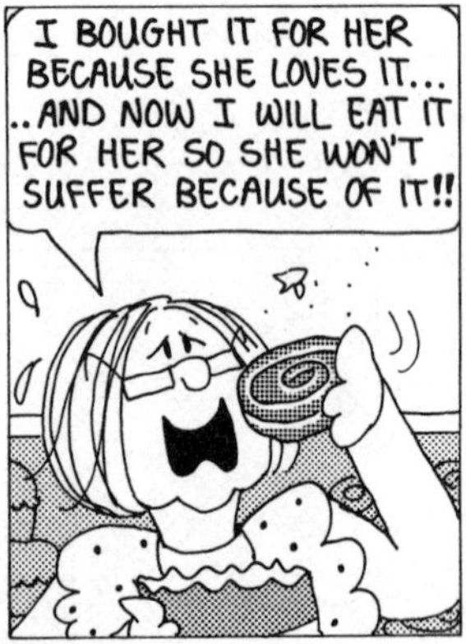

I BOUGHT IT FOR HER BECAUSE SHE LOVES IT... ..AND NOW I WILL EAT IT FOR HER SO SHE WON'T SUFFER BECAUSE OF IT!!

Food as Conversation Tool:

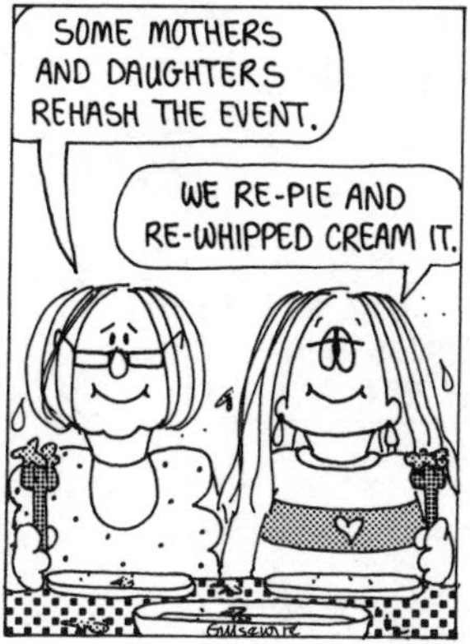

SOME MOTHERS AND DAUGHTERS REHASH THE EVENT.
WE RE-PIE AND RE-WHIPPED CREAM IT.

Food as Protection:

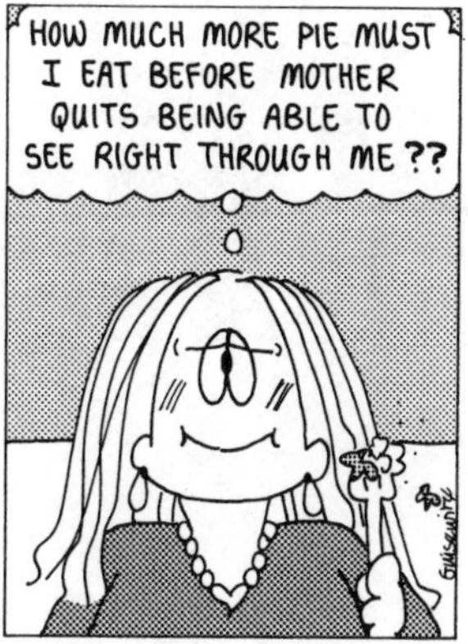

HOW MUCH MORE PIE MUST I EAT BEFORE MOTHER QUITS BEING ABLE TO SEE RIGHT THROUGH ME??

Food as I-Gave-Birth-Right:

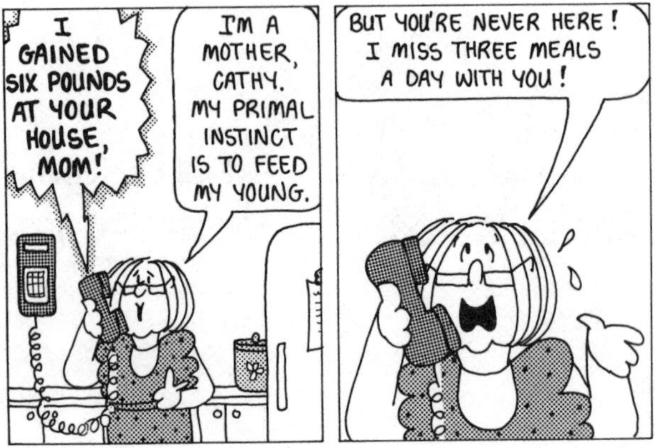
I GAINED SIX POUNDS AT YOUR HOUSE, MOM!
I'M A MOTHER, CATHY. MY PRIMAL INSTINCT IS TO FEED MY YOUNG.
BUT YOU'RE NEVER HERE! I MISS THREE MEALS A DAY WITH YOU!

ANY TIME I HAVE YOU BACK IN MY NEST, I'M GOING TO SPEND EVERY SECOND I CAN POPPING FOOD IN YOUR MOUTH, LIKE A MAMA BIRD REUNITED WITH HER HATCHLING!
MOM...
IF YOU SPREAD LAST WEEKEND'S FOOD OUT OVER THE LAST TWELVE MONTHS, IT WOULD HAVE ONLY BEEN ABOUT SIX CALORIES A FEEDING.
Guisewite

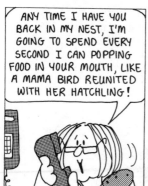

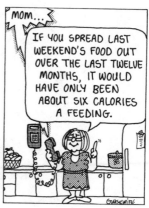

WHAT COINCIDENCE THAT THE UMBILICAL CORD IS LOCATED SO CLOSE TO THE STOMACH.
ICE CREAM
GUISEWITE

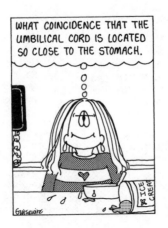

The Spark

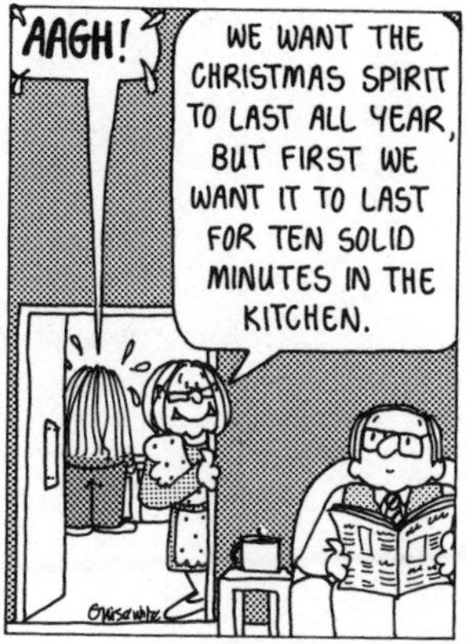
AAGH!
WE WANT THE CHRISTMAS SPIRIT TO LAST ALL YEAR, BUT FIRST WE WANT IT TO LAST FOR TEN SOLID MINUTES IN THE KITCHEN.

Mom can make me crazy faster than any human on earth.

Mom can make me crazy with a look.

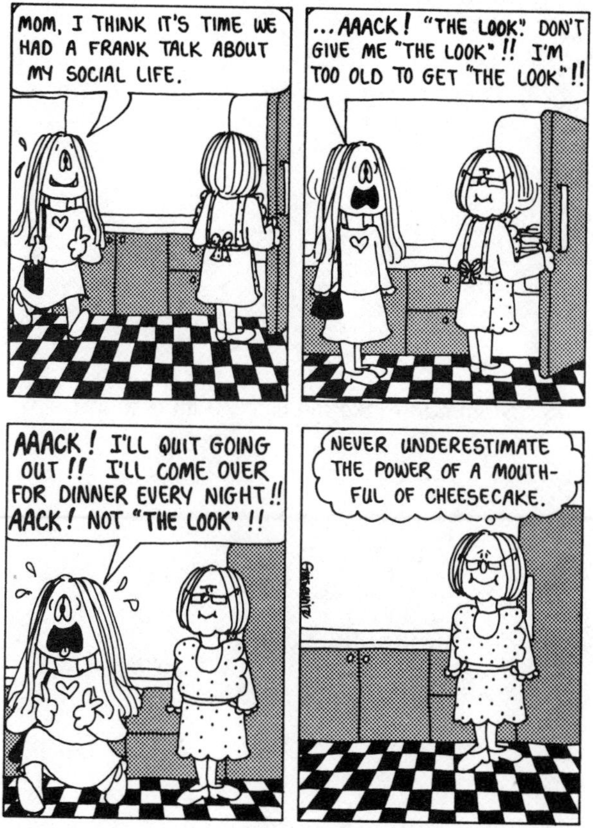
MOM, I THINK IT'S TIME WE HAD A FRANK TALK ABOUT MY SOCIAL LIFE.
...AAACK! "THE LOOK." DON'T GIVE ME "THE LOOK"!! I'M TOO OLD TO GET "THE LOOK"!!
AAACK! I'LL QUIT GOING OUT!! I'LL COME OVER FOR DINNER EVERY NIGHT!! AACK! NOT "THE LOOK"!!
NEVER UNDERESTIMATE THE POWER OF A MOUTH-FUL OF CHEESECAKE.

Mom can make me crazy with a sound.

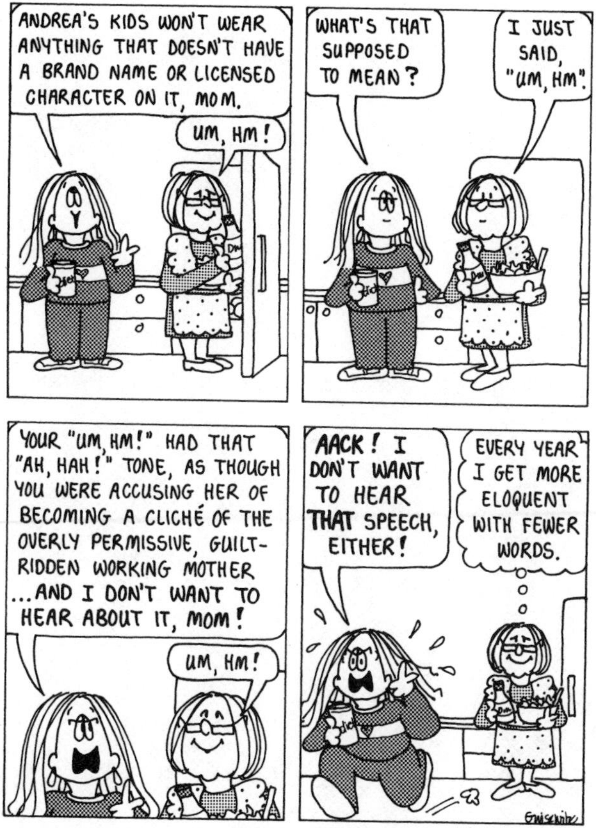
ANDREA'S KIDS WON'T WEAR ANYTHING THAT DOESN'T HAVE A BRAND NAME OR LICENSED CHARACTER ON IT, MOM.
UM, HM!
WHAT'S THAT SUPPOSED TO MEAN?
I JUST SAID, "UM, HM".
YOUR "UM, HM!" HAD THAT "AH, HAH!" TONE, AS THOUGH YOU WERE ACCUSING HER OF BECOMING A CLICHÉ OF THE OVERLY PERMISSIVE, GUILT-RIDDEN WORKING MOTHER ...AND I DON'T WANT TO HEAR ABOUT IT, MOM!
UM, HM!
AACK! I DON'T WANT TO HEAR THAT SPEECH, EITHER!
EVERY YEAR I GET MORE ELOQUENT WITH FEWER WORDS.

Mom can make me crazy by doing absolutely nothing.

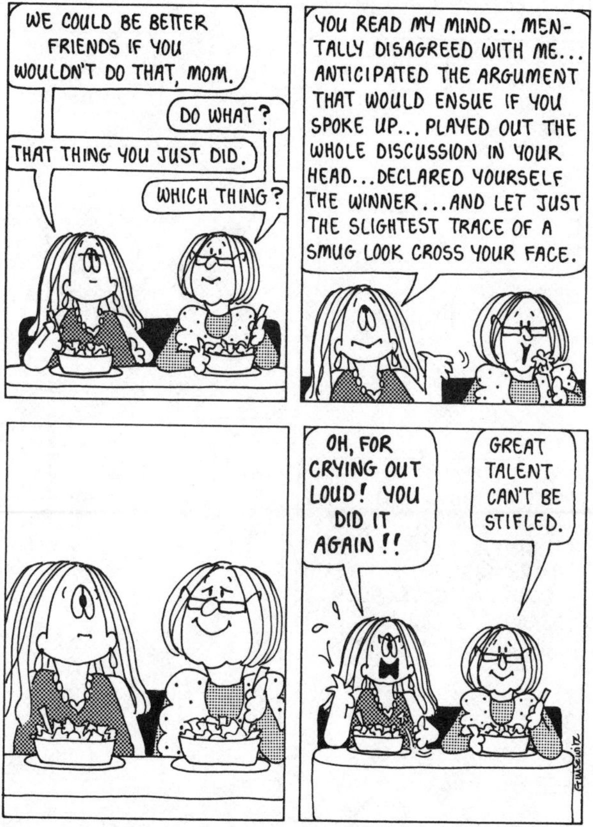
WE COULD BE BETTER FRIENDS IF YOU WOULDN'T DO THAT, MOM.
DO WHAT?
THAT THING YOU JUST DID.
WHICH THING?
YOU READ MY MIND... MENTALLY DISAGREED WITH ME... ANTICIPATED THE ARGUMENT THAT WOULD ENSUE IF YOU SPOKE UP... PLAYED OUT THE WHOLE DISCUSSION IN YOUR HEAD... DECLARED YOURSELF THE WINNER... AND LET JUST THE SLIGHTEST TRACE OF A SMUG LOOK CROSS YOUR FACE.
OH, FOR CRYING OUT LOUD! YOU DID IT AGAIN!!
GREAT TALENT CAN'T BE STIFLED.
GUISEWITE

Mom can encourage me, restore me, center me . . .

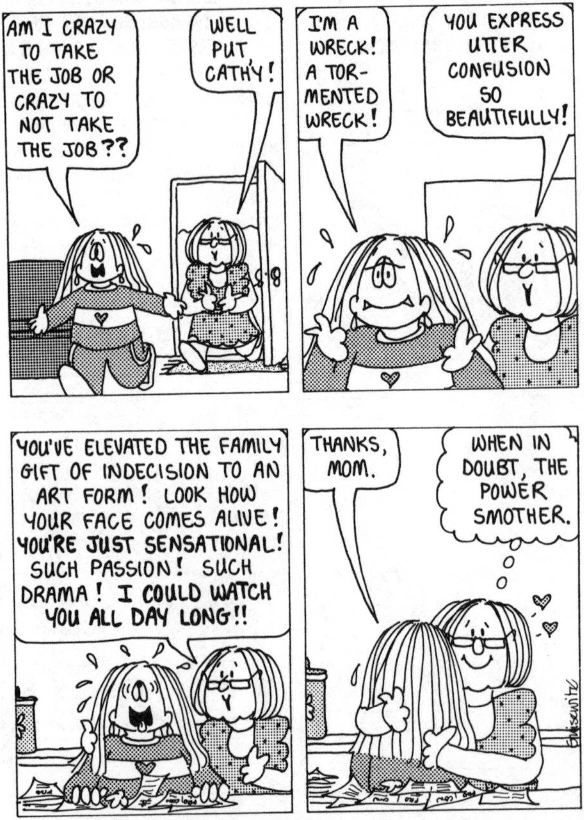
AM I CRAZY TO TAKE THE JOB OR CRAZY TO NOT TAKE THE JOB??
WELL PUT, CATHY!
I'M A WRECK! A TORMENTED WRECK!
YOU EXPRESS UTTER CONFUSION SO BEAUTIFULLY!
YOU'VE ELEVATED THE FAMILY GIFT OF INDECISION TO AN ART FORM! LOOK HOW YOUR FACE COMES ALIVE! YOU'RE JUST SENSATIONAL! SUCH PASSION! SUCH DRAMA! I COULD WATCH YOU ALL DAY LONG!!
THANKS, MOM.
WHEN IN DOUBT, THE POWER SMOTHER.
Guisewite

and then make me crazy by being polite.

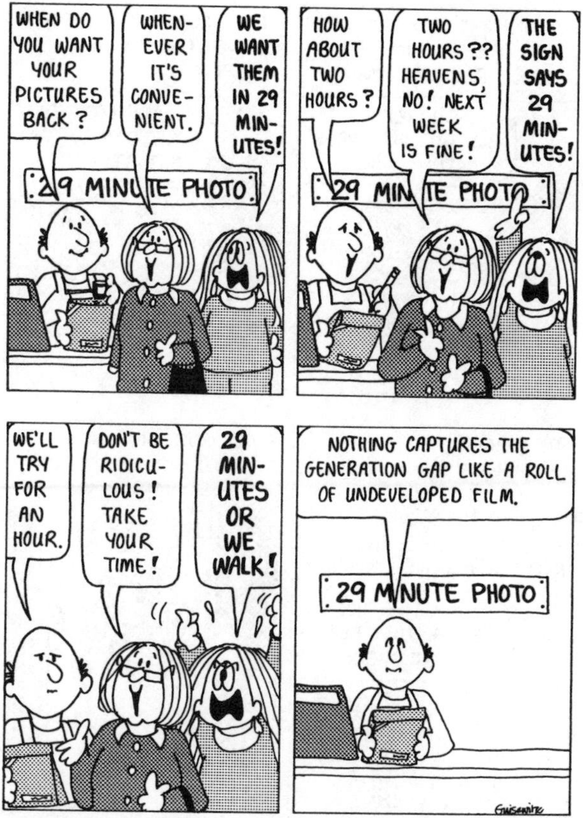
WHEN DO YOU WANT YOUR PICTURES BACK?
WHENEVER IT'S CONVENIENT.
WE WANT THEM IN 29 MINUTES!
29 MINUTE PHOTO
HOW ABOUT TWO HOURS?
TWO HOURS?? HEAVENS, NO! NEXT WEEK IS FINE!
THE SIGN SAYS 29 MINUTES!
29 MINUTE PHOTO
WE'LL TRY FOR AN HOUR.
DON'T BE RIDICULOUS! TAKE YOUR TIME!
29 MINUTES OR WE WALK!
NOTHING CAPTURES THE GENERATION GAP LIKE A ROLL OF UNDEVELOPED FILM.
29 MINUTE PHOTO
Guisewite

Mom can love me unconditionally . . .

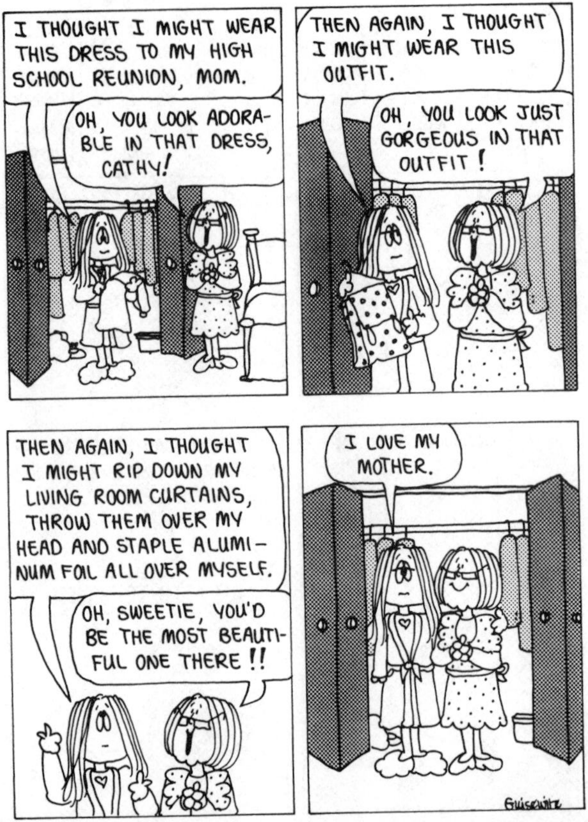
I THOUGHT I MIGHT WEAR THIS DRESS TO MY HIGH SCHOOL REUNION, MOM.
OH, YOU LOOK ADORABLE IN THAT DRESS, CATHY!
THEN AGAIN, I THOUGHT I MIGHT WEAR THIS OUTFIT.
OH, YOU LOOK JUST GORGEOUS IN THAT OUTFIT!
THEN AGAIN, I THOUGHT I MIGHT RIP DOWN MY LIVING ROOM CURTAINS, THROW THEM OVER MY HEAD AND STAPLE ALUMINUM FOIL ALL OVER MYSELF.
OH, SWEETIE, YOU'D BE THE MOST BEAUTIFUL ONE THERE!!
I LOVE MY MOTHER.
Guisewite

and then make me crazy on spec.

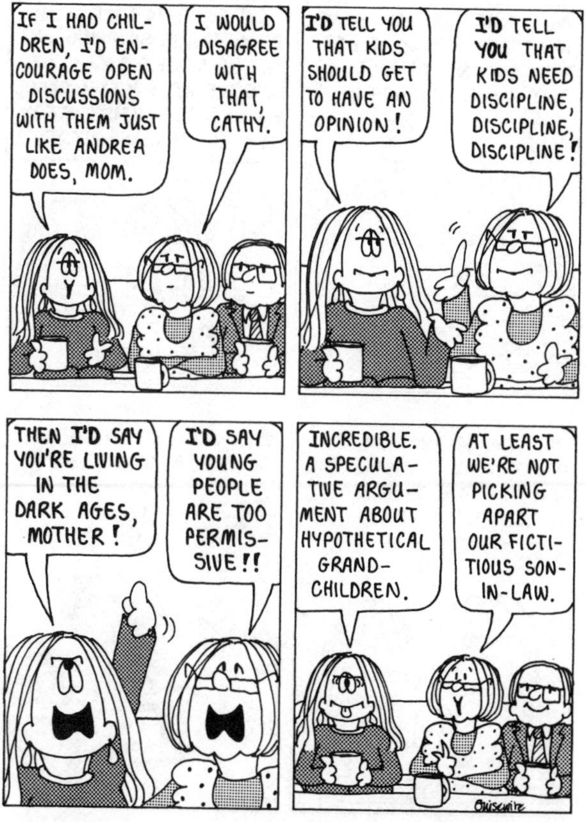
IF I HAD CHILDREN, I'D ENCOURAGE OPEN DISCUSSIONS WITH THEM JUST LIKE ANDREA DOES, MOM.
I WOULD DISAGREE WITH THAT, CATHY.
I'D TELL YOU THAT KIDS SHOULD GET TO HAVE AN OPINION!
I'D TELL YOU THAT KIDS NEED DISCIPLINE, DISCIPLINE, DISCIPLINE!
THEN I'D SAY YOU'RE LIVING IN THE DARK AGES, MOTHER!
I'D SAY YOUNG PEOPLE ARE TOO PERMISSIVE!!
INCREDIBLE. A SPECULATIVE ARGUMENT ABOUT HYPOTHETICAL GRANDCHILDREN.
AT LEAST WE'RE NOT PICKING APART OUR FICTITIOUS SON-IN-LAW.
Guisewite

Mom can propel me into the world . . .

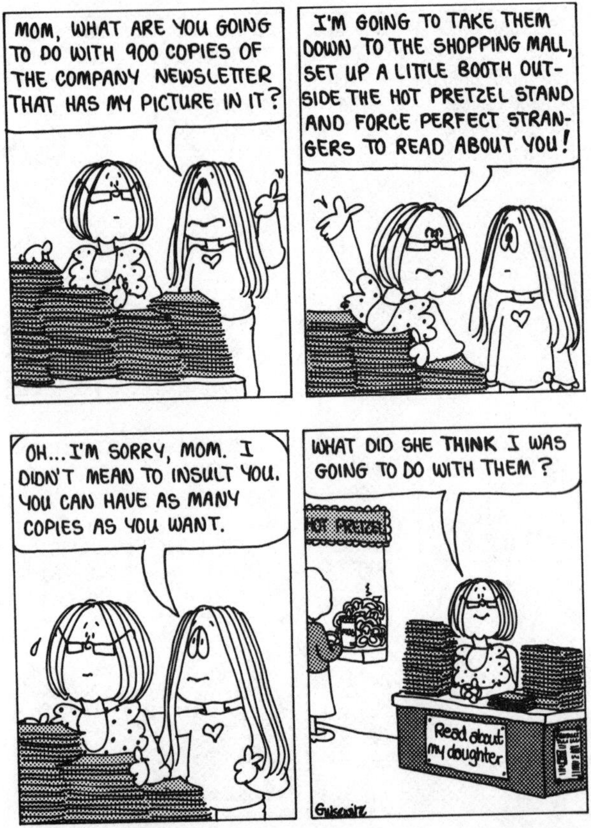

MOM, WHAT ARE YOU GOING TO DO WITH 900 COPIES OF THE COMPANY NEWSLETTER THAT HAS MY PICTURE IN IT?
I'M GOING TO TAKE THEM DOWN TO THE SHOPPING MALL, SET UP A LITTLE BOOTH OUT-SIDE THE HOT PRETZEL STAND AND FORCE PERFECT STRAN-GERS TO READ ABOUT YOU!
OH... I'M SORRY, MOM. I DIDN'T MEAN TO INSULT YOU. YOU CAN HAVE AS MANY COPIES AS YOU WANT.
WHAT DID SHE THINK I WAS GOING TO DO WITH THEM?
Read about my daughter

and then screech me to a halt in produce.

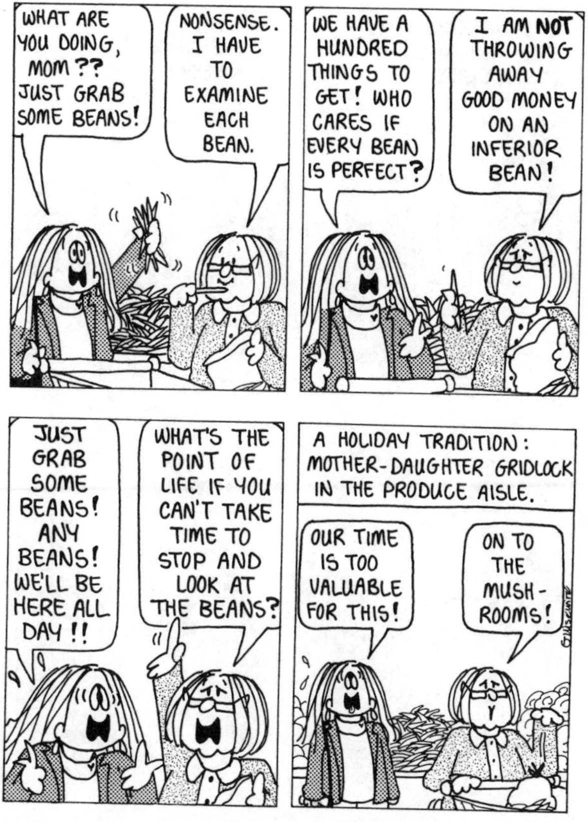
WHAT ARE YOU DOING, MOM?? JUST GRAB SOME BEANS!
NONSENSE. I HAVE TO EXAMINE EACH BEAN.
WE HAVE A HUNDRED THINGS TO GET! WHO CARES IF EVERY BEAN IS PERFECT?
I AM NOT THROWING AWAY GOOD MONEY ON AN INFERIOR BEAN!
JUST GRAB SOME BEANS! ANY BEANS! WE'LL BE HERE ALL DAY!!
WHAT'S THE POINT OF LIFE IF YOU CAN'T TAKE TIME TO STOP AND LOOK AT THE BEANS?
A HOLIDAY TRADITION: MOTHER-DAUGHTER GRIDLOCK IN THE PRODUCE AISLE.
OUR TIME IS TOO VALUABLE FOR THIS!
ON TO THE MUSH-ROOMS!
GUISEWITE

Mom always knows the exact right thing to say . . .

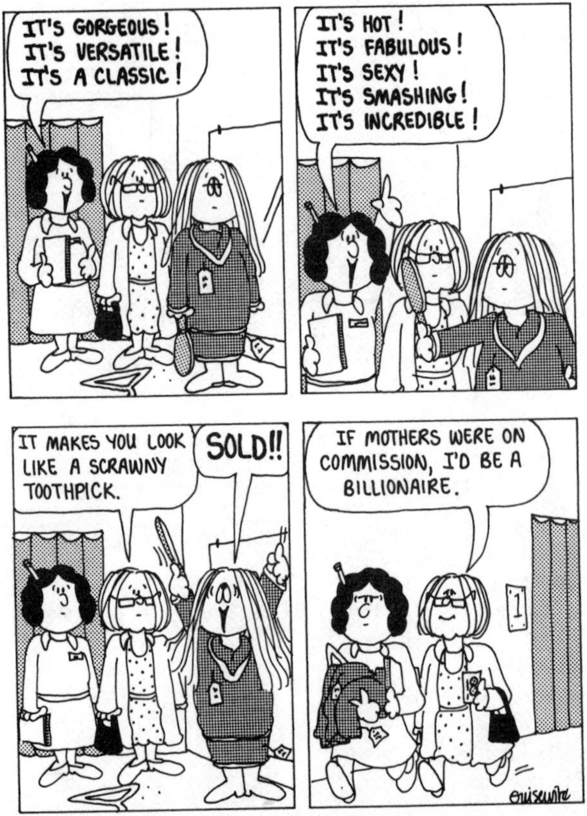

IT'S GORGEOUS! IT'S VERSATILE! IT'S A CLASSIC!
IT'S HOT! IT'S FABULOUS! IT'S SEXY! IT'S SMASHING! IT'S INCREDIBLE!
IT MAKES YOU LOOK LIKE A SCRAWNY TOOTHPICK.
SOLD!!
IF MOTHERS WERE ON COMMISSION, I'D BE A BILLIONAIRE.
1

and the exact wrong thing to say.

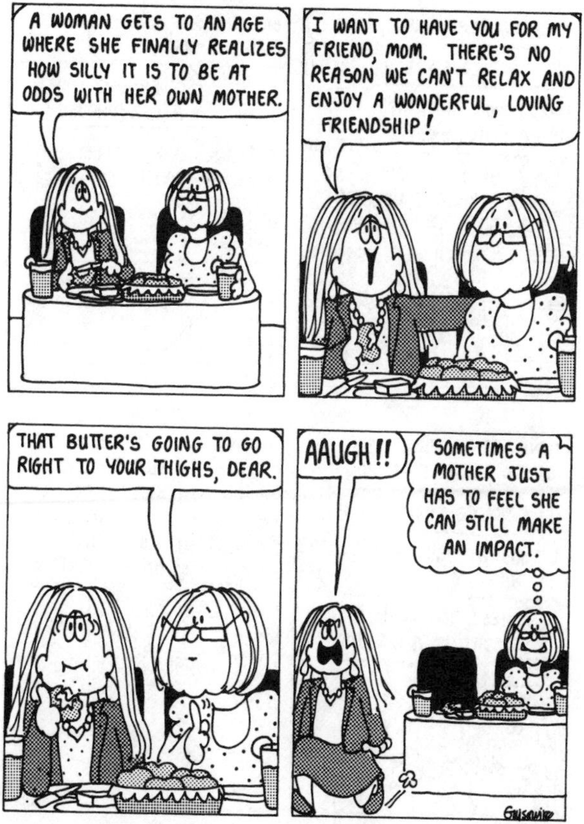
A WOMAN GETS TO AN AGE WHERE SHE FINALLY REALIZES HOW SILLY IT IS TO BE AT ODDS WITH HER OWN MOTHER.
I WANT TO HAVE YOU FOR MY FRIEND, MOM. THERE'S NO REASON WE CAN'T RELAX AND ENJOY A WONDERFUL, LOVING FRIENDSHIP!
THAT BUTTER'S GOING TO GO RIGHT TO YOUR THIGHS, DEAR.
AAUGH!!
SOMETIMES A MOTHER JUST HAS TO FEEL SHE CAN STILL MAKE AN IMPACT.

Mom can make me crazy by agreeing with me.

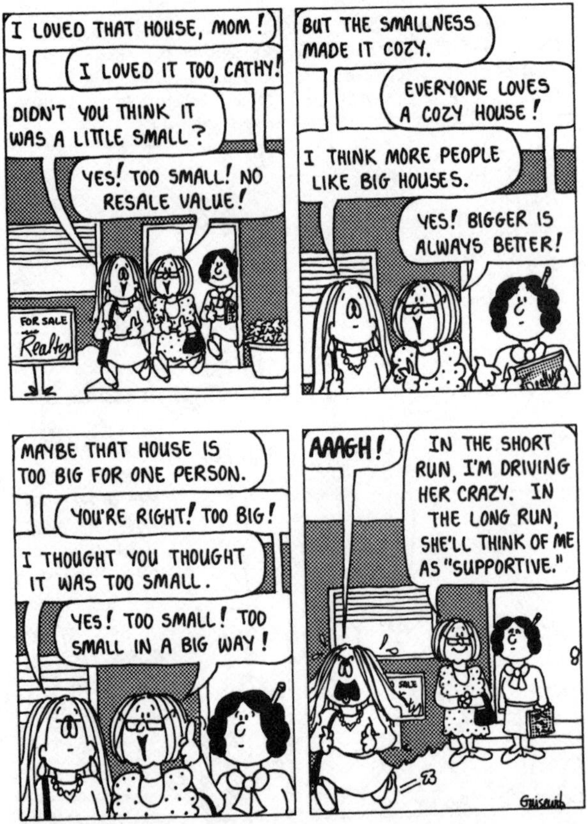
I LOVED THAT HOUSE, MOM!
I LOVED IT TOO, CATHY!
DIDN'T YOU THINK IT WAS A LITTLE SMALL?
YES! TOO SMALL! NO RESALE VALUE!
FOR SALE
Realty
BUT THE SMALLNESS MADE IT COZY.
EVERYONE LOVES A COZY HOUSE!
I THINK MORE PEOPLE LIKE BIG HOUSES.
YES! BIGGER IS ALWAYS BETTER!
MAYBE THAT HOUSE IS TOO BIG FOR ONE PERSON.
YOU'RE RIGHT! TOO BIG!
I THOUGHT YOU THOUGHT IT WAS TOO SMALL.
YES! TOO SMALL! TOO SMALL IN A BIG WAY!
AAAGH!
IN THE SHORT RUN, I'M DRIVING HER CRAZY. IN THE LONG RUN, SHE'LL THINK OF ME AS "SUPPORTIVE."
Guisewite

Mom can make all those around us crazy.

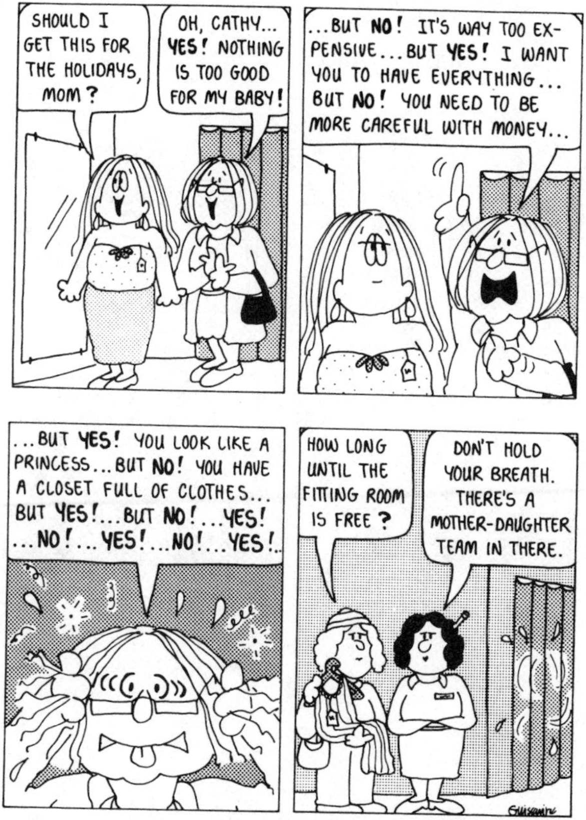
SHOULD I GET THIS FOR THE HOLIDAYS, MOM?
OH, CATHY... YES! NOTHING IS TOO GOOD FOR MY BABY!
...BUT NO! IT'S WAY TOO EXPENSIVE... BUT YES! I WANT YOU TO HAVE EVERYTHING... BUT NO! YOU NEED TO BE MORE CAREFUL WITH MONEY...
...BUT YES! YOU LOOK LIKE A PRINCESS... BUT NO! YOU HAVE A CLOSET FULL OF CLOTHES... BUT YES!... BUT NO!... YES! ...NO!... YES!... NO!... YES!...
HOW LONG UNTIL THE FITTING ROOM IS FREE?
DON'T HOLD YOUR BREATH. THERE'S A MOTHER-DAUGHTER TEAM IN THERE.
GUISEWITE

Mom can completely reconnect me with who I am . . .

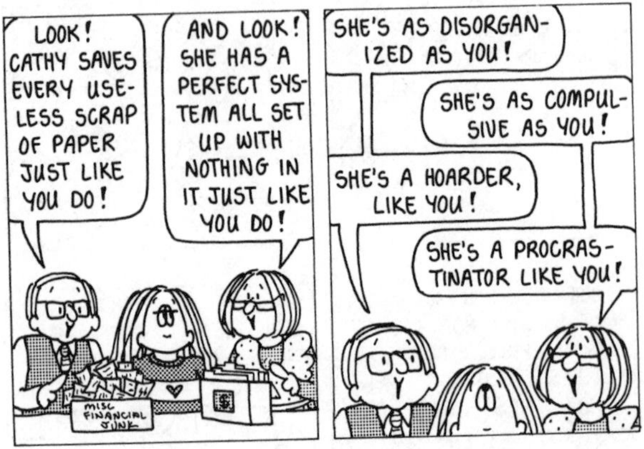
LOOK! CATHY SAVES EVERY USE-LESS SCRAP OF PAPER JUST LIKE YOU DO!
AND LOOK! SHE HAS A PERFECT SYS-TEM ALL SET UP WITH NOTHING IN IT JUST LIKE YOU DO!
MISC FINANCIAL JUNK
SHE'S AS DISORGAN-IZED AS YOU!
SHE'S AS COMPUL-SIVE AS YOU!
SHE'S A HOARDER, LIKE YOU!
SHE'S A PROCRAS-TINATOR LIKE YOU!

and then make me crazy when I see who it is.

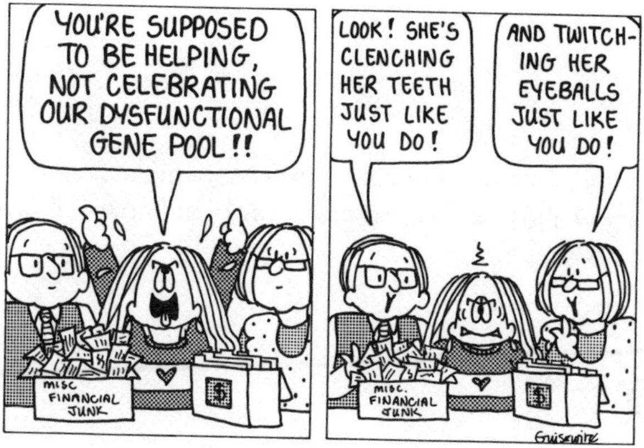
YOU'RE SUPPOSED TO BE HELPING, NOT CELEBRATING OUR DYSFUNCTIONAL GENE POOL!!
MISC FINANCIAL JUNK
LOOK! SHE'S CLENCHING HER TEETH JUST LIKE YOU DO!
AND TWITCHING HER EYEBALLS JUST LIKE YOU DO!
MISC. FINANCIAL JUNK
Guisewite

No matter how many times Mom makes me crazy, I know she'll always be there, and she knows I'll always come back for more.

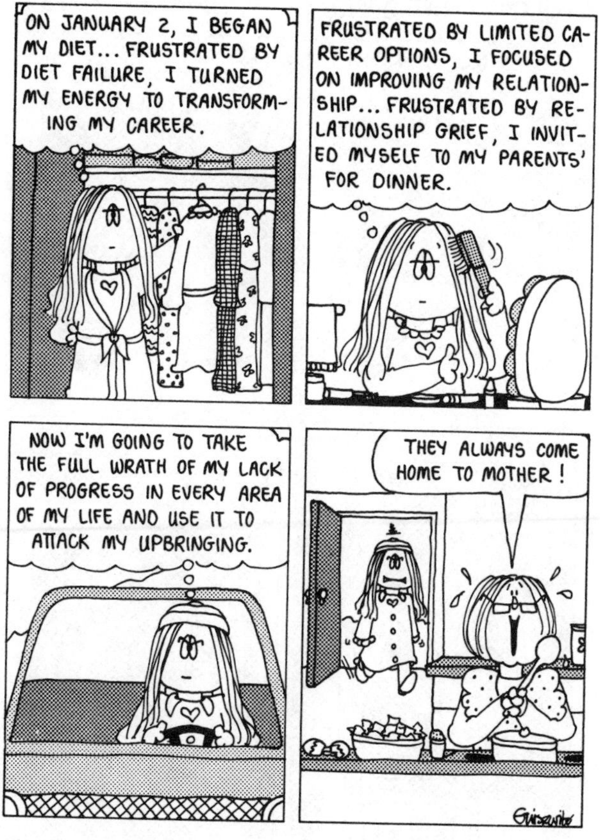
ON JANUARY 2, I BEGAN MY DIET... FRUSTRATED BY DIET FAILURE, I TURNED MY ENERGY TO TRANSFORMING MY CAREER.
FRUSTRATED BY LIMITED CAREER OPTIONS, I FOCUSED ON IMPROVING MY RELATIONSHIP... FRUSTRATED BY RELATIONSHIP GRIEF, I INVITED MYSELF TO MY PARENTS' FOR DINNER.
NOW I'M GOING TO TAKE THE FULL WRATH OF MY LACK OF PROGRESS IN EVERY AREA OF MY LIFE AND USE IT TO ATTACK MY UPBRINGING.
THEY ALWAYS COME HOME TO MOTHER!
Guisewite

Mom and I were going back and forth in 1978 . . .

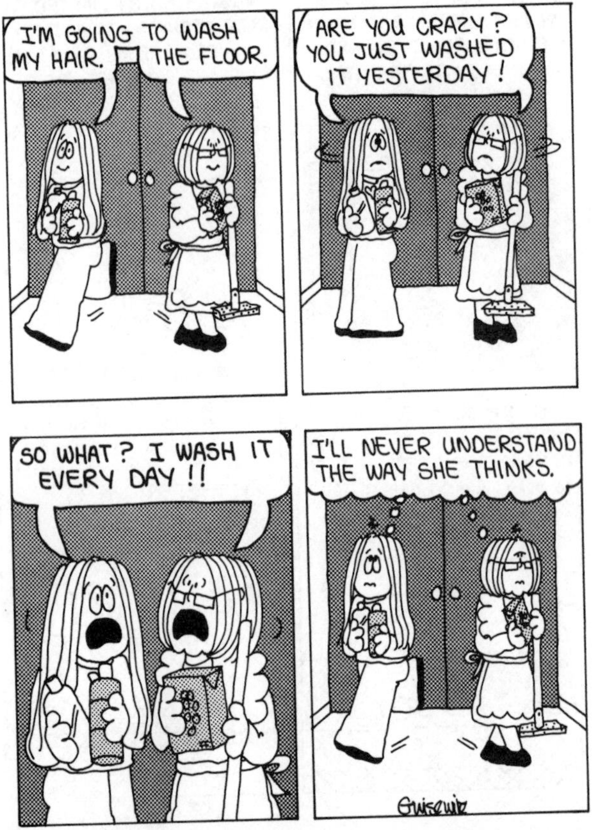
I'M GOING TO WASH MY HAIR.
THE FLOOR.
ARE YOU CRAZY? YOU JUST WASHED IT YESTERDAY!
SO WHAT? I WASH IT EVERY DAY!!
I'LL NEVER UNDERSTAND THE WAY SHE THINKS.
Guisewite

back and forth in 1984 . . .

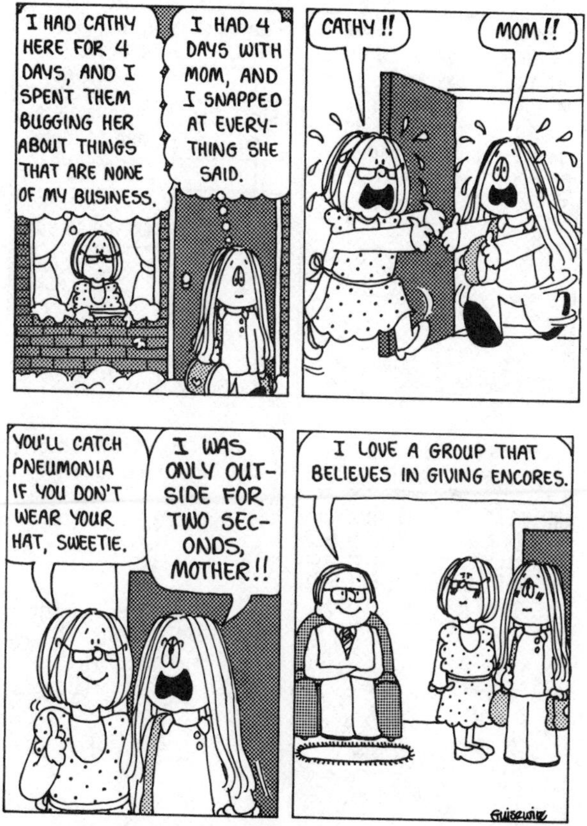
I HAD CATHY HERE FOR 4 DAYS, AND I SPENT THEM BUGGING HER ABOUT THINGS THAT ARE NONE OF MY BUSINESS.
I HAD 4 DAYS WITH MOM, AND I SNAPPED AT EVERY-THING SHE SAID.
CATHY !!
MOM !!
YOU'LL CATCH PNEUMONIA IF YOU DON'T WEAR YOUR HAT, SWEETIE.
I WAS ONLY OUT-SIDE FOR TWO SEC-ONDS, MOTHER!!
I LOVE A GROUP THAT BELIEVES IN GIVING ENCORES.
GUISEWITE

back and forth in 1987 . . .

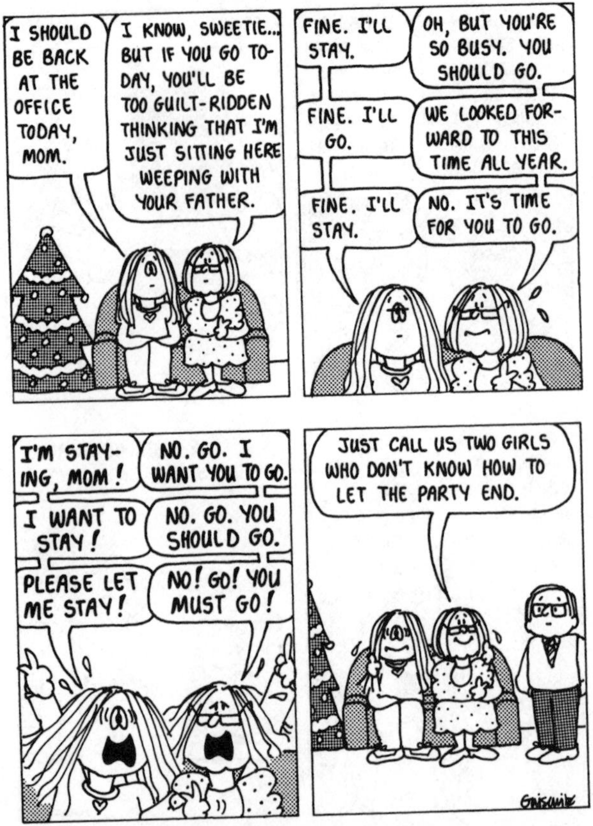
I SHOULD BE BACK AT THE OFFICE TODAY, MOM.
I KNOW, SWEETIE... BUT IF YOU GO TODAY, YOU'LL BE TOO GUILT-RIDDEN THINKING THAT I'M JUST SITTING HERE WEEPING WITH YOUR FATHER.
FINE. I'LL STAY.
OH, BUT YOU'RE SO BUSY. YOU SHOULD GO.
FINE. I'LL GO.
WE LOOKED FORWARD TO THIS TIME ALL YEAR.
FINE. I'LL STAY.
NO. IT'S TIME FOR YOU TO GO.
I'M STAYING, MOM!
NO. GO. I WANT YOU TO GO.
I WANT TO STAY!
NO. GO. YOU SHOULD GO.
PLEASE LET ME STAY!
NO! GO! YOU MUST GO!
JUST CALL US TWO GIRLS WHO DON'T KNOW HOW TO LET THE PARTY END.
GUISEWITE

back and forth in 1989 . . .

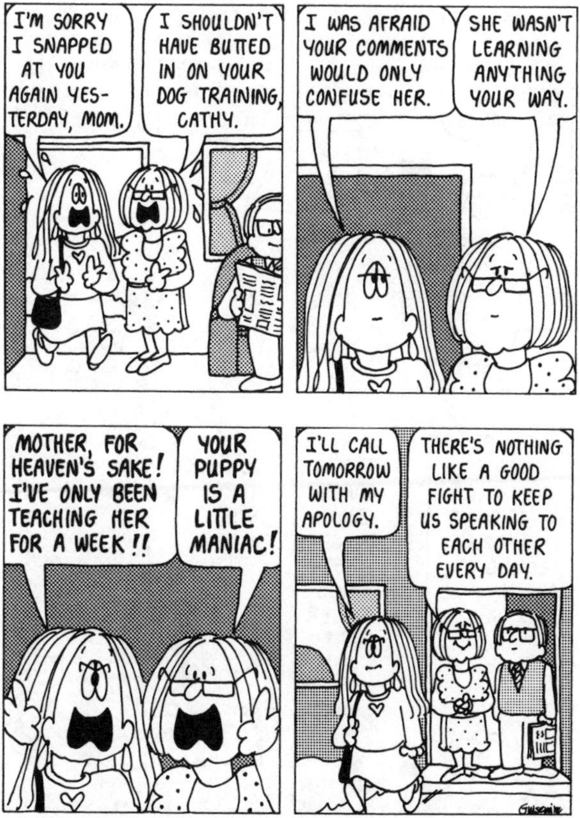
I'M SORRY I SNAPPED AT YOU AGAIN YESTERDAY, MOM.
I SHOULDN'T HAVE BUTTED IN ON YOUR DOG TRAINING, CATHY.
I WAS AFRAID YOUR COMMENTS WOULD ONLY CONFUSE HER.
SHE WASN'T LEARNING ANYTHING YOUR WAY.
MOTHER, FOR HEAVEN'S SAKE! I'VE ONLY BEEN TEACHING HER FOR A WEEK!!
YOUR PUPPY IS A LITTLE MANIAC!
I'LL CALL TOMORROW WITH MY APOLOGY.
THERE'S NOTHING LIKE A GOOD FIGHT TO KEEP US SPEAKING TO EACH OTHER EVERY DAY.
Guisewite

back and forth in 1996 . . .

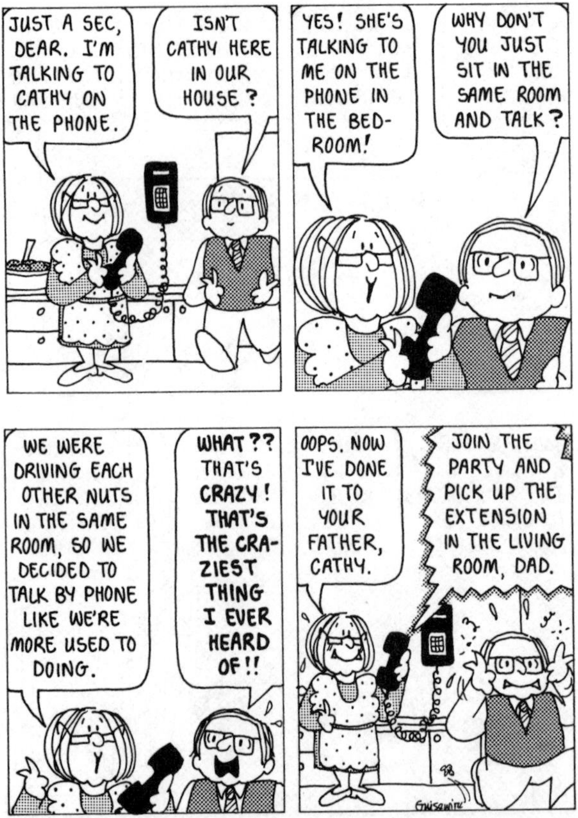
JUST A SEC, DEAR. I'M TALKING TO CATHY ON THE PHONE.
ISN'T CATHY HERE IN OUR HOUSE?
YES! SHE'S TALKING TO ME ON THE PHONE IN THE BED-ROOM!
WHY DON'T YOU JUST SIT IN THE SAME ROOM AND TALK?
WE WERE DRIVING EACH OTHER NUTS IN THE SAME ROOM, SO WE DECIDED TO TALK BY PHONE LIKE WE'RE MORE USED TO DOING.
WHAT?? THAT'S CRAZY! THAT'S THE CRA-ZIEST THING I EVER HEARD OF!!
OOPS. NOW I'VE DONE IT TO YOUR FATHER, CATHY.
JOIN THE PARTY AND PICK UP THE EXTENSION IN THE LIVING ROOM, DAD.
Guisewite

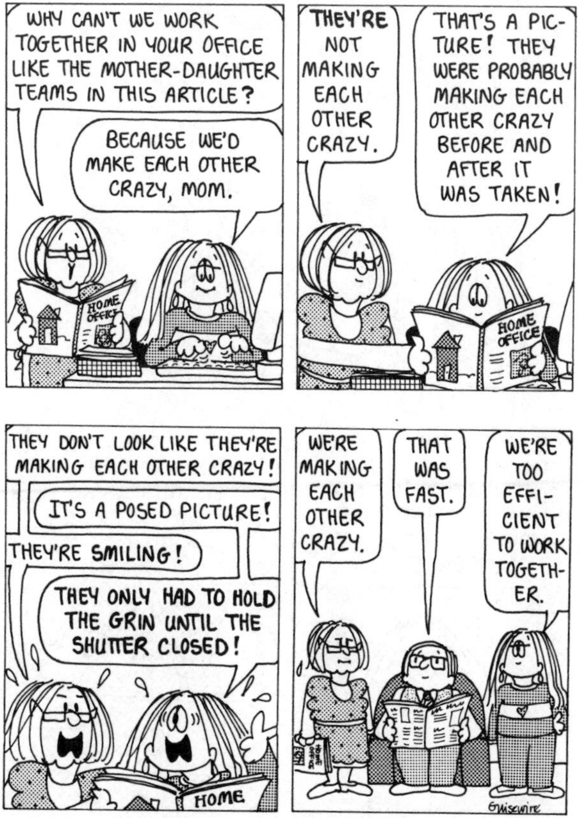
WHY CAN'T WE WORK TOGETHER IN YOUR OFFICE LIKE THE MOTHER-DAUGHTER TEAMS IN THIS ARTICLE?
BECAUSE WE'D MAKE EACH OTHER CRAZY, MOM.
HOME OFFICE
THEY'RE NOT MAKING EACH OTHER CRAZY.
THAT'S A PICTURE! THEY WERE PROBABLY MAKING EACH OTHER CRAZY BEFORE AND AFTER IT WAS TAKEN!
HOME OFFICE
THEY DON'T LOOK LIKE THEY'RE MAKING EACH OTHER CRAZY!
IT'S A POSED PICTURE!
THEY'RE SMILING!
THEY ONLY HAD TO HOLD THE GRIN UNTIL THE SHUTTER CLOSED!
HOME
WE'RE MAKING EACH OTHER CRAZY.
THAT WAS FAST.
WE'RE TOO EFFICIENT TO WORK TOGETHER.
Guisewite

back and forth in 1999 . . .

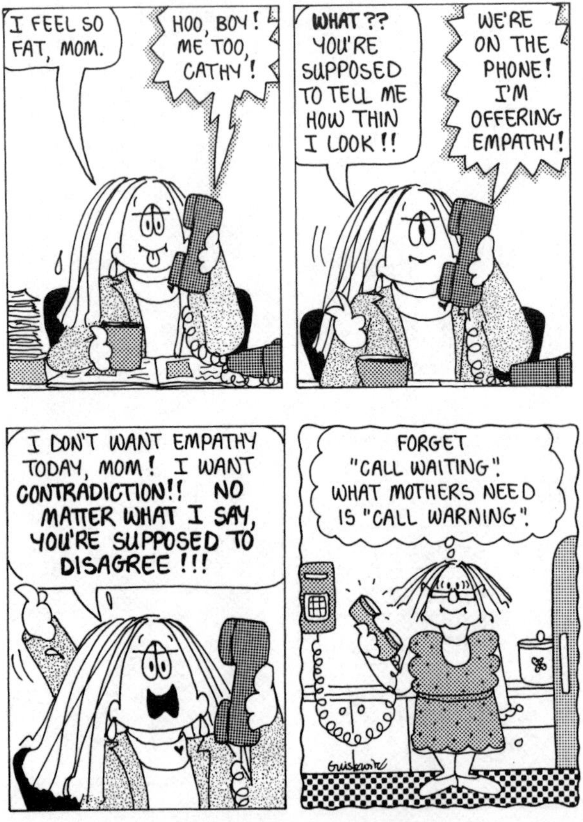

I FEEL SO FAT, MOM.
HOO, BOY! ME TOO, CATHY!
WHAT?? YOU'RE SUPPOSED TO TELL ME HOW THIN I LOOK!!
WE'RE ON THE PHONE! I'M OFFERING EMPATHY!
I DON'T WANT EMPATHY TODAY, MOM! I WANT CONTRADICTION!! NO MATTER WHAT I SAY, YOU'RE SUPPOSED TO DISAGREE!!!
FORGET "CALL WAITING". WHAT MOTHERS NEED IS "CALL WARNING".
Guisewite

back and forth 15 minutes ago.

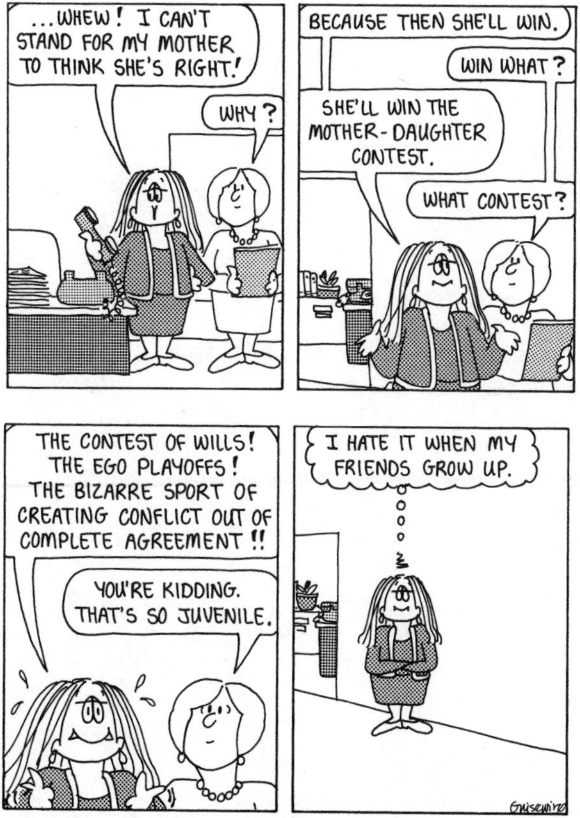

...WHEW! I CAN'T STAND FOR MY MOTHER TO THINK SHE'S RIGHT!
WHY?
BECAUSE THEN SHE'LL WIN.
WIN WHAT?
SHE'LL WIN THE MOTHER-DAUGHTER CONTEST.
WHAT CONTEST?
THE CONTEST OF WILLS! THE EGO PLAYOFFS! THE BIZARRE SPORT OF CREATING CONFLICT OUT OF COMPLETE AGREEMENT!!
YOU'RE KIDDING. THAT'S SO JUVENILE.
I HATE IT WHEN MY FRIENDS GROW UP.
Guisewite

For some, the mother-daughter sparks ignite a really long phase.

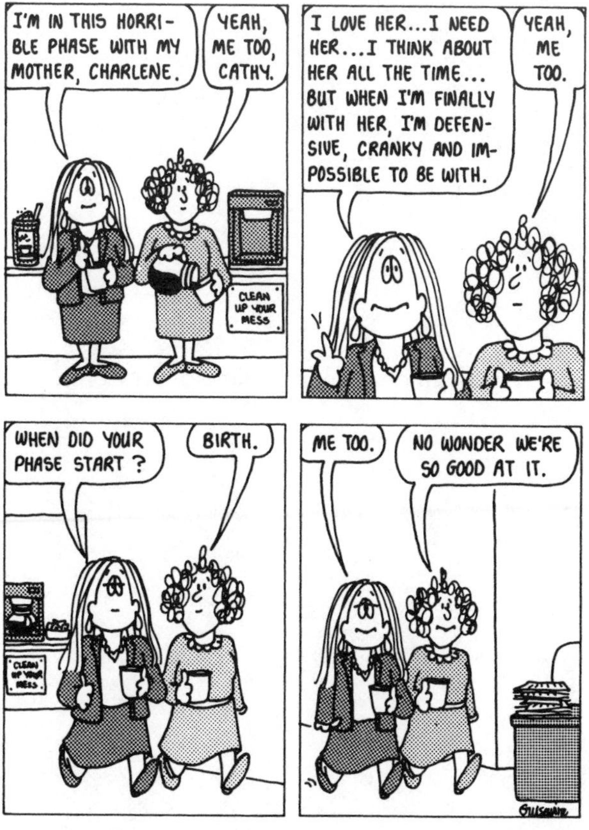
I'M IN THIS HORRIBLE PHASE WITH MY MOTHER, CHARLENE.
YEAH, ME TOO, CATHY.
CLEAN UP YOUR MESS
I LOVE HER...I NEED HER...I THINK ABOUT HER ALL THE TIME... BUT WHEN I'M FINALLY WITH HER, I'M DEFENSIVE, CRANKY AND IMPOSSIBLE TO BE WITH.
YEAH, ME TOO.
WHEN DID YOUR PHASE START ?
BIRTH.
CLEAN UP YOUR MESS
ME TOO.
NO WONDER WE'RE SO GOOD AT IT.

For Mom and me, a lifetime of fireworks.

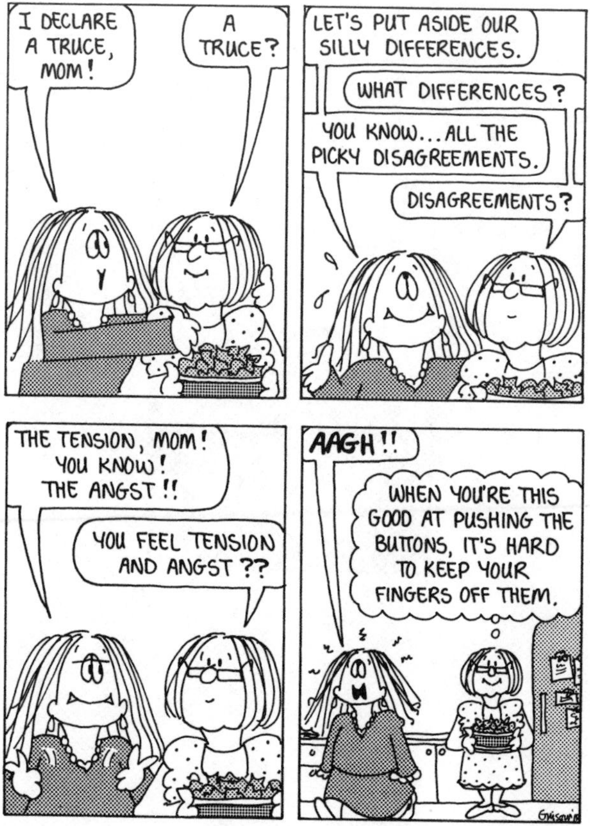
I DECLARE A TRUCE, MOM!
A TRUCE?
LET'S PUT ASIDE OUR SILLY DIFFERENCES.
WHAT DIFFERENCES?
YOU KNOW... ALL THE PICKY DISAGREEMENTS.
DISAGREEMENTS?
THE TENSION, MOM! YOU KNOW! THE ANGST!!
YOU FEEL TENSION AND ANGST??
AAGH!!
WHEN YOU'RE THIS GOOD AT PUSHING THE BUTTONS, IT'S HARD TO KEEP YOUR FINGERS OFF THEM.

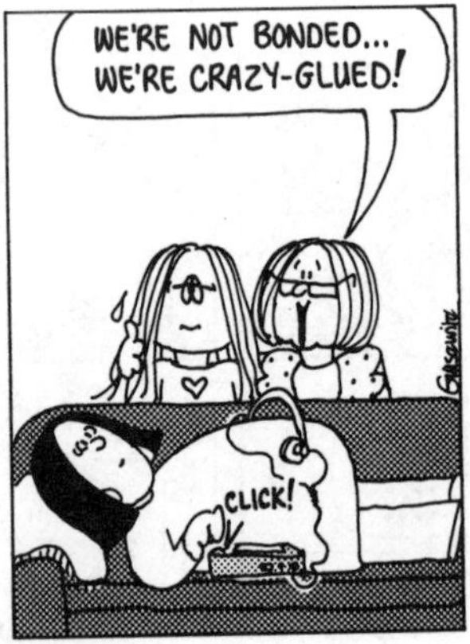
WE'RE NOT BONDED...
WE'RE CRAZY-GLUED!
CLICK!

The Action Figure

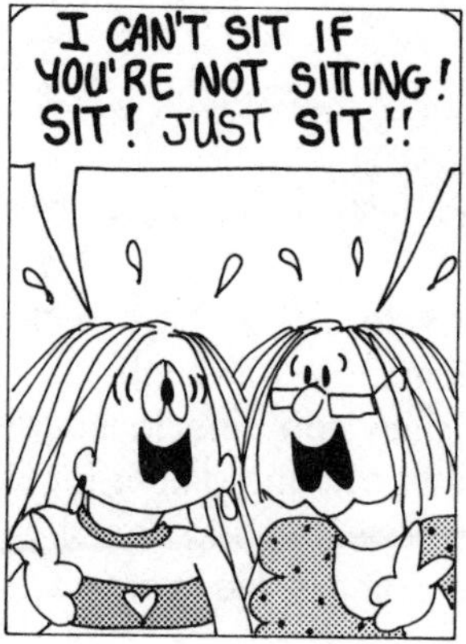
I CAN'T SIT IF YOU'RE NOT SITTING! SIT! JUST SIT!!

My mother can't sit down. Okay, she can sit, but she can't *just* sit. She can't sit unless she's doing at least one, and usually 16, things while she's sitting.

She sits in front of the TV with a sewing box and two years of mending.

Sits on a plane with six months of correspondence to catch up on.

Sits in the car with bills, bank statements, and the last month of newspapers to go through.

Sits on the kitchen stool simultaneously helping a friend on the phone, cooking dinner for Dad, cutting coupons from the paper, writing dental appointments in her calendar, and doing ankle stretches.

Because Mom can't sit without doing anything, she can't go anywhere without taking everything. Bags of reading material in case she has to sit. Folders of things to organize in case she sits. Calendars and stationery systems in case there's a moment to sit.

She packs to walk into the living room to watch the six o'clock news like some pack for Europe: pants to hem . . . shirts to iron . . . thank-you notes to write . . . Christmas cards to answer . . . a bag of buttons to organize . . . potatoes to peel.

Then she packs to walk back into the bedroom in case she accidentally sits on the bed: articles to read . . . anniversary cards to send . . . clothes to fold . . . lists to make . . . a purse to clean . . . an address book to update.

As far as we know, Mom has never sat on the beach in her life. The packing job would be too overwhelming.

It should come as no surprise that, just in case Mom is going to have a moment where her hands are idle, she always fully packs her brain.

50 years of potential things to worry about.
5,000 different disaster scenarios.
50,000 possible things that could go wrong .

Not a little mental tote bag of concerns, but the cerebral equivalent of a baggage car of Speculative Parental Angst.

My mother can't just sit.

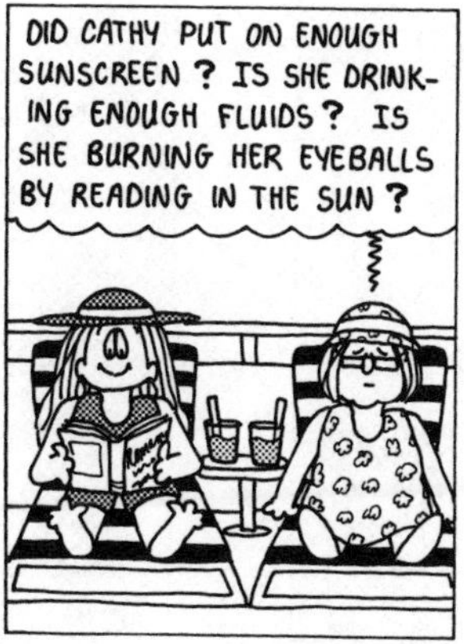
DID CATHY PUT ON ENOUGH SUNSCREEN? IS SHE DRINKING ENOUGH FLUIDS? IS SHE BURNING HER EYEBALLS BY READING IN THE SUN?

. . .

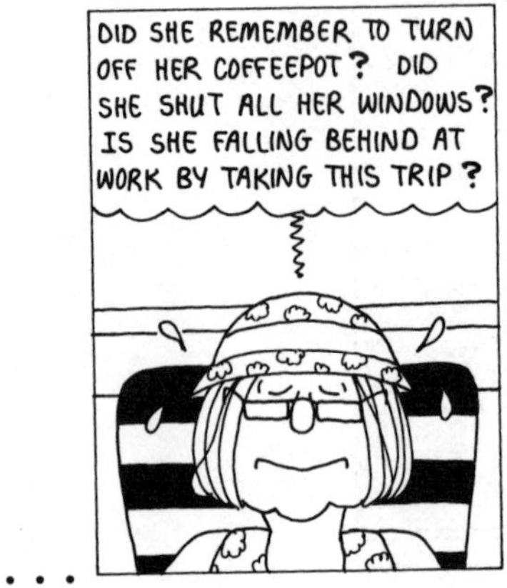
DID SHE REMEMBER TO TURN OFF HER COFFEEPOT? DID SHE SHUT ALL HER WINDOWS? IS SHE FALLING BEHIND AT WORK BY TAKING THIS TRIP?

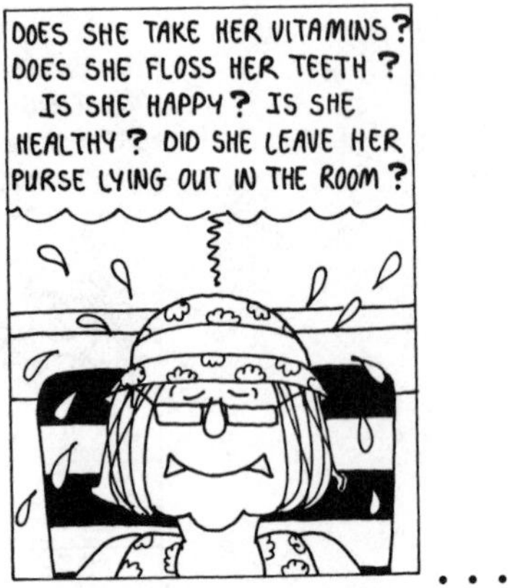
DOES SHE TAKE HER VITAMINS? DOES SHE FLOSS HER TEETH? IS SHE HAPPY? IS SHE HEALTHY? DID SHE LEAVE HER PURSE LYING OUT IN THE ROOM?

. . .

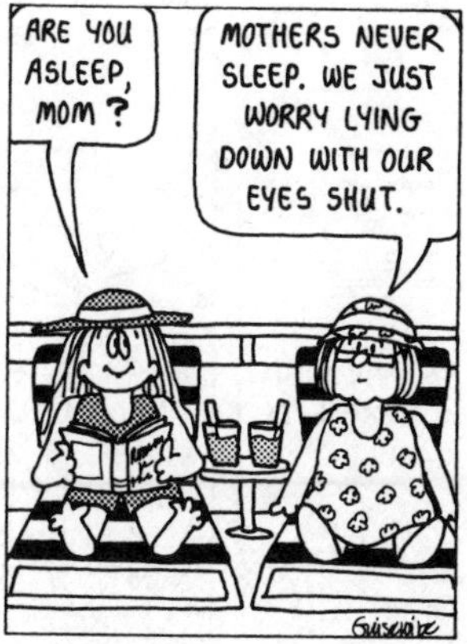
ARE YOU ASLEEP, MOM?
MOTHERS NEVER SLEEP. WE JUST WORRY LYING DOWN WITH OUR EYES SHUT.

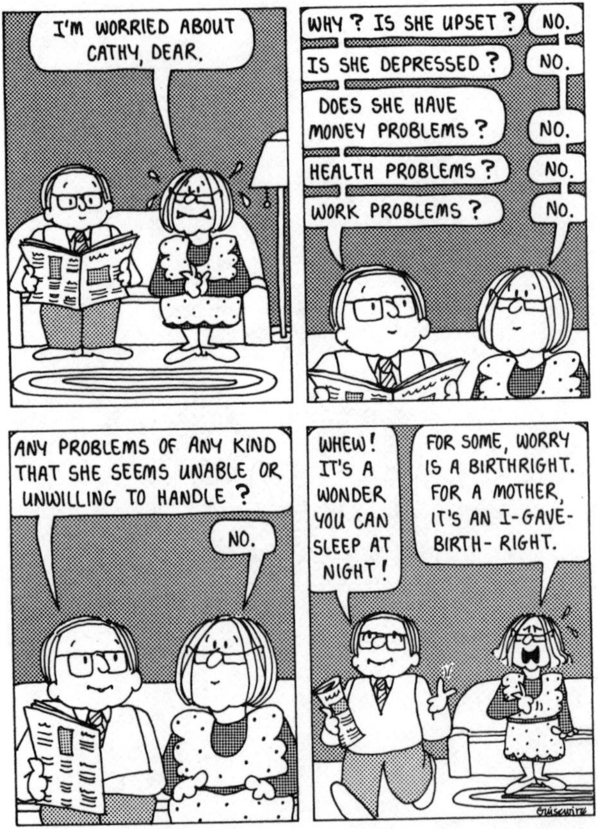
I'M WORRIED ABOUT CATHY, DEAR.
WHY? IS SHE UPSET?
NO.
IS SHE DEPRESSED?
NO.
DOES SHE HAVE MONEY PROBLEMS?
NO.
HEALTH PROBLEMS?
NO.
WORK PROBLEMS?
NO.
ANY PROBLEMS OF ANY KIND THAT SHE SEEMS UNABLE OR UNWILLING TO HANDLE?
NO.
WHEW! IT'S A WONDER YOU CAN SLEEP AT NIGHT!
FOR SOME, WORRY IS A BIRTHRIGHT. FOR A MOTHER, IT'S AN I-GAVE-BIRTH-RIGHT.

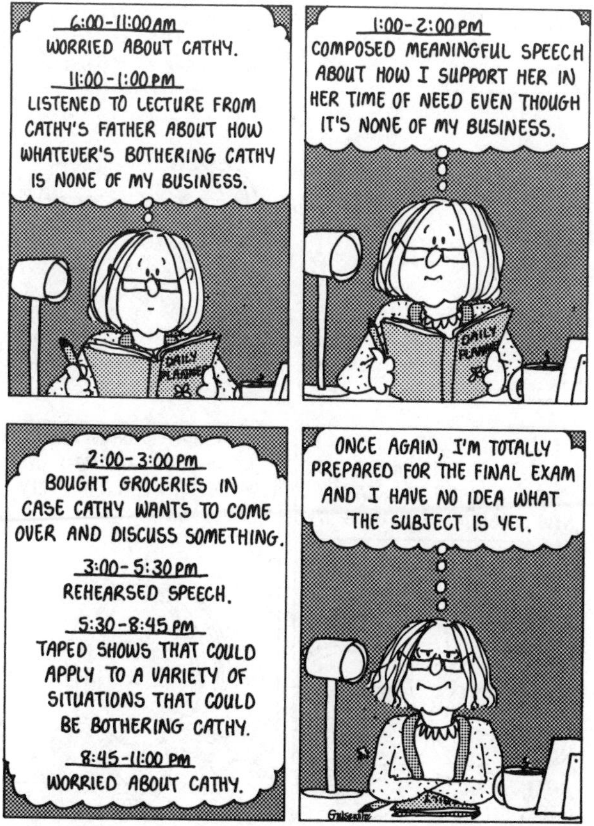
6:00-11:00 AM
WORRIED ABOUT CATHY.
11:00-1:00 PM
LISTENED TO LECTURE FROM CATHY'S FATHER ABOUT HOW WHATEVER'S BOTHERING CATHY IS NONE OF MY BUSINESS.
DAILY PLANNER
1:00-2:00 PM
COMPOSED MEANINGFUL SPEECH ABOUT HOW I SUPPORT HER IN HER TIME OF NEED EVEN THOUGH IT'S NONE OF MY BUSINESS.
DAILY PLANNER
2:00-3:00 PM
BOUGHT GROCERIES IN CASE CATHY WANTS TO COME OVER AND DISCUSS SOMETHING.
3:00-5:30 PM
REHEARSED SPEECH.
5:30-8:45 PM
TAPED SHOWS THAT COULD APPLY TO A VARIETY OF SITUATIONS THAT COULD BE BOTHERING CATHY.
8:45-11:00 PM
WORRIED ABOUT CATHY.
ONCE AGAIN, I'M TOTALLY PREPARED FOR THE FINAL EXAM AND I HAVE NO IDEA WHAT THE SUBJECT IS YET.

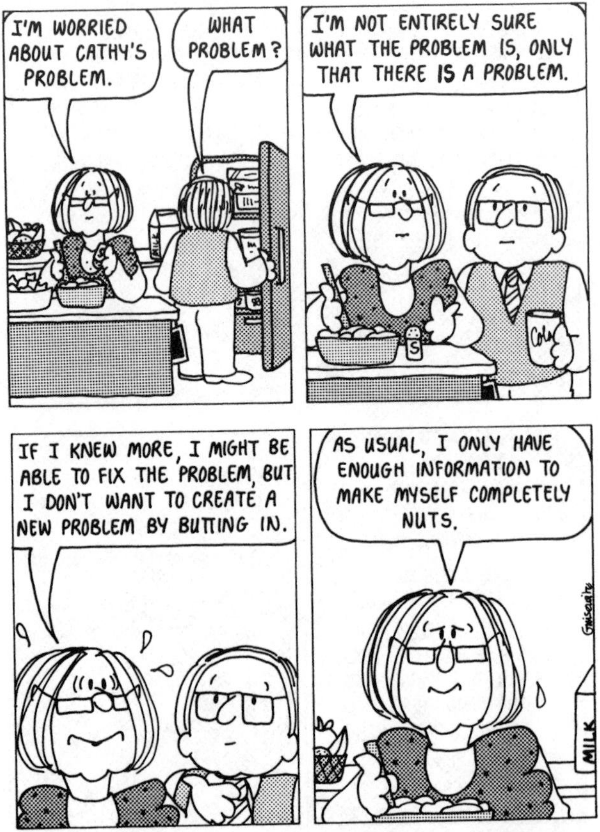
I'M WORRIED ABOUT CATHY'S PROBLEM.
WHAT PROBLEM?
I'M NOT ENTIRELY SURE WHAT THE PROBLEM IS, ONLY THAT THERE IS A PROBLEM.
IF I KNEW MORE, I MIGHT BE ABLE TO FIX THE PROBLEM, BUT I DON'T WANT TO CREATE A NEW PROBLEM BY BUTTING IN.
AS USUAL, I ONLY HAVE ENOUGH INFORMATION TO MAKE MYSELF COMPLETELY NUTS.

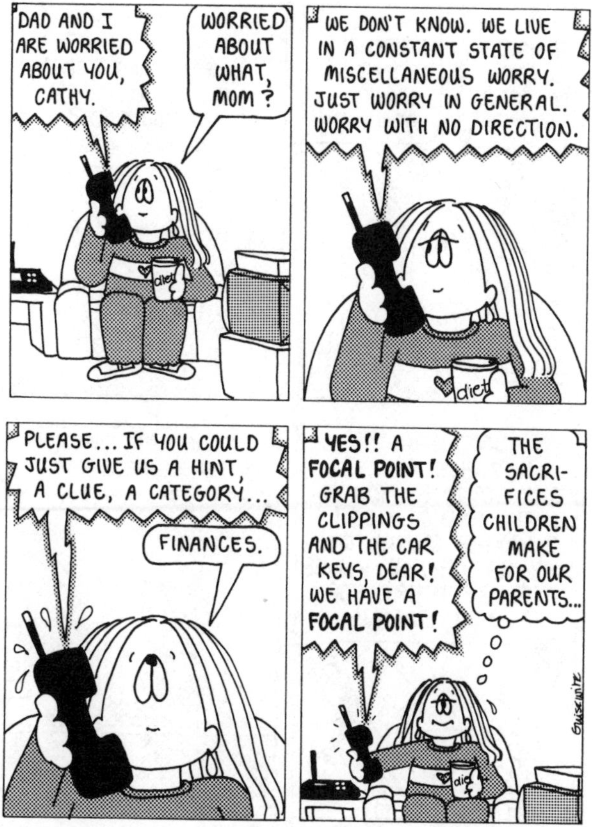
DAD AND I ARE WORRIED ABOUT YOU, CATHY.
WORRIED ABOUT WHAT, MOM?
WE DON'T KNOW. WE LIVE IN A CONSTANT STATE OF MISCELLANEOUS WORRY. JUST WORRY IN GENERAL. WORRY WITH NO DIRECTION.
diet
PLEASE... IF YOU COULD JUST GIVE US A HINT, A CLUE, A CATEGORY...
FINANCES.
YES!! A FOCAL POINT! GRAB THE CLIPPINGS AND THE CAR KEYS, DEAR! WE HAVE A FOCAL POINT!
THE SACRIFICES CHILDREN MAKE FOR OUR PARENTS...
GUISEWITE

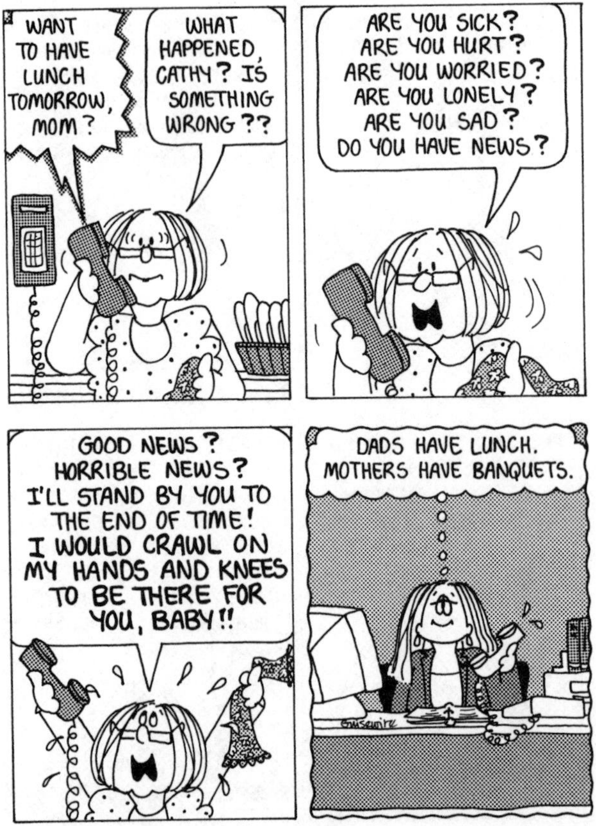
WANT TO HAVE LUNCH TOMORROW, MOM?
WHAT HAPPENED, CATHY? IS SOMETHING WRONG??
ARE YOU SICK? ARE YOU HURT? ARE YOU WORRIED? ARE YOU LONELY? ARE YOU SAD? DO YOU HAVE NEWS?
GOOD NEWS? HORRIBLE NEWS? I'LL STAND BY YOU TO THE END OF TIME! I WOULD CRAWL ON MY HANDS AND KNEES TO BE THERE FOR YOU, BABY!!
DADS HAVE LUNCH. MOTHERS HAVE BANQUETS.

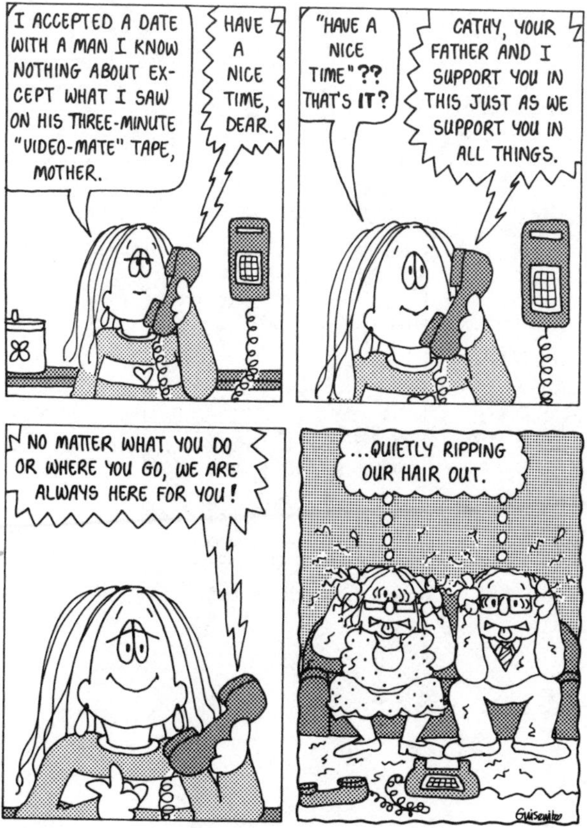
I ACCEPTED A DATE WITH A MAN I KNOW NOTHING ABOUT EXCEPT WHAT I SAW ON HIS THREE-MINUTE "VIDEO-MATE" TAPE, MOTHER.
HAVE A NICE TIME, DEAR.
"HAVE A NICE TIME"?? THAT'S IT?
CATHY, YOUR FATHER AND I SUPPORT YOU IN THIS JUST AS WE SUPPORT YOU IN ALL THINGS.
NO MATTER WHAT YOU DO OR WHERE YOU GO, WE ARE ALWAYS HERE FOR YOU!
...QUIETLY RIPPING OUR HAIR OUT.
Guisewite

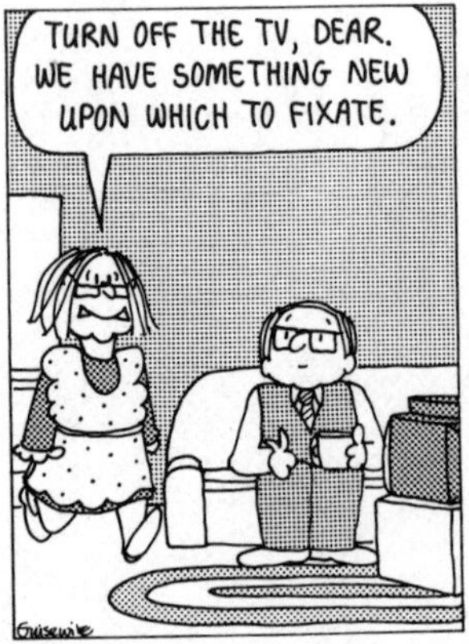
TURN OFF THE TV, DEAR. WE HAVE SOMETHING NEW UPON WHICH TO FIXATE.
Guisewite

The Mother of the Potential Bride

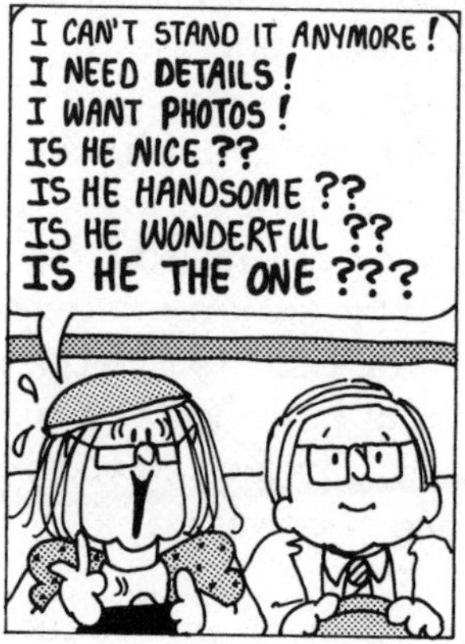
I CAN'T STAND IT ANYMORE!
I NEED DETAILS!
I WANT PHOTOS!
IS HE NICE??
IS HE HANDSOME??
IS HE WONDERFUL??
IS HE THE ONE???

My mother got a coffee cake covered in aluminum foil in 1953 and has been reusing that same piece of aluminum foil ever since.

She rinses out plastic sandwich bags and hangs them on a little rack in the kitchen to dry. She reuses coffee filters until they deteriorate.

Plastic silverware is hand-washed and reused.

Gift wrap is flattened and reused.

Ribbons are ironed and reused.

Cardboard boxes are treated like gold.

Empty jars are treated like fine china.

Twist ties are collected like rare coins.

Used paper cups have their own cupboard.

A box of paper clips lasts 40 years.

A rubber band is forever.

In my mother's home, there's no such thing as "disposable."

For a long time, I thought it was about not wasting money. Then I realized it was also about not wasting resources—a natural act of conservation from a genuine "earth mother."

But as time has gone on, I've realized my mom's refusal to get rid of things that could still work if given a chance also comes from an even deeper belief system:

My mother is a woman who commits.

The "perfectly nice sofa" she and Dad bought in 1958 will be their "perfectly nice sofa" until the end of time.

Their lamp was their lamp when they got married, is their lamp now, and will be their lamp in the year 3001 . . . no matter how many new lamp designs are made . . . no matter how many "Spectacular Lamp Sales" there are . . . no matter how many "Lamp Warehouse Superstores" spring up.

Once a bathroom towel enters Mom's house, it's there for life. It's a bathroom towel for the first 20 or so years . . . then cut into a dishtowel . . . then cut into a rag . . . then stuffing for a pillow. Then the teeny leftover scraps are folded and enshrined in a "perfectly good" 35-year-old shoe box "in case there's a grandchild someday who wants a little piece of something for a dollhouse."

If buying an oven mitt represents a lifelong vow of loyalty and devotion, try and imagine how invested Mom is in the institution of marriage.

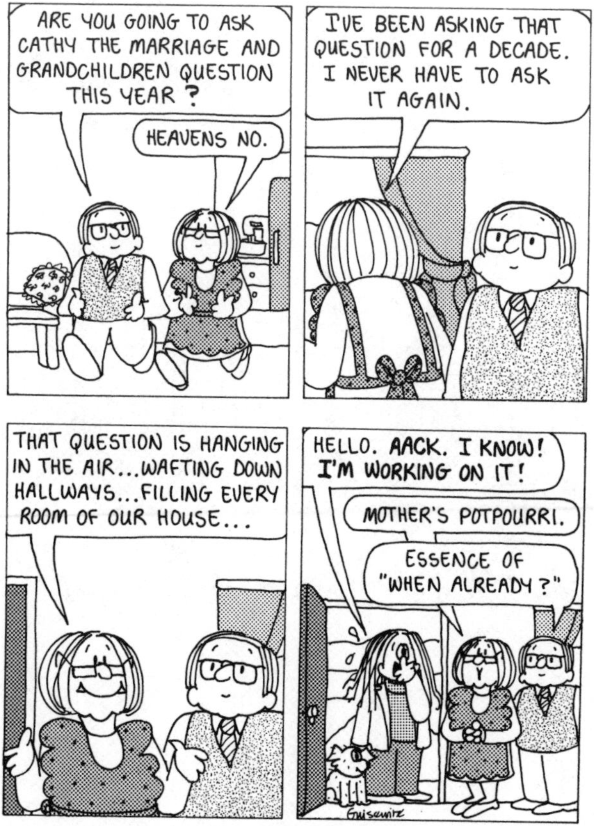
ARE YOU GOING TO ASK CATHY THE MARRIAGE AND GRANDCHILDREN QUESTION THIS YEAR?
HEAVENS NO.
I'VE BEEN ASKING THAT QUESTION FOR A DECADE. I NEVER HAVE TO ASK IT AGAIN.
THAT QUESTION IS HANGING IN THE AIR...WAFTING DOWN HALLWAYS...FILLING EVERY ROOM OF OUR HOUSE...
HELLO. AACK. I KNOW! I'M WORKING ON IT!
MOTHER'S POTPOURRI.
ESSENCE OF "WHEN ALREADY?"
Guisewite

Imagine how much Mom believes in trying to make something work.

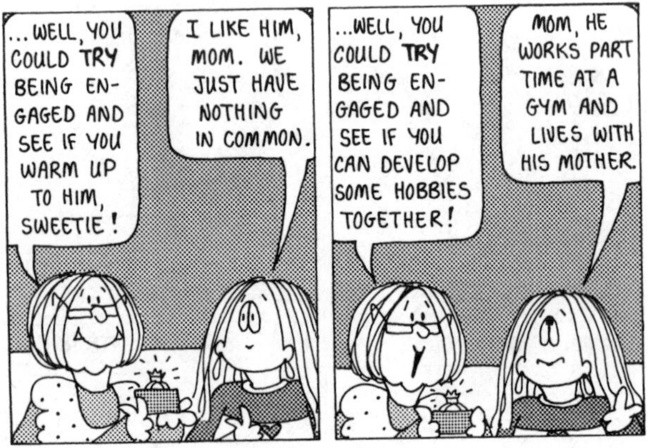
...WELL, YOU COULD TRY BEING ENGAGED AND SEE IF YOU WARM UP TO HIM, SWEETIE!
I LIKE HIM, MOM. WE JUST HAVE NOTHING IN COMMON.
...WELL, YOU COULD TRY BEING ENGAGED AND SEE IF YOU CAN DEVELOP SOME HOBBIES TOGETHER!
MOM, HE WORKS PART TIME AT A GYM AND LIVES WITH HIS MOTHER.

WELL, YOU COULD JUST TRY BEING ENGAGED!! THE RING IS RIGHT HERE! LOOK HOW SPARKLY IT IS!! JUST TRY! TRY FOR YOUR MAMA!!
WHICH IS WORSE, A WOMAN BLINDED BY LOVE, OR A MOTHER BLINDED BY CUBIC ZIRCONIA...
Guisewite

Imagine how challenging the selection process was, considering how long Mom's version of "forever" is going to last.

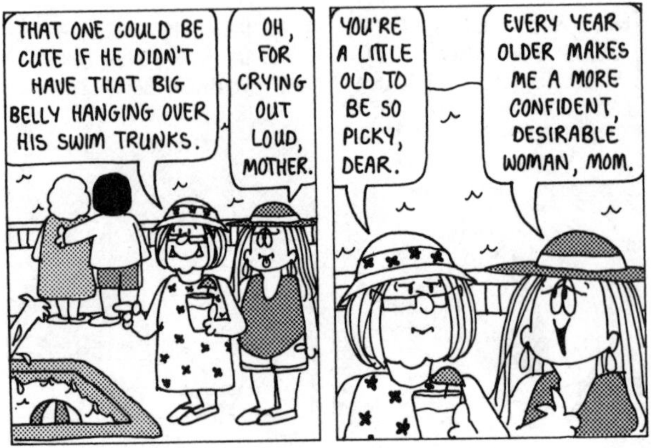
THAT ONE COULD BE CUTE IF HE DIDN'T HAVE THAT BIG BELLY HANGING OVER HIS SWIM TRUNKS.
OH, FOR CRYING OUT LOUD, MOTHER.
YOU'RE A LITTLE OLD TO BE SO PICKY, DEAR.
EVERY YEAR OLDER MAKES ME A MORE CONFIDENT, DESIRABLE WOMAN, MOM.

THAT MAN IS NOT GOOD ENOUGH FOR ME! VIRTUALLY NO MAN ON EARTH IS WORTHY OF THE BRILLIANT, BEAUTIFUL, LOVING AND INCREDIBLE PACKAGE I HAVE BECOME!!!
I'D SCREAM EXCEPT SHE'S QUOTING ME.
Guisewite

Mom picked out my silver pattern when I was one day old and slowly, lovingly, spoon by spoon, collected a six-piece place setting for 12, over 22 years.

In 1972, Mom's beautiful, classic wedding gift was complete and ready to present to me.

1972—the same year I graduated from college with a class of women who were declaring that men were "pigs" and "marriage was dead" and announcing that we were free, independent spirits who were never going to sacrifice our potential for the suffocating, stifling, repressing role of "wife."

Mom's a patient woman.

In real life, my mother was always a champion of having it all. It was Mom who sent me my first subscription to Ms. Magazine . . . Mom who cheered me on to my first job interviews . . . Mom who helped me feel so proud of my first single apartment . . . Mom who, in 1978— when the whole world was changing for women—made me believe I could do anything.

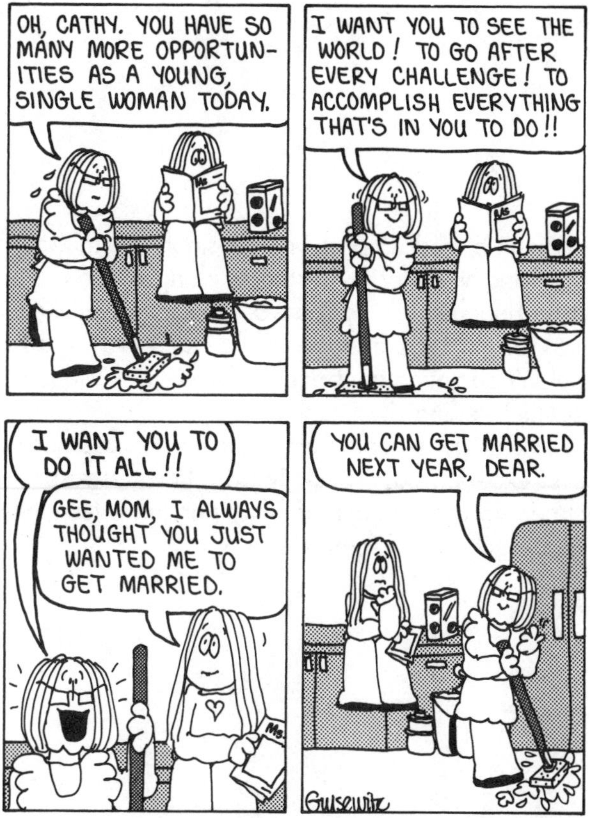
OH, CATHY. YOU HAVE SO MANY MORE OPPORTUNITIES AS A YOUNG, SINGLE WOMAN TODAY.
Ms.
I WANT YOU TO SEE THE WORLD! TO GO AFTER EVERY CHALLENGE! TO ACCOMPLISH EVERYTHING THAT'S IN YOU TO DO!!
I WANT YOU TO DO IT ALL!!
GEE, MOM, I ALWAYS THOUGHT YOU JUST WANTED ME TO GET MARRIED.
Ms.
YOU CAN GET MARRIED NEXT YEAR, DEAR.
Guisewite

When I turned 35 and was still single, Mom gave me my wedding silver for my birthday, along with a beautiful speech about how proud she was of me, that all she wanted was for me to be happy, and that there was no reason I shouldn't be eating my frozen single-serving dinners with a beautiful sterling silver fork.

It was as generous an act of motherly acceptance as I'd ever experienced, especially since I always suspected that deep down, she thought I might be just a teeny-weeny bit happier if I found someone.

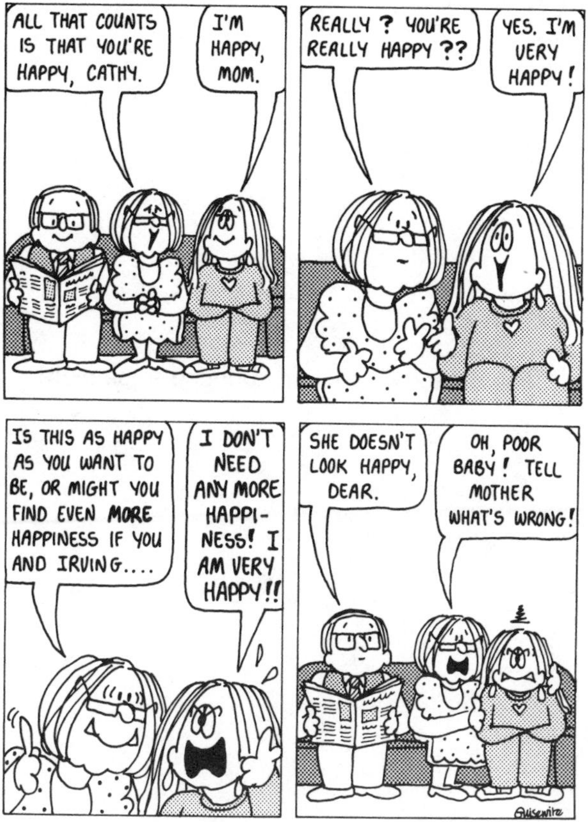
ALL THAT COUNTS IS THAT YOU'RE HAPPY, CATHY.
I'M HAPPY, MOM.
REALLY ? YOU'RE REALLY HAPPY ??
YES. I'M VERY HAPPY !
IS THIS AS HAPPY AS YOU WANT TO BE, OR MIGHT YOU FIND EVEN MORE HAPPINESS IF YOU AND IRVING....
I DON'T NEED ANY MORE HAPPI-NESS! I AM VERY HAPPY!!
SHE DOESN'T LOOK HAPPY, DEAR.
OH, POOR BABY! TELL MOTHER WHAT'S WRONG!
Guisewite

Time passed. The world changed some more.

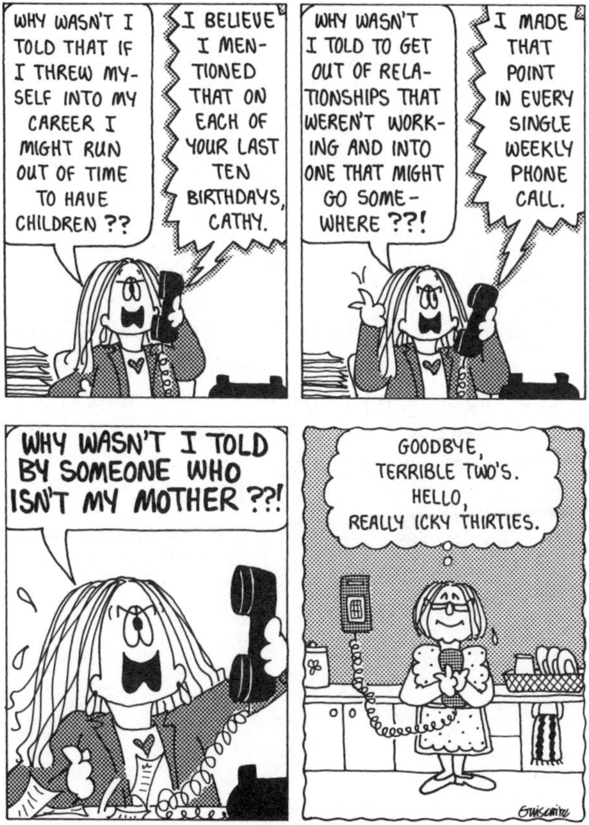
WHY WASN'T I TOLD THAT IF I THREW MYSELF INTO MY CAREER I MIGHT RUN OUT OF TIME TO HAVE CHILDREN??
I BELIEVE I MENTIONED THAT ON EACH OF YOUR LAST TEN BIRTHDAYS, CATHY.
WHY WASN'T I TOLD TO GET OUT OF RELATIONSHIPS THAT WEREN'T WORKING AND INTO ONE THAT MIGHT GO SOMEWHERE??!
I MADE THAT POINT IN EVERY SINGLE WEEKLY PHONE CALL.
WHY WASN'T I TOLD BY SOMEONE WHO ISN'T MY MOTHER??!
GOODBYE, TERRIBLE TWO'S. HELLO, REALLY ICKY THIRTIES.
Guisewite

I got married for the first time at age 47, a miracle of love for me, a triumph of stamina for my mother.

Looking back, my single years were never that "single" anyway. I always had Mom by my side, on the phone, and in my brain.

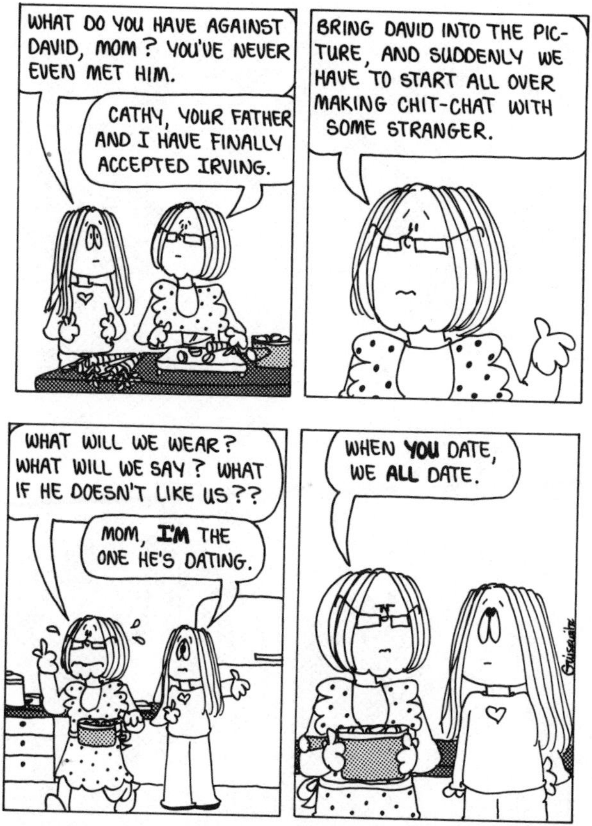
WHAT DO YOU HAVE AGAINST DAVID, MOM? YOU'VE NEVER EVEN MET HIM.
CATHY, YOUR FATHER AND I HAVE FINALLY ACCEPTED IRVING.
BRING DAVID INTO THE PIC-TURE, AND SUDDENLY WE HAVE TO START ALL OVER MAKING CHIT-CHAT WITH SOME STRANGER.
WHAT WILL WE WEAR? WHAT WILL WE SAY? WHAT IF HE DOESN'T LIKE US??
MOM, **I'M** THE ONE HE'S DATING.
WHEN **YOU** DATE, WE **ALL** DATE.
Guisewite

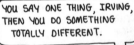

YOU SAY ONE THING, IRVING, THEN YOU DO SOMETHING TOTALLY DIFFERENT.

YOU MAKE ME GUESS WHAT YOU'RE THINKING, AND WHEN I GUESS WRONG YOU SAY I DON'T UNDERSTAND YOU.

ONE DAY YOU ACT LIKE I'M THE MOST IMPORTANT THING IN YOUR LIFE... THE NEXT DAY YOU LOOK AT ME LIKE I'M FROM MARS.

WHAT ARE YOU TRYING TO DO TO ME, IRVING ?!!

HE'S PRE-PARING YOU FOR MOTHERHOOD.

IRVING! WHAT A JOY TO HAVE YOU WITH US FOR A HOLIDAY MEAL!!!

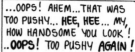

...OOPS! AHEM...THAT WAS TOO PUSHY... HEE, HEE... MY, HOW HANDSOME YOU LOOK! ..OOPS! TOO PUSHY AGAIN!

...HEE HEE..WAIT, WAIT! I HAD A WHOLE ENTRANCE SPEECH PRACTICED AND NOW I FORGOT IT... HEE HEE WAIT I...

COME HERE A SECOND, MOM.

HOW ON EARTH DO YOU YOUNG PEOPLE DATE??

PANT PANT

FAN FAN FAN

1984

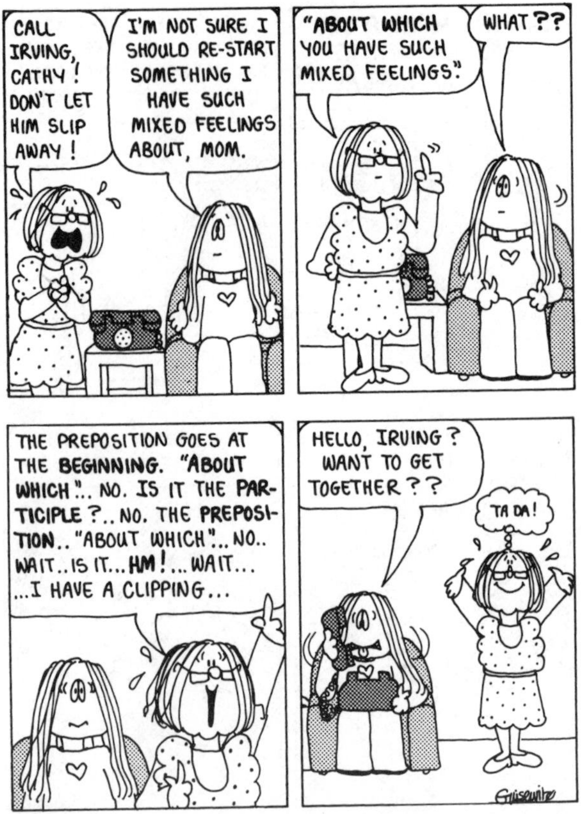
CALL IRVING, CATHY! DON'T LET HIM SLIP AWAY!
I'M NOT SURE I SHOULD RE-START SOMETHING I HAVE SUCH MIXED FEELINGS ABOUT, MOM.
"ABOUT WHICH YOU HAVE SUCH MIXED FEELINGS."
WHAT??
THE PREPOSITION GOES AT THE BEGINNING. "ABOUT WHICH"... NO. IS IT THE PARTICIPLE?.. NO. THE PREPOSITION.. "ABOUT WHICH"... NO.. WAIT.. IS IT... HM!... WAIT... ...I HAVE A CLIPPING...
HELLO, IRVING? WANT TO GET TOGETHER??
TA DA!
Guisewite

1984

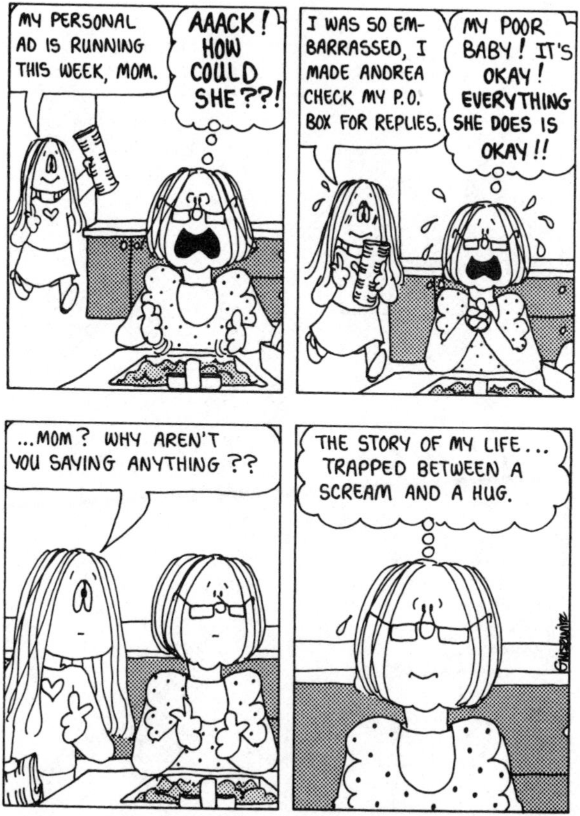
MY PERSONAL AD IS RUNNING THIS WEEK, MOM.
AAACK! HOW COULD SHE??!
I WAS SO EMBARRASSED, I MADE ANDREA CHECK MY P.O. BOX FOR REPLIES.
MY POOR BABY! IT'S OKAY! EVERYTHING SHE DOES IS OKAY!!
...MOM? WHY AREN'T YOU SAYING ANYTHING??
THE STORY OF MY LIFE... TRAPPED BETWEEN A SCREAM AND A HUG.

1984

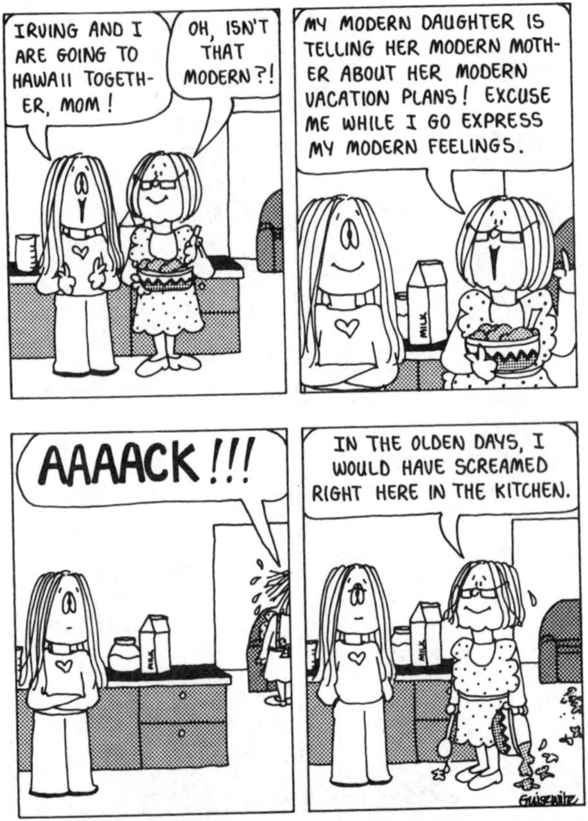

IRVING AND I ARE GOING TO HAWAII TOGETH- ER, MOM!
OH, ISN'T THAT MODERN?!
MY MODERN DAUGHTER IS TELLING HER MODERN MOTH- ER ABOUT HER MODERN VACATION PLANS! EXCUSE ME WHILE I GO EXPRESS MY MODERN FEELINGS.
MILK
AAAACK!!!
MILK
IN THE OLDEN DAYS, I WOULD HAVE SCREAMED RIGHT HERE IN THE KITCHEN.
MILK
Guisewite

1984

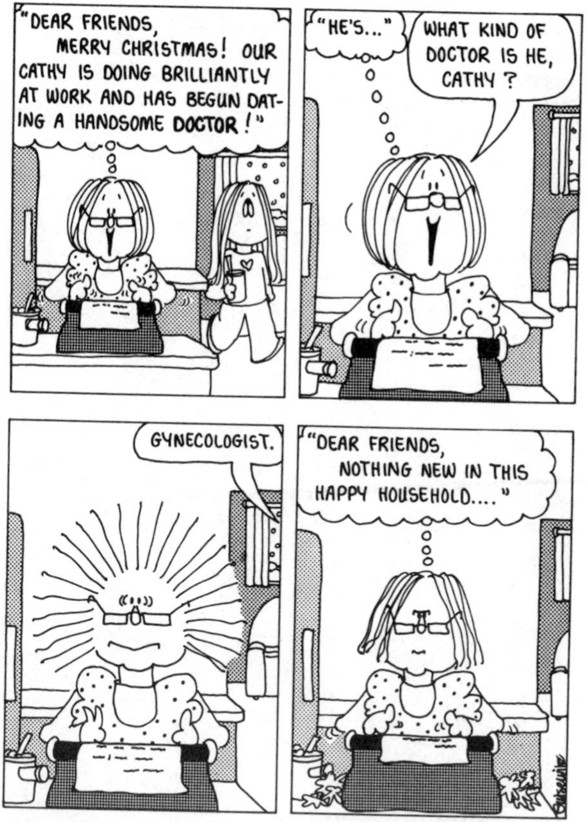
"DEAR FRIENDS,
MERRY CHRISTMAS! OUR CATHY IS DOING BRILLIANTLY AT WORK AND HAS BEGUN DATING A HANDSOME DOCTOR!"
"HE'S..."
WHAT KIND OF DOCTOR IS HE, CATHY ?
GYNECOLOGIST.
"DEAR FRIENDS,
NOTHING NEW IN THIS HAPPY HOUSEHOLD...."

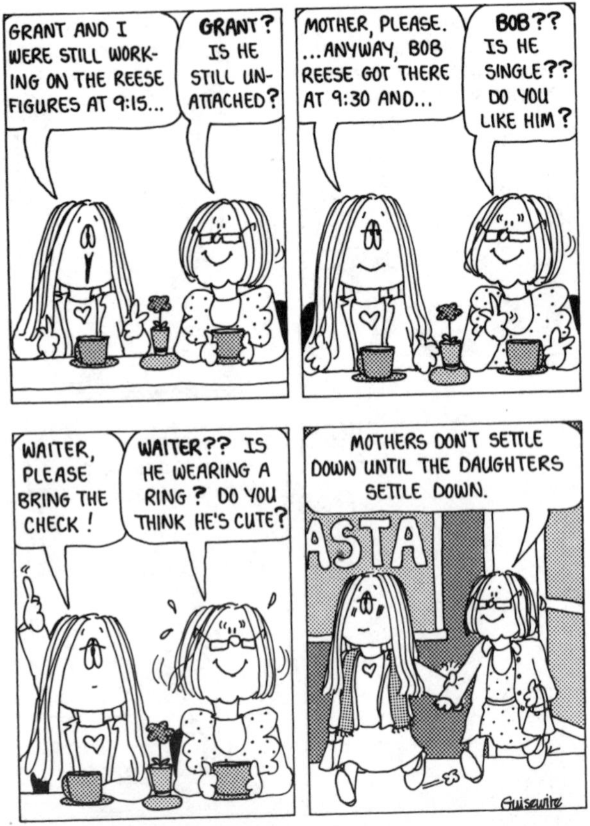
GRANT AND I WERE STILL WORKING ON THE REESE FIGURES AT 9:15...
GRANT? IS HE STILL UNATTACHED?
MOTHER, PLEASE. ...ANYWAY, BOB REESE GOT THERE AT 9:30 AND...
BOB?? IS HE SINGLE?? DO YOU LIKE HIM?
WAITER, PLEASE BRING THE CHECK!
WAITER?? IS HE WEARING A RING? DO YOU THINK HE'S CUTE?
MOTHERS DON'T SETTLE DOWN UNTIL THE DAUGHTERS SETTLE DOWN.
ASTA
Guisewite

1986

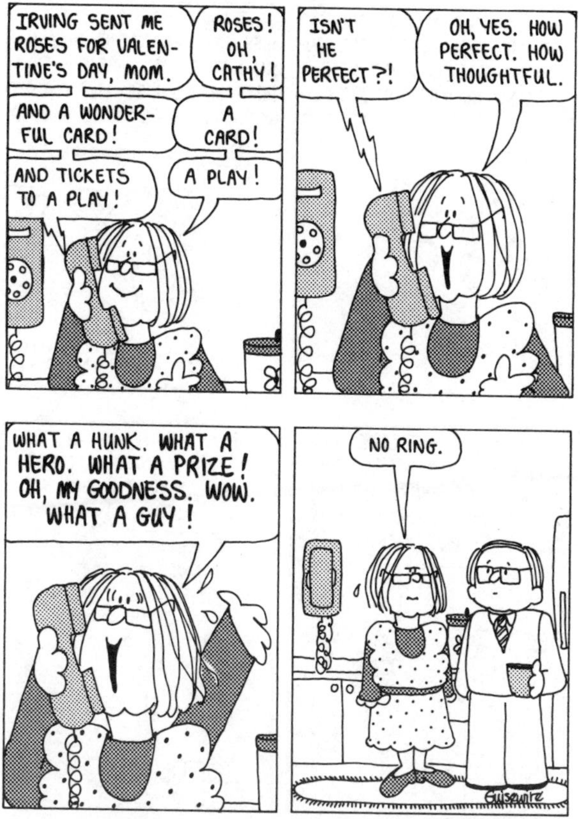
IRVING SENT ME ROSES FOR VALENTINE'S DAY, MOM.
ROSES! OH, CATHY!
AND A WONDERFUL CARD!
A CARD!
AND TICKETS TO A PLAY!
A PLAY!
ISN'T HE PERFECT?!
OH, YES. HOW PERFECT. HOW THOUGHTFUL.
WHAT A HUNK. WHAT A HERO. WHAT A PRIZE! OH, MY GOODNESS. WOW. WHAT A GUY!
NO RING.
Guisewite

1988

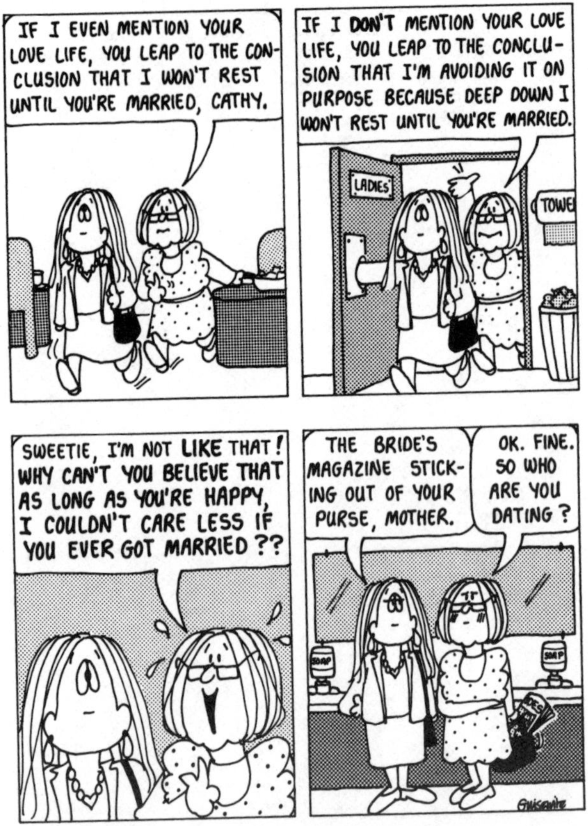

IF I EVEN MENTION YOUR LOVE LIFE, YOU LEAP TO THE CONCLUSION THAT I WON'T REST UNTIL YOU'RE MARRIED, CATHY.
IF I DON'T MENTION YOUR LOVE LIFE, YOU LEAP TO THE CONCLUSION THAT I'M AVOIDING IT ON PURPOSE BECAUSE DEEP DOWN I WON'T REST UNTIL YOU'RE MARRIED.
LADIES
SWEETIE, I'M NOT LIKE THAT! WHY CAN'T YOU BELIEVE THAT AS LONG AS YOU'RE HAPPY, I COULDN'T CARE LESS IF YOU EVER GOT MARRIED??
THE BRIDE'S MAGAZINE STICKING OUT OF YOUR PURSE, MOTHER.
OK. FINE. SO WHO ARE YOU DATING?
SOAP
SOAP
GUISEWITE

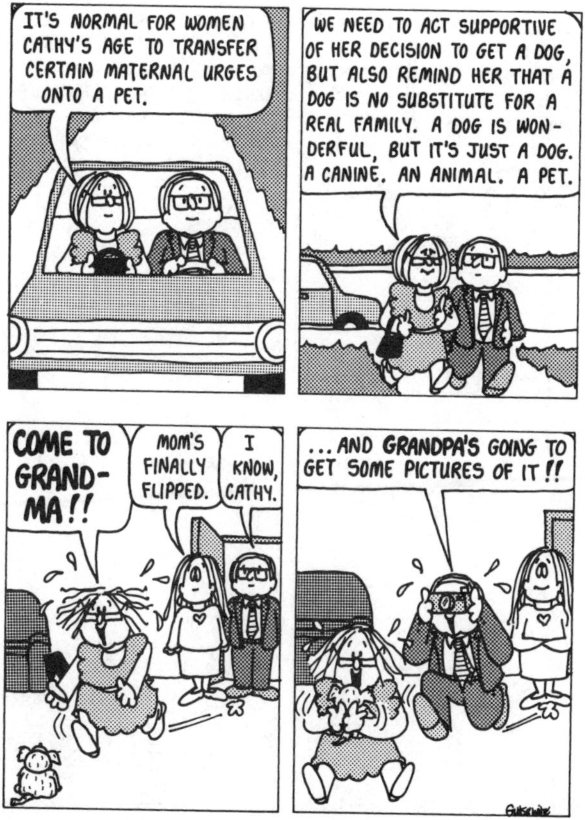
IT'S NORMAL FOR WOMEN CATHY'S AGE TO TRANSFER CERTAIN MATERNAL URGES ONTO A PET.
WE NEED TO ACT SUPPORTIVE OF HER DECISION TO GET A DOG, BUT ALSO REMIND HER THAT A DOG IS NO SUBSTITUTE FOR A REAL FAMILY. A DOG IS WONDERFUL, BUT IT'S JUST A DOG. A CANINE. AN ANIMAL. A PET.
COME TO GRANDMA!!
MOM'S FINALLY FLIPPED.
I KNOW, CATHY.
...AND GRANDPA'S GOING TO GET SOME PICTURES OF IT!!
Guisewite

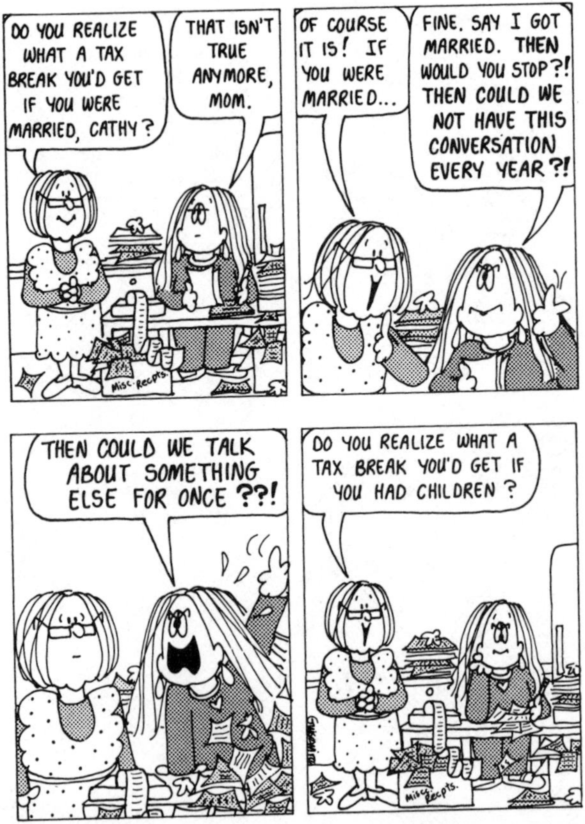
DO YOU REALIZE WHAT A TAX BREAK YOU'D GET IF YOU WERE MARRIED, CATHY?
THAT ISN'T TRUE ANYMORE, MOM.
Misc. Recpts.
OF COURSE IT IS! IF YOU WERE MARRIED...
FINE. SAY I GOT MARRIED. THEN WOULD YOU STOP?! THEN COULD WE NOT HAVE THIS CONVERSATION EVERY YEAR?!
THEN COULD WE TALK ABOUT SOMETHING ELSE FOR ONCE??!
DO YOU REALIZE WHAT A TAX BREAK YOU'D GET IF YOU HAD CHILDREN?
Misc. Recpts.

1989

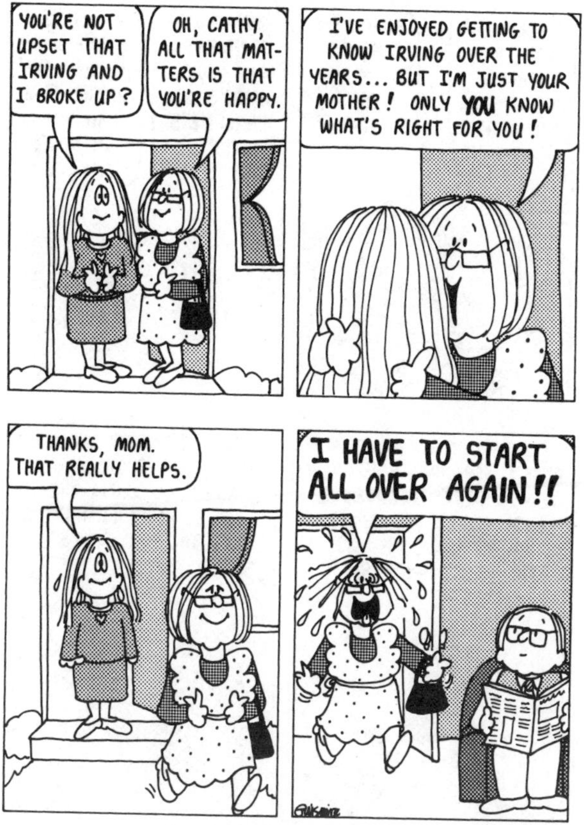
YOU'RE NOT UPSET THAT IRVING AND I BROKE UP?
OH, CATHY, ALL THAT MATTERS IS THAT YOU'RE HAPPY.
I'VE ENJOYED GETTING TO KNOW IRVING OVER THE YEARS... BUT I'M JUST YOUR MOTHER! ONLY YOU KNOW WHAT'S RIGHT FOR YOU!
THANKS, MOM. THAT REALLY HELPS.
I HAVE TO START ALL OVER AGAIN!!

1990

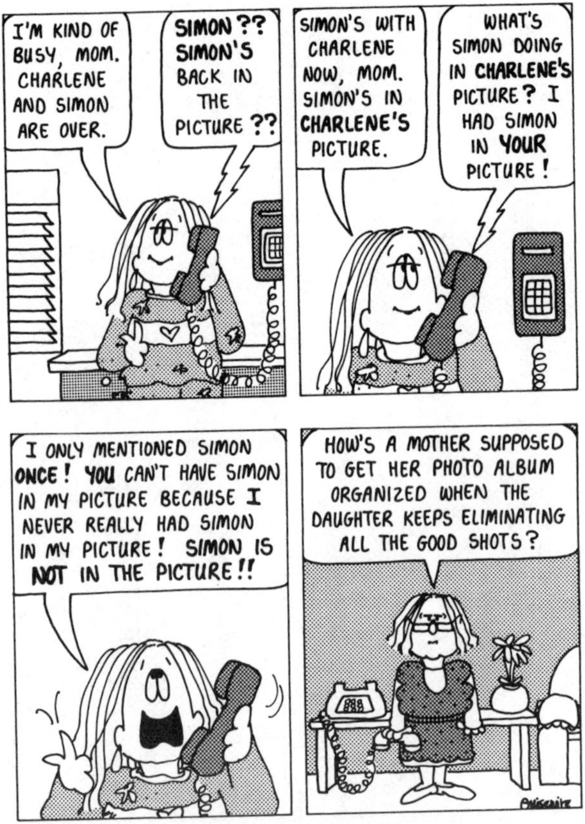

I'M KIND OF BUSY, MOM. CHARLENE AND SIMON ARE OVER.
SIMON?? SIMON'S BACK IN THE PICTURE??
SIMON'S WITH CHARLENE NOW, MOM. SIMON'S IN CHARLENE'S PICTURE.
WHAT'S SIMON DOING IN CHARLENE'S PICTURE? I HAD SIMON IN YOUR PICTURE!
I ONLY MENTIONED SIMON ONCE! YOU CAN'T HAVE SIMON IN MY PICTURE BECAUSE I NEVER REALLY HAD SIMON IN MY PICTURE! SIMON IS NOT IN THE PICTURE!!
HOW'S A MOTHER SUPPOSED TO GET HER PHOTO ALBUM ORGANIZED WHEN THE DAUGHTER KEEPS ELIMINATING ALL THE GOOD SHOTS?

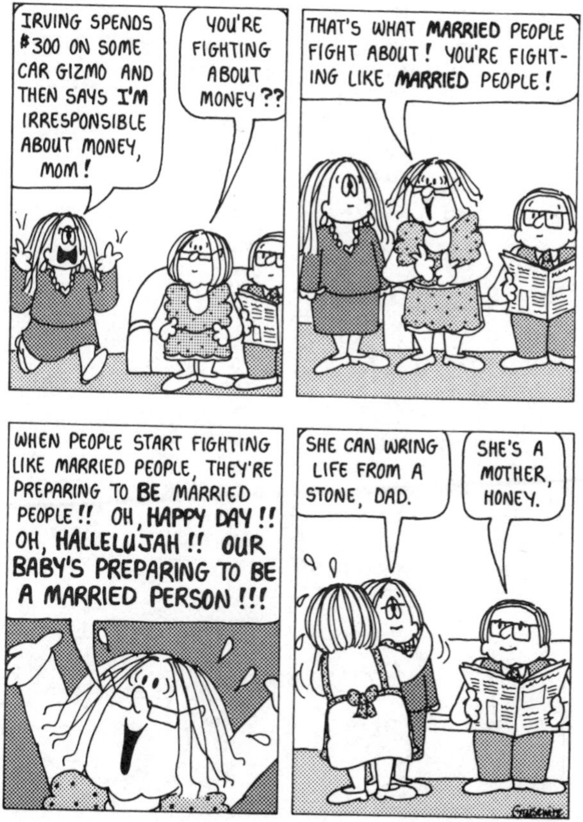
IRVING SPENDS $300 ON SOME CAR GIZMO AND THEN SAYS I'M IRRESPONSIBLE ABOUT MONEY, MOM!
YOU'RE FIGHTING ABOUT MONEY??
THAT'S WHAT MARRIED PEOPLE FIGHT ABOUT! YOU'RE FIGHTING LIKE MARRIED PEOPLE!
WHEN PEOPLE START FIGHTING LIKE MARRIED PEOPLE, THEY'RE PREPARING TO BE MARRIED PEOPLE!! OH, HAPPY DAY!! OH, HALLELUJAH!! OUR BABY'S PREPARING TO BE A MARRIED PERSON!!!
SHE CAN WRING LIFE FROM A STONE, DAD.
SHE'S A MOTHER, HONEY.

1992

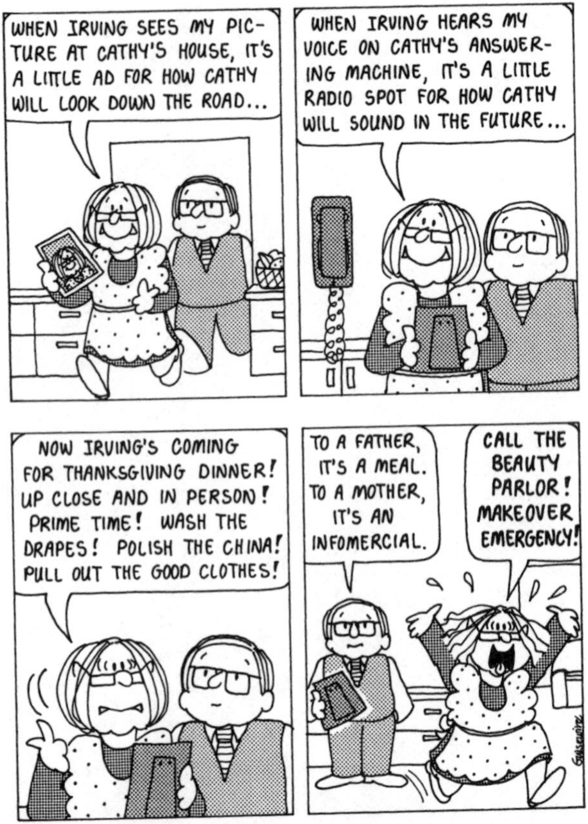

WHEN IRVING SEES MY PICTURE AT CATHY'S HOUSE, IT'S A LITTLE AD FOR HOW CATHY WILL LOOK DOWN THE ROAD...
WHEN IRVING HEARS MY VOICE ON CATHY'S ANSWERING MACHINE, IT'S A LITTLE RADIO SPOT FOR HOW CATHY WILL SOUND IN THE FUTURE...
NOW IRVING'S COMING FOR THANKSGIVING DINNER! UP CLOSE AND IN PERSON! PRIME TIME! WASH THE DRAPES! POLISH THE CHINA! PULL OUT THE GOOD CLOTHES!
TO A FATHER, IT'S A MEAL. TO A MOTHER, IT'S AN INFOMERCIAL.
CALL THE BEAUTY PARLOR! MAKEOVER EMERGENCY!

1993

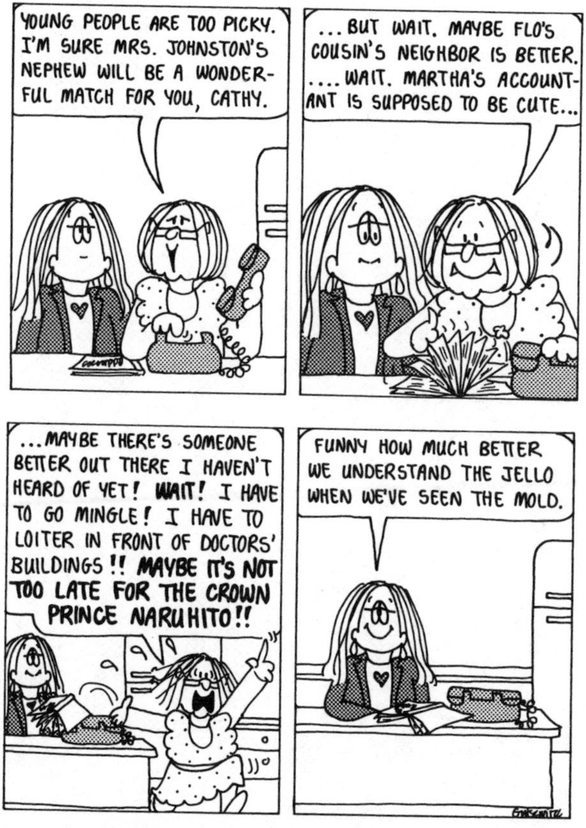
YOUNG PEOPLE ARE TOO PICKY. I'M SURE MRS. JOHNSTON'S NEPHEW WILL BE A WONDERFUL MATCH FOR YOU, CATHY.
... BUT WAIT. MAYBE FLO'S COUSIN'S NEIGHBOR IS BETTER. .... WAIT. MARTHA'S ACCOUNTANT IS SUPPOSED TO BE CUTE...
... MAYBE THERE'S SOMEONE BETTER OUT THERE I HAVEN'T HEARD OF YET! WAIT! I HAVE TO GO MINGLE! I HAVE TO LOITER IN FRONT OF DOCTORS' BUILDINGS!! MAYBE IT'S NOT TOO LATE FOR THE CROWN PRINCE NARUHITO!!
FUNNY HOW MUCH BETTER WE UNDERSTAND THE JELLO WHEN WE'VE SEEN THE MOLD.

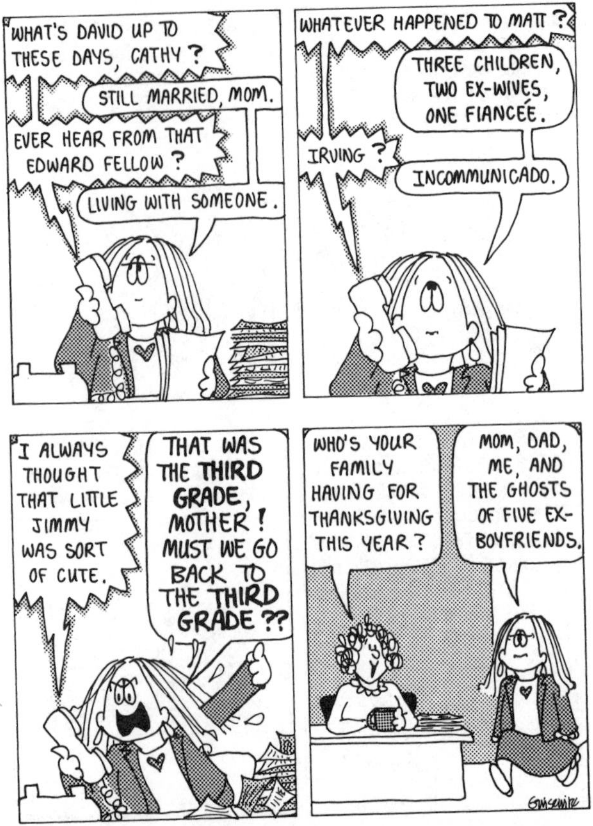
WHAT'S DAVID UP TO THESE DAYS, CATHY?
STILL MARRIED, MOM.
EVER HEAR FROM THAT EDWARD FELLOW?
LIVING WITH SOMEONE.
WHATEVER HAPPENED TO MATT?
THREE CHILDREN, TWO EX-WIVES, ONE FIANCÉE.
IRVING?
INCOMMUNICADO.
I ALWAYS THOUGHT THAT LITTLE JIMMY WAS SORT OF CUTE.
THAT WAS THE THIRD GRADE, MOTHER! MUST WE GO BACK TO THE THIRD GRADE??
WHO'S YOUR FAMILY HAVING FOR THANKSGIVING THIS YEAR?
MOM, DAD, ME, AND THE GHOSTS OF FIVE EX-BOYFRIENDS.

1994

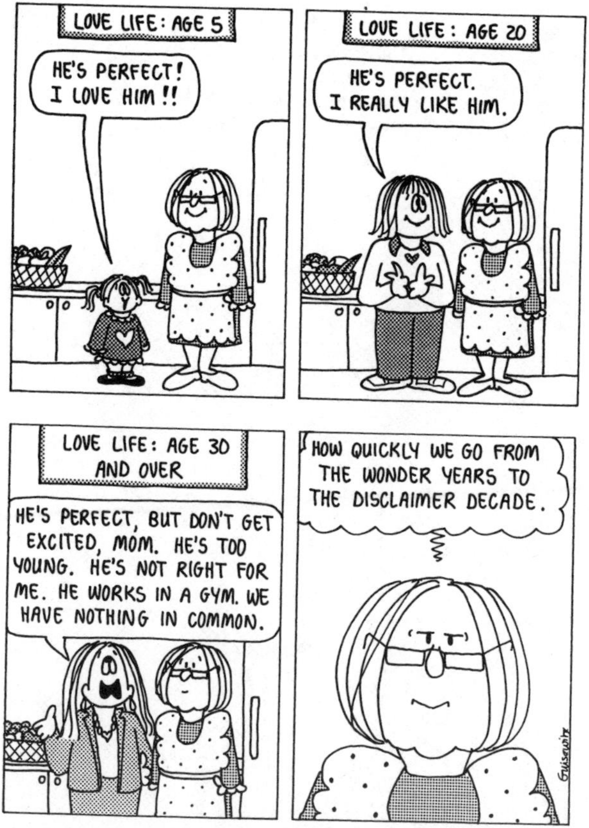

LOVE LIFE: AGE 5
HE'S PERFECT! I LOVE HIM!!
LOVE LIFE: AGE 20
HE'S PERFECT. I REALLY LIKE HIM.
LOVE LIFE: AGE 30 AND OVER
HE'S PERFECT, BUT DON'T GET EXCITED, MOM. HE'S TOO YOUNG. HE'S NOT RIGHT FOR ME. HE WORKS IN A GYM. WE HAVE NOTHING IN COMMON.
HOW QUICKLY WE GO FROM THE WONDER YEARS TO THE DISCLAIMER DECADE.

1994

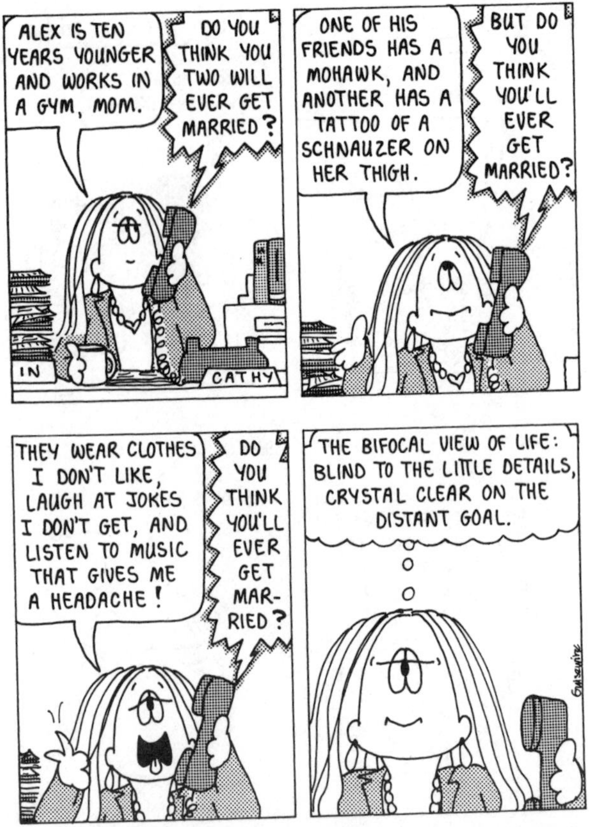
ALEX IS TEN YEARS YOUNGER AND WORKS IN A GYM, MOM.
DO YOU THINK YOU TWO WILL EVER GET MARRIED?
IN
CATHY
ONE OF HIS FRIENDS HAS A MOHAWK, AND ANOTHER HAS A TATTOO OF A SCHNAUZER ON HER THIGH.
BUT DO YOU THINK YOU'LL EVER GET MARRIED?
THEY WEAR CLOTHES I DON'T LIKE, LAUGH AT JOKES I DON'T GET, AND LISTEN TO MUSIC THAT GIVES ME A HEADACHE!
DO YOU THINK YOU'LL EVER GET MAR-RIED?
THE BIFOCAL VIEW OF LIFE: BLIND TO THE LITTLE DETAILS, CRYSTAL CLEAR ON THE DISTANT GOAL.

1994

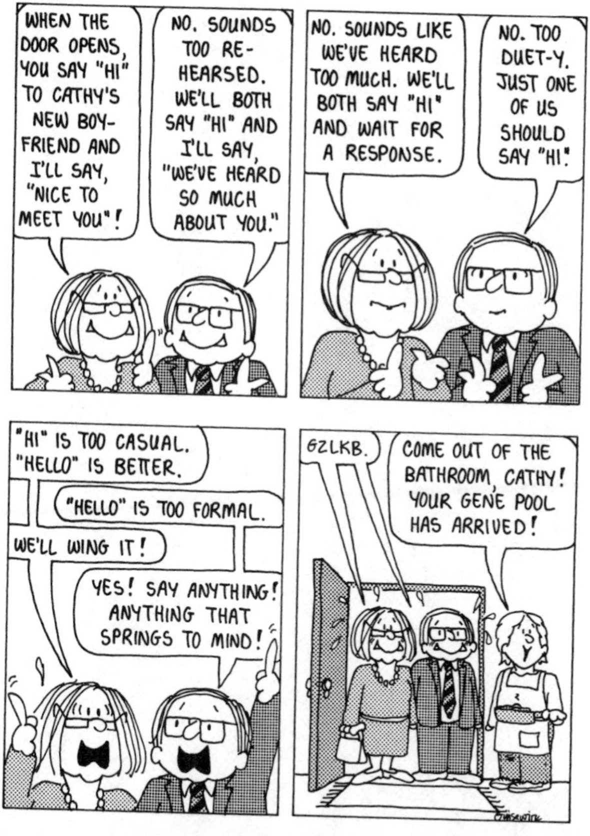

WHEN THE DOOR OPENS, YOU SAY "HI" TO CATHY'S NEW BOY-FRIEND AND I'LL SAY, "NICE TO MEET YOU"!
NO. SOUNDS TOO RE-HEARSED. WE'LL BOTH SAY "HI" AND I'LL SAY, "WE'VE HEARD SO MUCH ABOUT YOU."
NO. SOUNDS LIKE WE'VE HEARD TOO MUCH. WE'LL BOTH SAY "HI" AND WAIT FOR A RESPONSE.
NO. TOO DUET-Y. JUST ONE OF US SHOULD SAY "HI."
"HI" IS TOO CASUAL. "HELLO" IS BETTER.
"HELLO" IS TOO FORMAL.
WE'LL WING IT!
YES! SAY ANYTHING! ANYTHING THAT SPRINGS TO MIND!
GZLKB.
COME OUT OF THE BATHROOM, CATHY! YOUR GENE POOL HAS ARRIVED!

1995

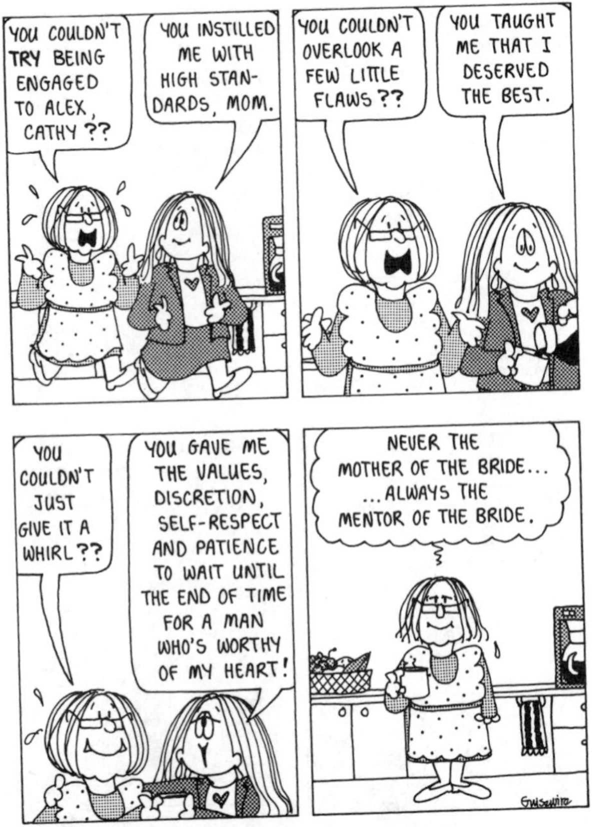
YOU COULDN'T TRY BEING ENGAGED TO ALEX, CATHY??
YOU INSTILLED ME WITH HIGH STANDARDS, MOM.
YOU COULDN'T OVERLOOK A FEW LITTLE FLAWS??
YOU TAUGHT ME THAT I DESERVED THE BEST.
YOU COULDN'T JUST GIVE IT A WHIRL??
YOU GAVE ME THE VALUES, DISCRETION, SELF-RESPECT AND PATIENCE TO WAIT UNTIL THE END OF TIME FOR A MAN WHO'S WORTHY OF MY HEART!
NEVER THE MOTHER OF THE BRIDE... ...ALWAYS THE MENTOR OF THE BRIDE.
Guisewite

1995

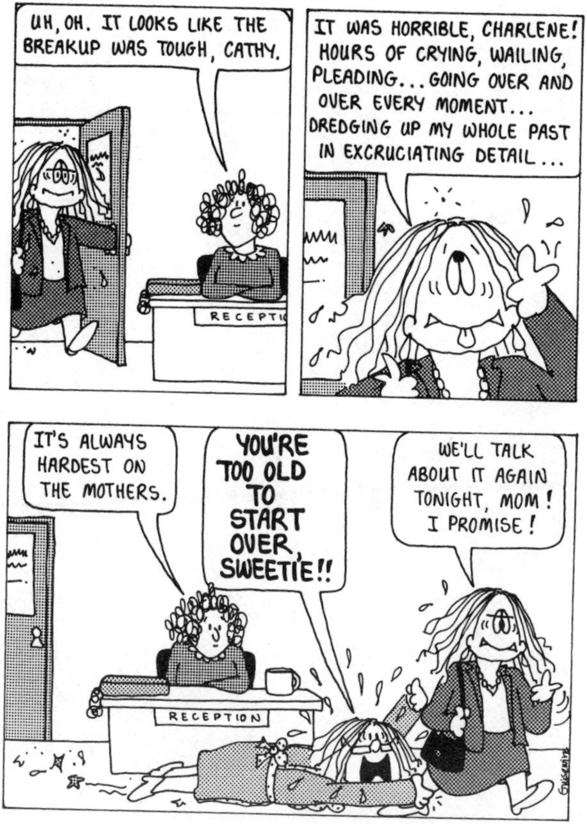

UH, OH. IT LOOKS LIKE THE BREAKUP WAS TOUGH, CATHY.
RECEPTI
IT WAS HORRIBLE, CHARLENE! HOURS OF CRYING, WAILING, PLEADING... GOING OVER AND OVER EVERY MOMENT... DREDGING UP MY WHOLE PAST IN EXCRUCIATING DETAIL...
IT'S ALWAYS HARDEST ON THE MOTHERS.
YOU'RE TOO OLD TO START OVER, SWEETIE!!
WE'LL TALK ABOUT IT AGAIN TONIGHT, MOM! I PROMISE!
RECEPTION

1995

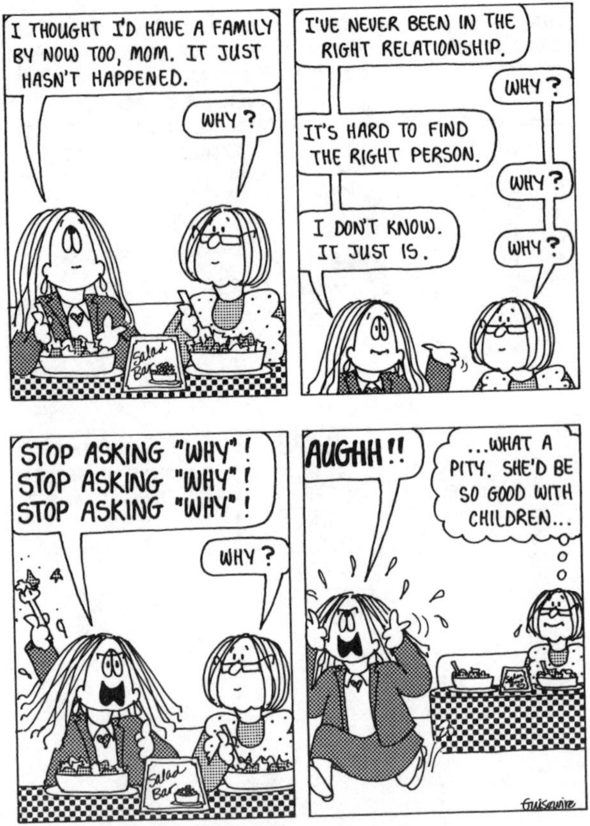
I THOUGHT I'D HAVE A FAMILY BY NOW TOO, MOM. IT JUST HASN'T HAPPENED.
WHY?
Salad Bar
I'VE NEVER BEEN IN THE RIGHT RELATIONSHIP.
WHY?
IT'S HARD TO FIND THE RIGHT PERSON.
WHY?
I DON'T KNOW. IT JUST IS.
WHY?
STOP ASKING "WHY"! STOP ASKING "WHY"! STOP ASKING "WHY"!
WHY?
Salad Bar
AUGHH!!
...WHAT A PITY. SHE'D BE SO GOOD WITH CHILDREN...
Guisewite

1995

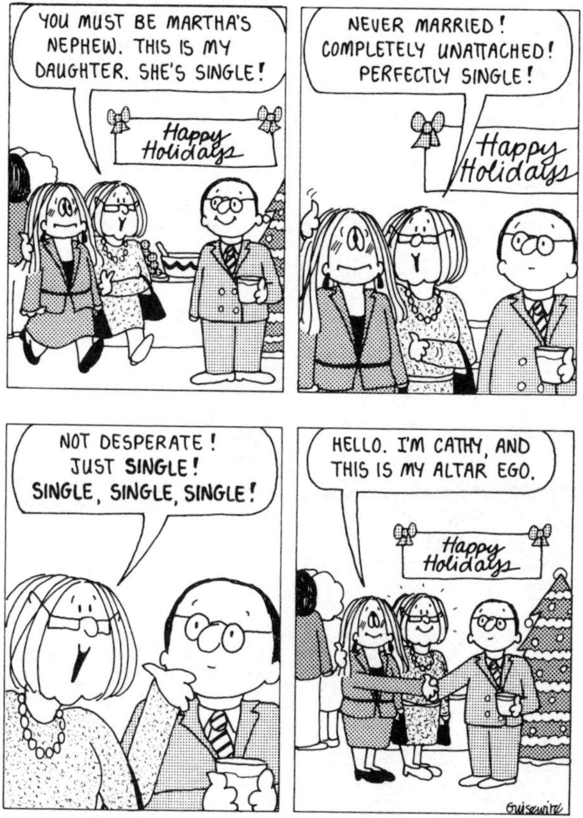
YOU MUST BE MARTHA'S NEPHEW. THIS IS MY DAUGHTER. SHE'S SINGLE!
Happy Holidays
NEVER MARRIED! COMPLETELY UNATTACHED! PERFECTLY SINGLE!
Happy Holidays
NOT DESPERATE! JUST SINGLE! SINGLE, SINGLE, SINGLE!
HELLO. I'M CATHY, AND THIS IS MY ALTAR EGO.
Happy Holidays
Guisewite

1996

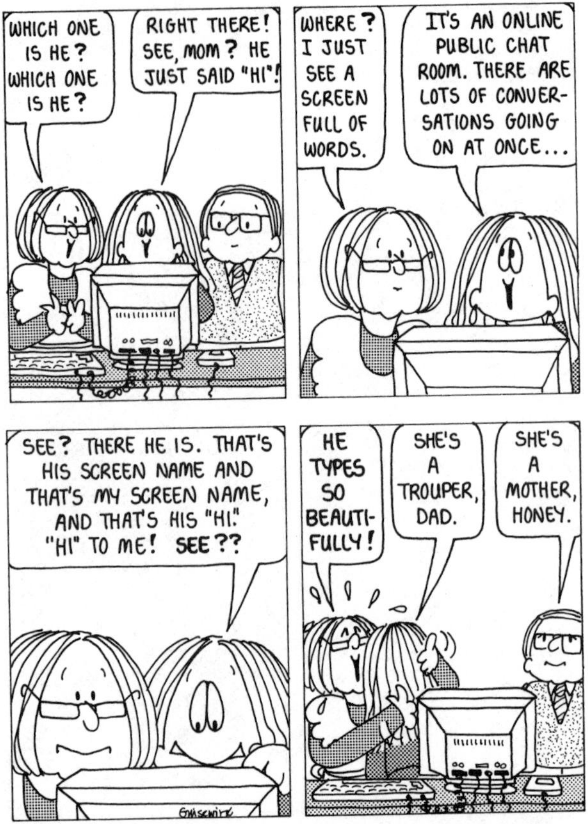
WHICH ONE IS HE? WHICH ONE IS HE?
RIGHT THERE! SEE, MOM? HE JUST SAID "HI"!
WHERE? I JUST SEE A SCREEN FULL OF WORDS.
IT'S AN ONLINE PUBLIC CHAT ROOM. THERE ARE LOTS OF CONVER-SATIONS GOING ON AT ONCE...
SEE? THERE HE IS. THAT'S HIS SCREEN NAME AND THAT'S MY SCREEN NAME, AND THAT'S HIS "HI." "HI" TO ME! SEE??
HE TYPES SO BEAUTI-FULLY!
SHE'S A TROUPER, DAD.
SHE'S A MOTHER, HONEY.

1996

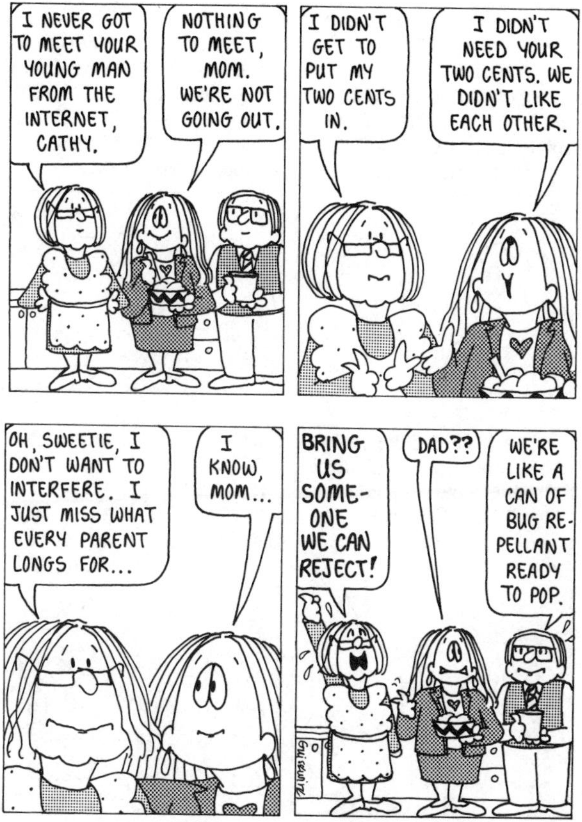

I NEVER GOT TO MEET YOUR YOUNG MAN FROM THE INTERNET, CATHY.
NOTHING TO MEET, MOM. WE'RE NOT GOING OUT.
I DIDN'T GET TO PUT MY TWO CENTS IN.
I DIDN'T NEED YOUR TWO CENTS. WE DIDN'T LIKE EACH OTHER.
OH, SWEETIE, I DON'T WANT TO INTERFERE. I JUST MISS WHAT EVERY PARENT LONGS FOR...
I KNOW, MOM...
BRING US SOME-ONE WE CAN REJECT!
DAD??
WE'RE LIKE A CAN OF BUG RE-PELLANT READY TO POP.

1996

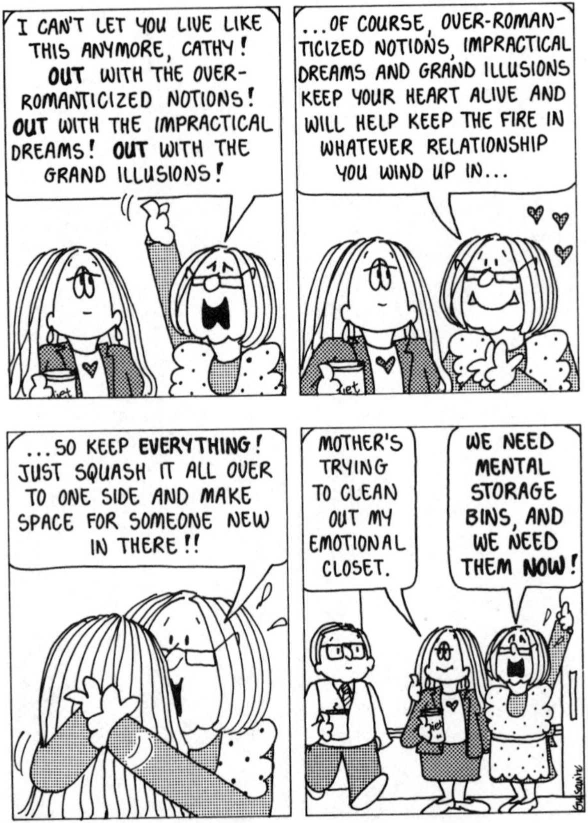
I CAN'T LET YOU LIVE LIKE THIS ANYMORE, CATHY! OUT WITH THE OVER-ROMANTICIZED NOTIONS! OUT WITH THE IMPRACTICAL DREAMS! OUT WITH THE GRAND ILLUSIONS!
...OF COURSE, OVER-ROMANTICIZED NOTIONS, IMPRACTICAL DREAMS AND GRAND ILLUSIONS KEEP YOUR HEART ALIVE AND WILL HELP KEEP THE FIRE IN WHATEVER RELATIONSHIP YOU WIND UP IN...
...SO KEEP EVERYTHING! JUST SQUASH IT ALL OVER TO ONE SIDE AND MAKE SPACE FOR SOMEONE NEW IN THERE!!
MOTHER'S TRYING TO CLEAN OUT MY EMOTIONAL CLOSET.
WE NEED MENTAL STORAGE BINS, AND WE NEED THEM NOW!

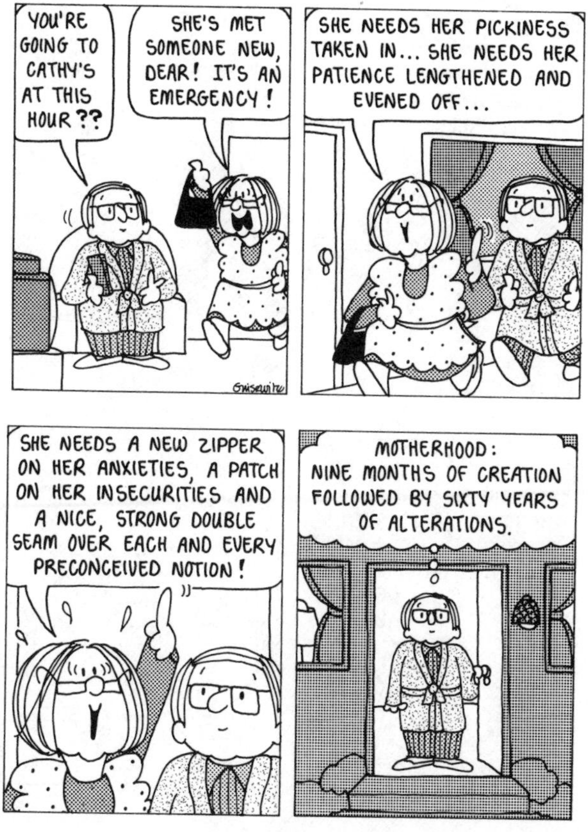
YOU'RE GOING TO CATHY'S AT THIS HOUR??
SHE'S MET SOMEONE NEW, DEAR! IT'S AN EMERGENCY!
SHE NEEDS HER PICKINESS TAKEN IN... SHE NEEDS HER PATIENCE LENGTHENED AND EVENED OFF...
SHE NEEDS A NEW ZIPPER ON HER ANXIETIES, A PATCH ON HER INSECURITIES AND A NICE, STRONG DOUBLE SEAM OVER EACH AND EVERY PRECONCEIVED NOTION!
MOTHERHOOD: NINE MONTHS OF CREATION FOLLOWED BY SIXTY YEARS OF ALTERATIONS.

1997

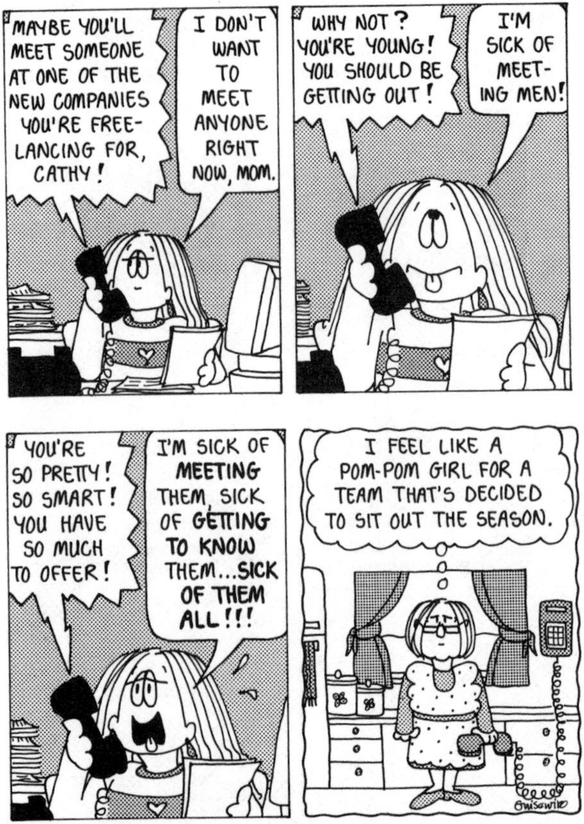
MAYBE YOU'LL MEET SOMEONE AT ONE OF THE NEW COMPANIES YOU'RE FREE-LANCING FOR, CATHY!
I DON'T WANT TO MEET ANYONE RIGHT NOW, MOM.
WHY NOT? YOU'RE YOUNG! YOU SHOULD BE GETTING OUT!
I'M SICK OF MEET-ING MEN!
YOU'RE SO PRETTY! SO SMART! YOU HAVE SO MUCH TO OFFER!
I'M SICK OF MEETING THEM, SICK OF GETTING TO KNOW THEM...SICK OF THEM ALL!!!
I FEEL LIKE A POM-POM GIRL FOR A TEAM THAT'S DECIDED TO SIT OUT THE SEASON.
Guisewite

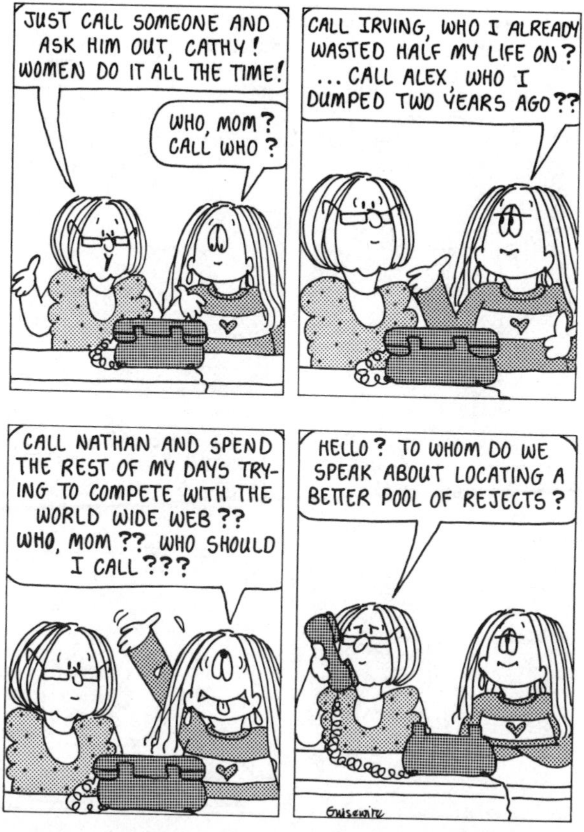
JUST CALL SOMEONE AND ASK HIM OUT, CATHY! WOMEN DO IT ALL THE TIME!
WHO, MOM? CALL WHO?
CALL IRVING, WHO I ALREADY WASTED HALF MY LIFE ON? ...CALL ALEX, WHO I DUMPED TWO YEARS AGO??
CALL NATHAN AND SPEND THE REST OF MY DAYS TRYING TO COMPETE WITH THE WORLD WIDE WEB?? WHO, MOM?? WHO SHOULD I CALL???
HELLO? TO WHOM DO WE SPEAK ABOUT LOCATING A BETTER POOL OF REJECTS?
Guisewite

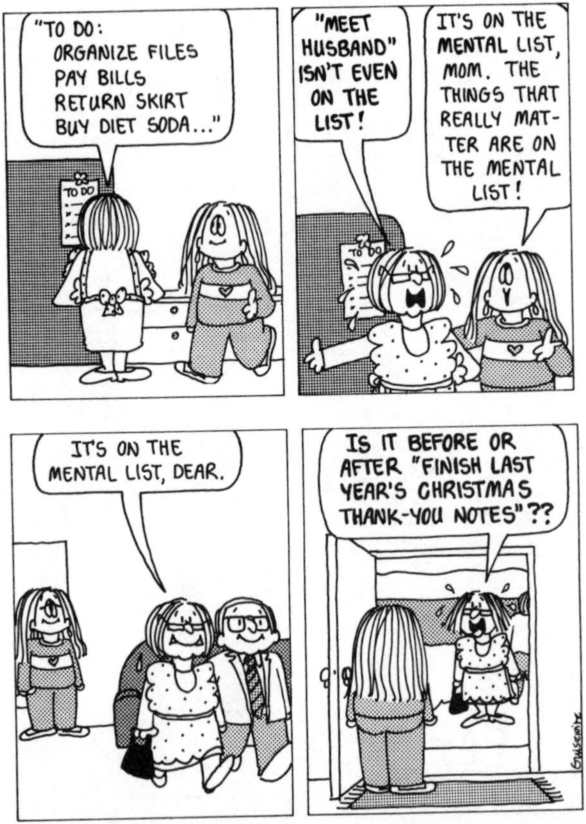
"TO DO:
ORGANIZE FILES
PAY BILLS
RETURN SKIRT
BUY DIET SODA..."
TO DO
"MEET HUSBAND" ISN'T EVEN ON THE LIST!
IT'S ON THE MENTAL LIST, MOM. THE THINGS THAT REALLY MATTER ARE ON THE MENTAL LIST!
TO DO
IT'S ON THE MENTAL LIST, DEAR.
IS IT BEFORE OR AFTER "FINISH LAST YEAR'S CHRISTMAS THANK-YOU NOTES"??
GUISEWITE

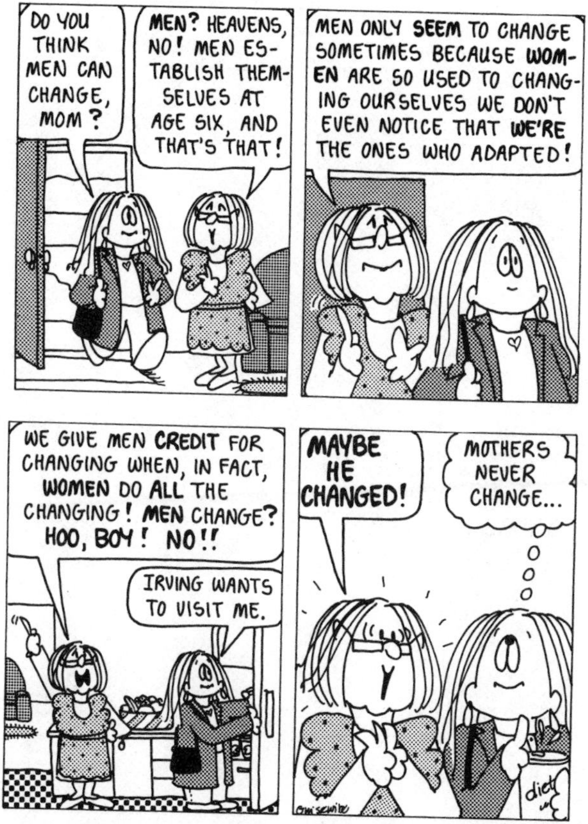
DO YOU THINK MEN CAN CHANGE, MOM?
MEN? HEAVENS, NO! MEN ESTABLISH THEMSELVES AT AGE SIX, AND THAT'S THAT!
MEN ONLY SEEM TO CHANGE SOMETIMES BECAUSE WOMEN ARE SO USED TO CHANGING OURSELVES WE DON'T EVEN NOTICE THAT WE'RE THE ONES WHO ADAPTED!
WE GIVE MEN CREDIT FOR CHANGING WHEN, IN FACT, WOMEN DO ALL THE CHANGING! MEN CHANGE? HOO, BOY! NO!!
IRVING WANTS TO VISIT ME.
MAYBE HE CHANGED!
MOTHERS NEVER CHANGE...
diet

1997

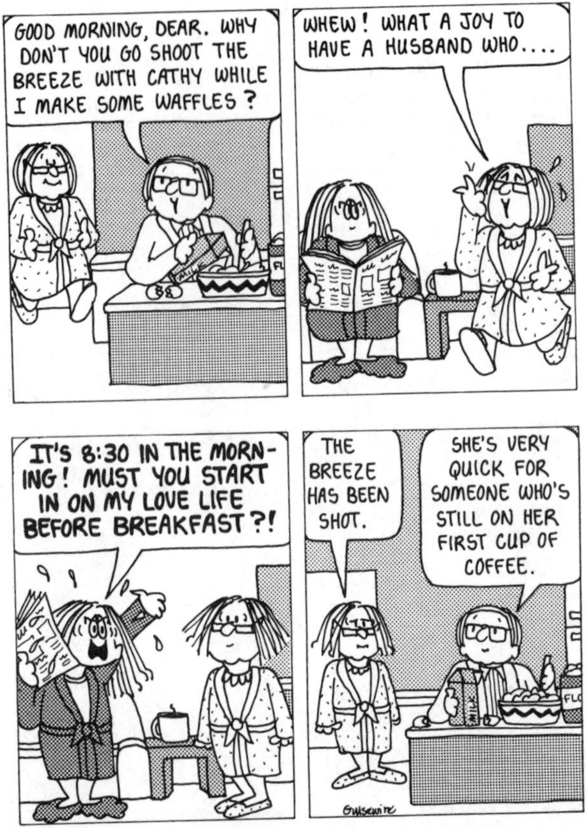
GOOD MORNING, DEAR. WHY DON'T YOU GO SHOOT THE BREEZE WITH CATHY WHILE I MAKE SOME WAFFLES?
WHEW! WHAT A JOY TO HAVE A HUSBAND WHO....
IT'S 8:30 IN THE MORNING! MUST YOU START IN ON MY LOVE LIFE BEFORE BREAKFAST?!
THE BREEZE HAS BEEN SHOT.
SHE'S VERY QUICK FOR SOMEONE WHO'S STILL ON HER FIRST CUP OF COFFEE.
Guisewite

1998

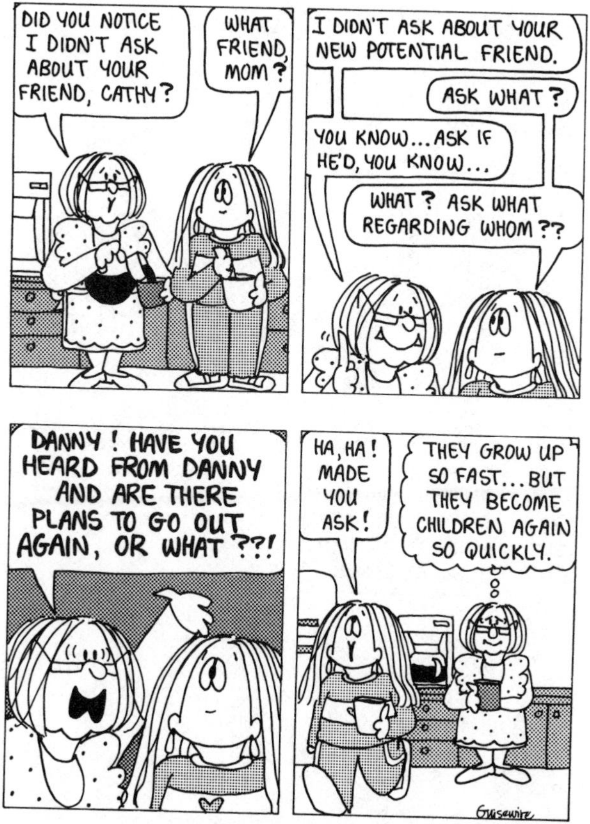
DID YOU NOTICE I DIDN'T ASK ABOUT YOUR FRIEND, CATHY?
WHAT FRIEND, MOM?
I DIDN'T ASK ABOUT YOUR NEW POTENTIAL FRIEND.
ASK WHAT?
YOU KNOW... ASK IF HE'D, YOU KNOW...
WHAT? ASK WHAT REGARDING WHOM??
DANNY! HAVE YOU HEARD FROM DANNY AND ARE THERE PLANS TO GO OUT AGAIN, OR WHAT??!
HA, HA! MADE YOU ASK!
THEY GROW UP SO FAST... BUT THEY BECOME CHILDREN AGAIN SO QUICKLY.
Guisewite

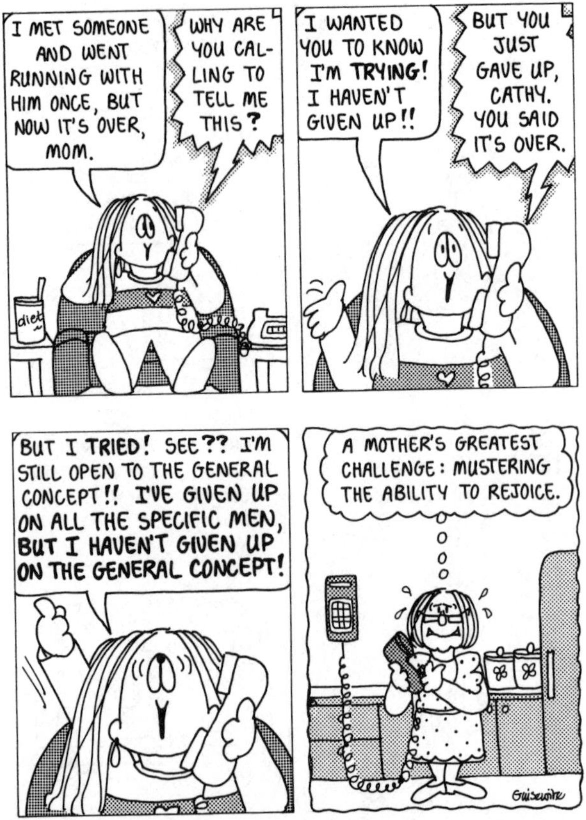
I MET SOMEONE AND WENT RUNNING WITH HIM ONCE, BUT NOW IT'S OVER, MOM.
WHY ARE YOU CALLING TO TELL ME THIS?
I WANTED YOU TO KNOW I'M TRYING! I HAVEN'T GIVEN UP!!
BUT YOU JUST GAVE UP, CATHY. YOU SAID IT'S OVER.
BUT I TRIED! SEE?? I'M STILL OPEN TO THE GENERAL CONCEPT!! I'VE GIVEN UP ON ALL THE SPECIFIC MEN, BUT I HAVEN'T GIVEN UP ON THE GENERAL CONCEPT!
A MOTHER'S GREATEST CHALLENGE: MUSTERING THE ABILITY TO REJOICE.
diet
Guisewite

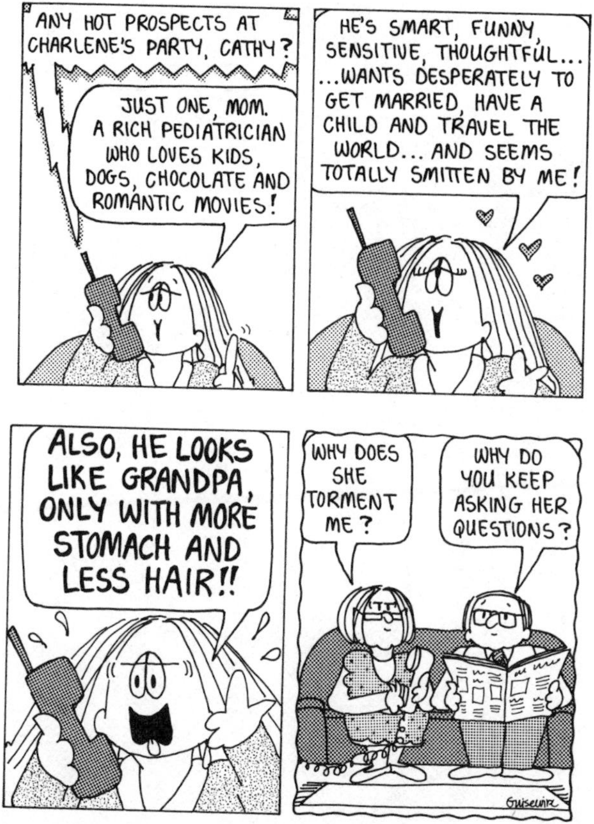
ANY HOT PROSPECTS AT CHARLENE'S PARTY, CATHY?
JUST ONE, MOM. A RICH PEDIATRICIAN WHO LOVES KIDS, DOGS, CHOCOLATE AND ROMANTIC MOVIES!
HE'S SMART, FUNNY, SENSITIVE, THOUGHTFUL... ...WANTS DESPERATELY TO GET MARRIED, HAVE A CHILD AND TRAVEL THE WORLD... AND SEEMS TOTALLY SMITTEN BY ME!
ALSO, HE LOOKS LIKE GRANDPA, ONLY WITH MORE STOMACH AND LESS HAIR!!
WHY DOES SHE TORMENT ME?
WHY DO YOU KEEP ASKING HER QUESTIONS?
Guisewite

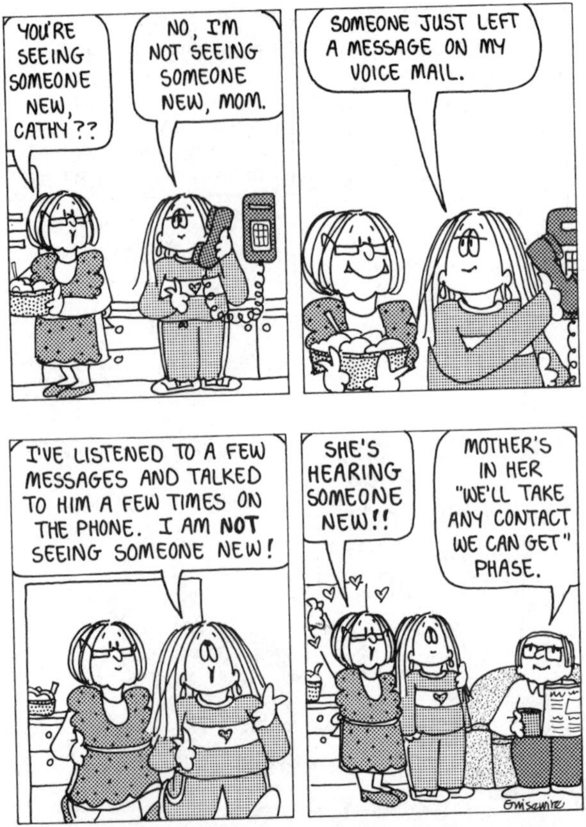
YOU'RE SEEING SOMEONE NEW, CATHY??
NO, I'M NOT SEEING SOMEONE NEW, MOM.
SOMEONE JUST LEFT A MESSAGE ON MY VOICE MAIL.
I'VE LISTENED TO A FEW MESSAGES AND TALKED TO HIM A FEW TIMES ON THE PHONE. I AM NOT SEEING SOMEONE NEW!
SHE'S HEARING SOMEONE NEW!!
MOTHER'S IN HER "WE'LL TAKE ANY CONTACT WE CAN GET" PHASE.
Guisewite

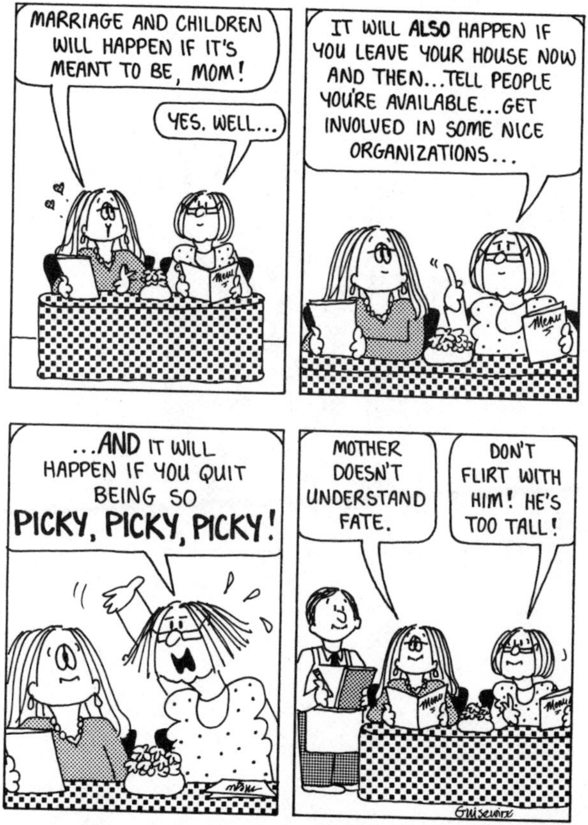
MARRIAGE AND CHILDREN WILL HAPPEN IF IT'S MEANT TO BE, MOM!
YES. WELL...
IT WILL ALSO HAPPEN IF YOU LEAVE YOUR HOUSE NOW AND THEN...TELL PEOPLE YOU'RE AVAILABLE...GET INVOLVED IN SOME NICE ORGANIZATIONS...
...AND IT WILL HAPPEN IF YOU QUIT BEING SO PICKY, PICKY, PICKY!
MOTHER DOESN'T UNDERSTAND FATE.
DON'T FLIRT WITH HIM! HE'S TOO TALL!
Guisewite

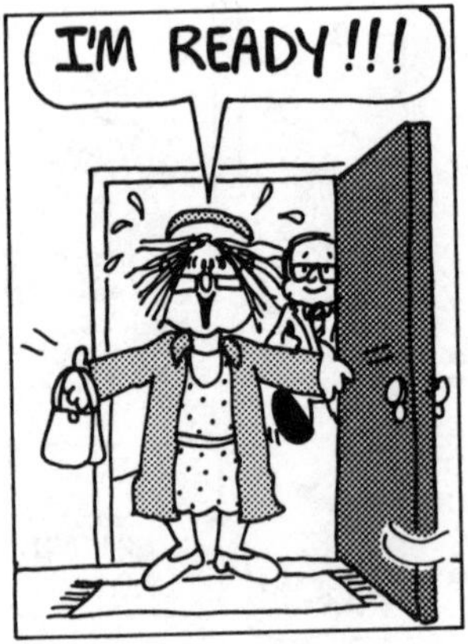
I'M READY!!!

The Miracle Worker

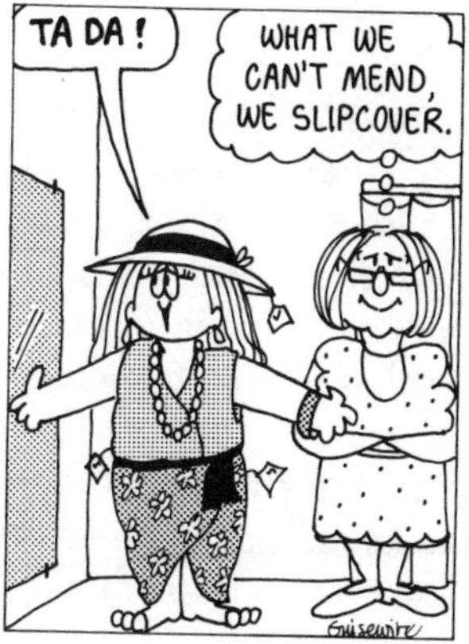
TA DA!
WHAT WE CAN'T MEND, WE SLIPCOVER.

I've seen my mother take a piece of cheese, a leftover yogurt, and some wilted lettuce out of my refrigerator and whip them into a three-course meal.

I've seen her turn a half-eaten melon, some peas, a box of whole wheat crackers, and some Cocoa Puffs into an hors d'oeuvres platter that rivals the best restaurant's in town when unexpected company popped in.

I've seen her pull an ancient, ripped shirt out of the "rag" box and transform it into a chic 20-piece Barbie wardrobe.

I've watched her march into her laundry room with a stain that the entire city of dry cleaners gave up on and emerge an hour later with a dress that looked brand new.

I've heard Mom solve the problems of the country in a few short sentences.

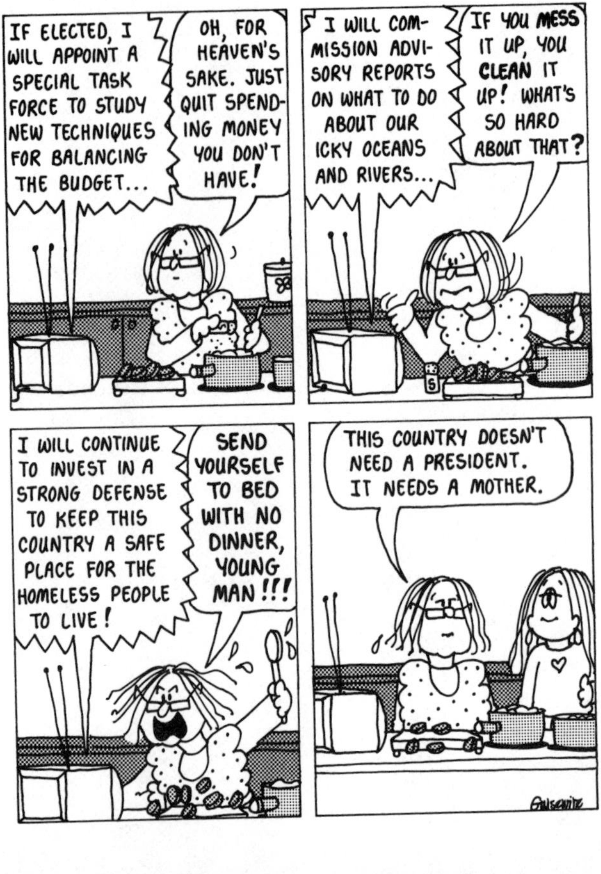
IF ELECTED, I WILL APPOINT A SPECIAL TASK FORCE TO STUDY NEW TECHNIQUES FOR BALANCING THE BUDGET...
OH, FOR HEAVEN'S SAKE. JUST QUIT SPENDING MONEY YOU DON'T HAVE!
I WILL COMMISSION ADVISORY REPORTS ON WHAT TO DO ABOUT OUR ICKY OCEANS AND RIVERS...
IF YOU MESS IT UP, YOU CLEAN IT UP! WHAT'S SO HARD ABOUT THAT?
I WILL CONTINUE TO INVEST IN A STRONG DEFENSE TO KEEP THIS COUNTRY A SAFE PLACE FOR THE HOMELESS PEOPLE TO LIVE!
SEND YOURSELF TO BED WITH NO DINNER, YOUNG MAN!!!
THIS COUNTRY DOESN'T NEED A PRESIDENT. IT NEEDS A MOTHER.
GUISEWITE

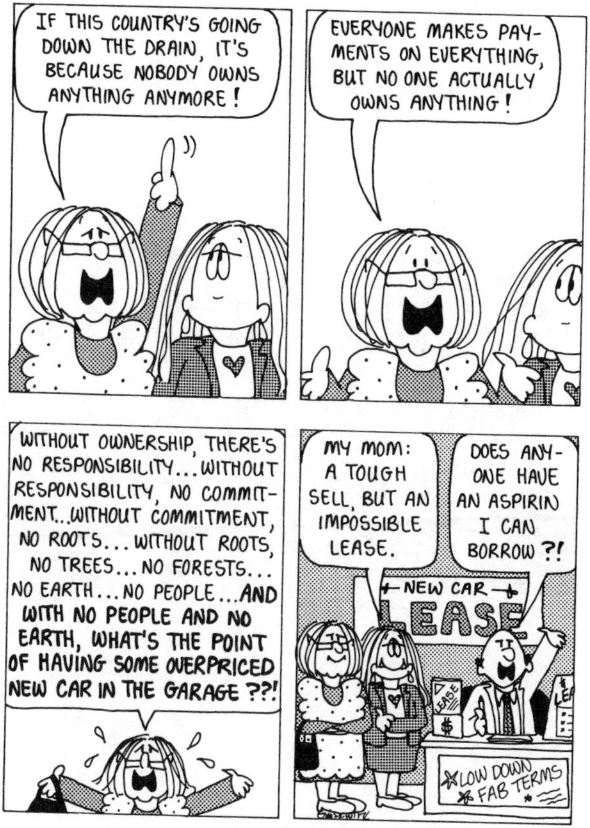

IF THIS COUNTRY'S GOING DOWN THE DRAIN, IT'S BECAUSE NOBODY OWNS ANYTHING ANYMORE!
EVERYONE MAKES PAYMENTS ON EVERYTHING, BUT NO ONE ACTUALLY OWNS ANYTHING!
WITHOUT OWNERSHIP, THERE'S NO RESPONSIBILITY... WITHOUT RESPONSIBILITY, NO COMMITMENT... WITHOUT COMMITMENT, NO ROOTS... WITHOUT ROOTS, NO TREES... NO FORESTS... NO EARTH... NO PEOPLE... AND WITH NO PEOPLE AND NO EARTH, WHAT'S THE POINT OF HAVING SOME OVERPRICED NEW CAR IN THE GARAGE??!
MY MOM: A TOUGH SELL, BUT AN IMPOSSIBLE LEASE.
DOES ANYONE HAVE AN ASPIRIN I CAN BORROW?!
NEW CAR
LEASE
LEASE
$
LOW DOWN
FAB TERMS

I've seen Mom undo a 25-year-long speech in 25 seconds.

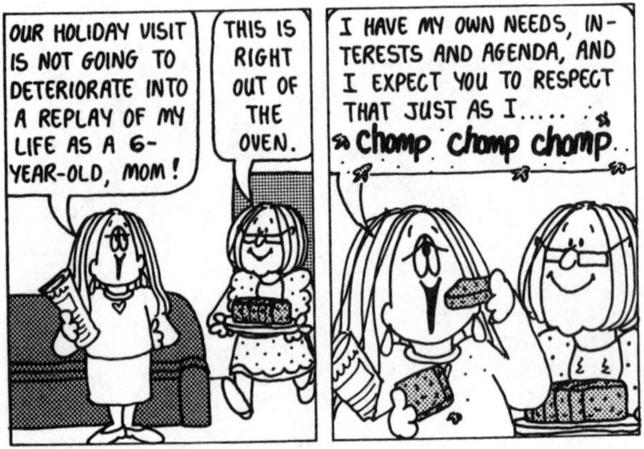

OUR HOLIDAY VISIT IS NOT GOING TO DETERIORATE INTO A REPLAY OF MY LIFE AS A 6-YEAR-OLD, MOM!
THIS IS RIGHT OUT OF THE OVEN.
I HAVE MY OWN NEEDS, INTERESTS AND AGENDA, AND I EXPECT YOU TO RESPECT THAT JUST AS I.....
chomp chomp chomp

HERE. LET ME PULL ALL THAT HAIR AWAY FROM YOUR PRETTY FACE, SWEETIE.
OK
...ANOTHER PROFESSIONAL DYNAMO, LEVELED BY MOM'S HOLIDAY NUTBREAD.

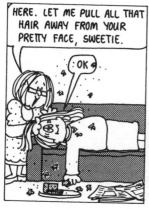

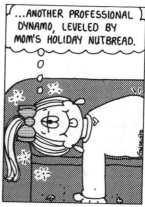

I've seen Mom take one job—"Mom"—and parlay it into a thousand different roles.

The Chameleon

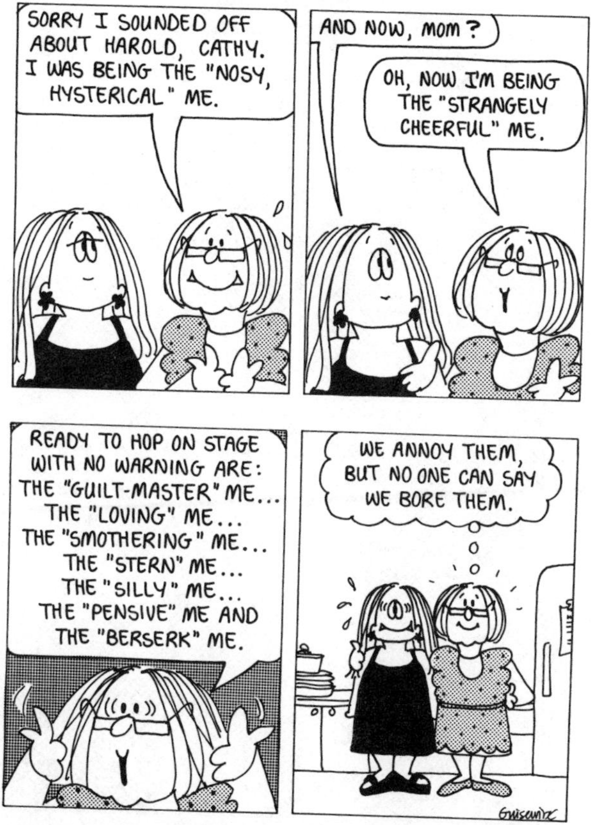

SORRY I SOUNDED OFF ABOUT HAROLD, CATHY. I WAS BEING THE "NOSY, HYSTERICAL" ME.
AND NOW, MOM?
OH, NOW I'M BEING THE "STRANGELY CHEERFUL" ME.
READY TO HOP ON STAGE WITH NO WARNING ARE: THE "GUILT-MASTER" ME... THE "LOVING" ME... THE "SMOTHERING" ME... THE "STERN" ME... THE "SILLY" ME... THE "PENSIVE" ME AND THE "BERSERK" ME.
WE ANNOY THEM, BUT NO ONE CAN SAY WE BORE THEM.
Guisewite

The Heroine

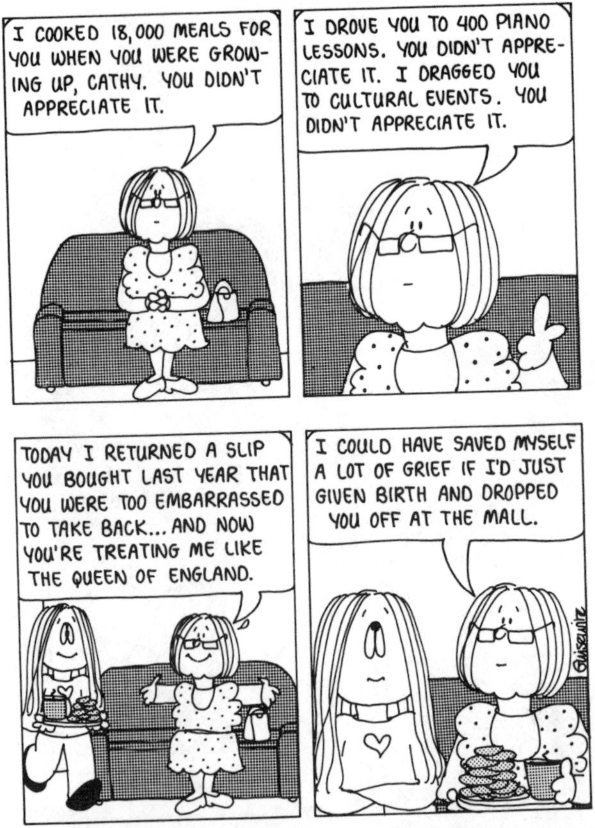
I COOKED 18,000 MEALS FOR YOU WHEN YOU WERE GROWING UP, CATHY. YOU DIDN'T APPRECIATE IT.
I DROVE YOU TO 400 PIANO LESSONS. YOU DIDN'T APPRECIATE IT. I DRAGGED YOU TO CULTURAL EVENTS. YOU DIDN'T APPRECIATE IT.
TODAY I RETURNED A SLIP YOU BOUGHT LAST YEAR THAT YOU WERE TOO EMBARRASSED TO TAKE BACK... AND NOW YOU'RE TREATING ME LIKE THE QUEEN OF ENGLAND.
I COULD HAVE SAVED MYSELF A LOT OF GRIEF IF I'D JUST GIVEN BIRTH AND DROPPED YOU OFF AT THE MALL.
GUISEWITE

The Advocate

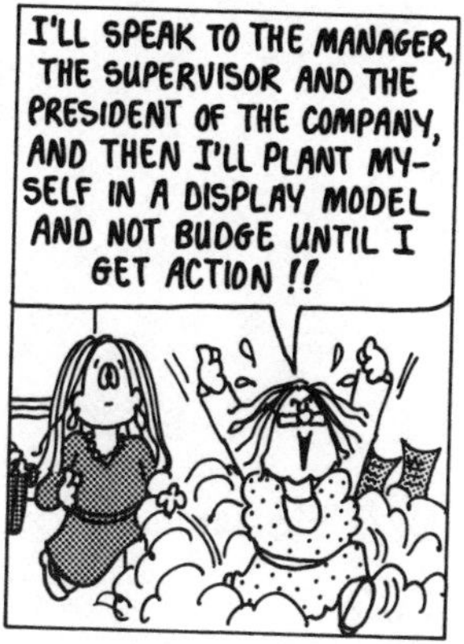
I'LL SPEAK TO THE MANAGER, THE SUPERVISOR AND THE PRESIDENT OF THE COMPANY, AND THEN I'LL PLANT MY-SELF IN A DISPLAY MODEL AND NOT BUDGE UNTIL I GET ACTION !!

The Healer

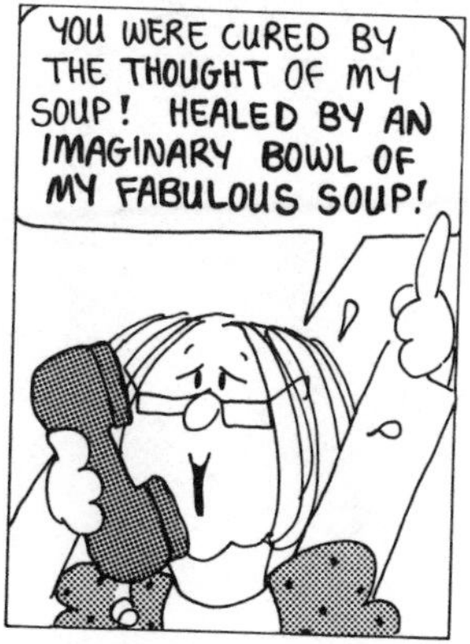
YOU WERE CURED BY THE THOUGHT OF MY SOUP! HEALED BY AN IMAGINARY BOWL OF MY FABULOUS SOUP!

The 24-Hour Hotline

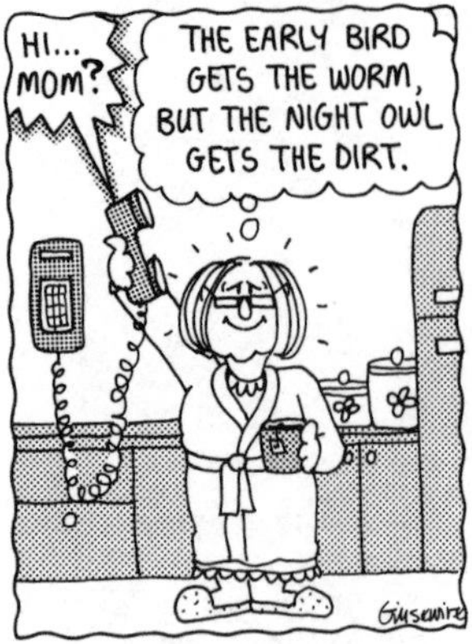
HI... MOM?
THE EARLY BIRD GETS THE WORM, BUT THE NIGHT OWL GETS THE DIRT.
Guisewite

The Teacher

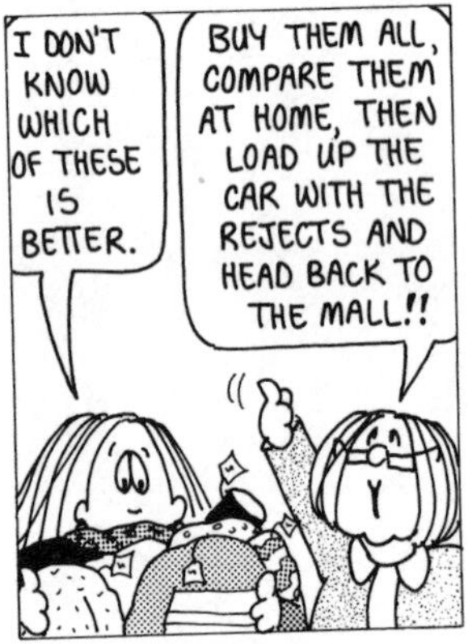
I DON'T KNOW WHICH OF THESE IS BETTER.
BUY THEM ALL, COMPARE THEM AT HOME, THEN LOAD UP THE CAR WITH THE REJECTS AND HEAD BACK TO THE MALL!!

The Convenience Store

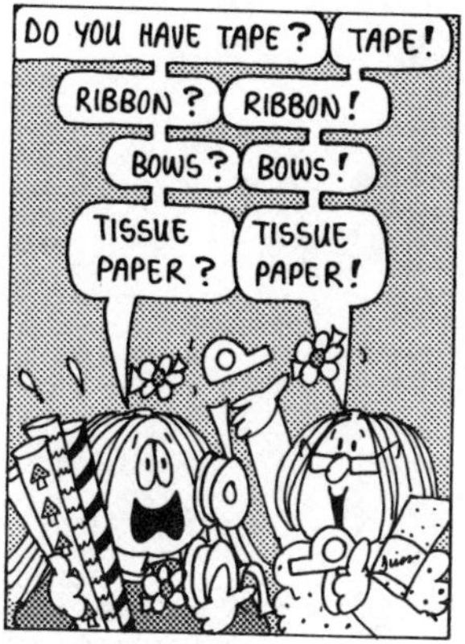
DO YOU HAVE TAPE?
TAPE!
RIBBON?
RIBBON!
BOWS?
BOWS!
TISSUE PAPER?
TISSUE PAPER!

The Conscience

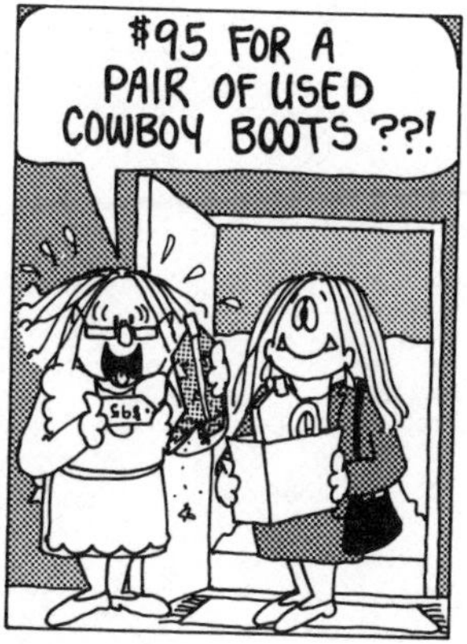
$95 FOR A PAIR OF USED COWBOY BOOTS??!

The Spokesperson

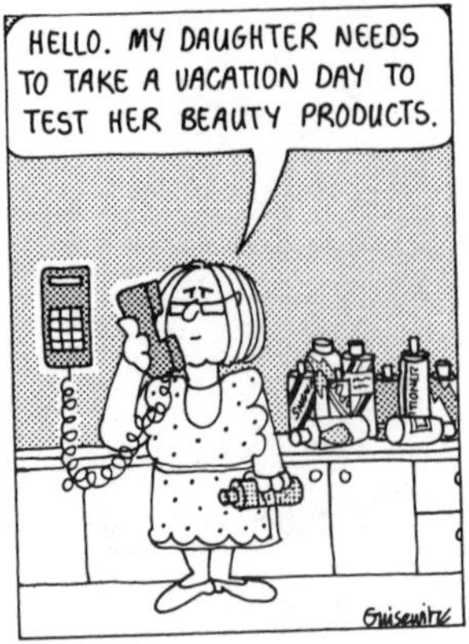
HELLO. MY DAUGHTER NEEDS TO TAKE A VACATION DAY TO TEST HER BEAUTY PRODUCTS.

The Idea Person

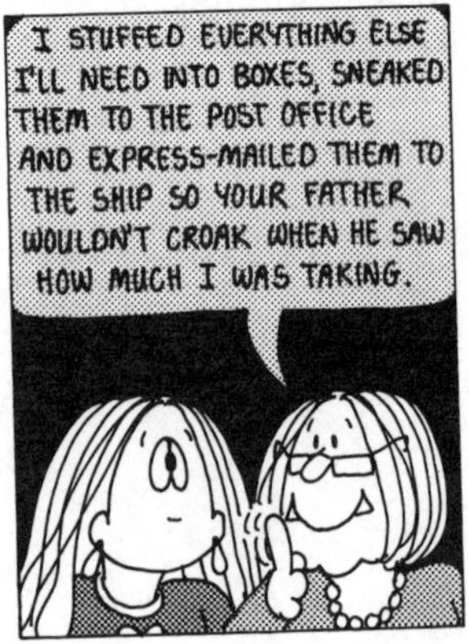
I STUFFED EVERYTHING ELSE I'LL NEED INTO BOXES, SNEAKED THEM TO THE POST OFFICE AND EXPRESS-MAILED THEM TO THE SHIP SO YOUR FATHER WOULDN'T CROAK WHEN HE SAW HOW MUCH I WAS TAKING.

The Personal Assistant

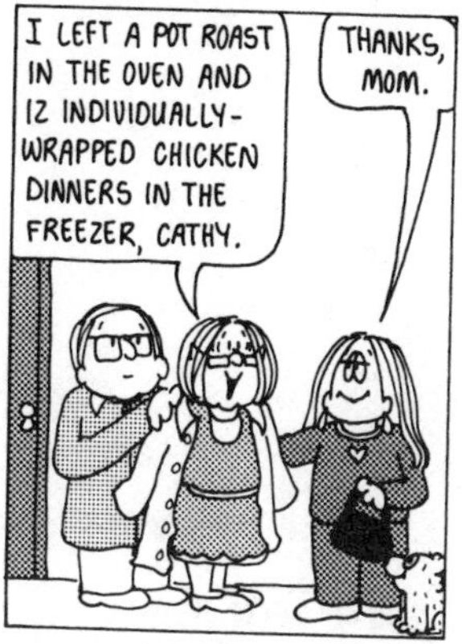
I LEFT A POT ROAST IN THE OVEN AND 12 INDIVIDUALLY-WRAPPED CHICKEN DINNERS IN THE FREEZER, CATHY.
THANKS, MOM.

The Prophet

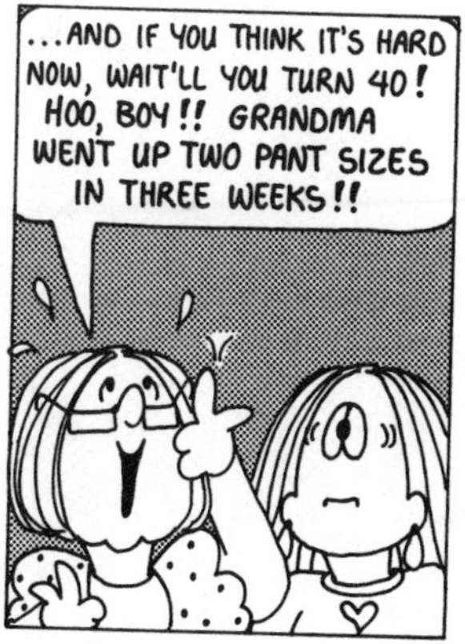
...AND IF YOU THINK IT'S HARD NOW, WAIT'LL YOU TURN 40! HOO, BOY!! GRANDMA WENT UP TWO PANT SIZES IN THREE WEEKS!!

The Team Player

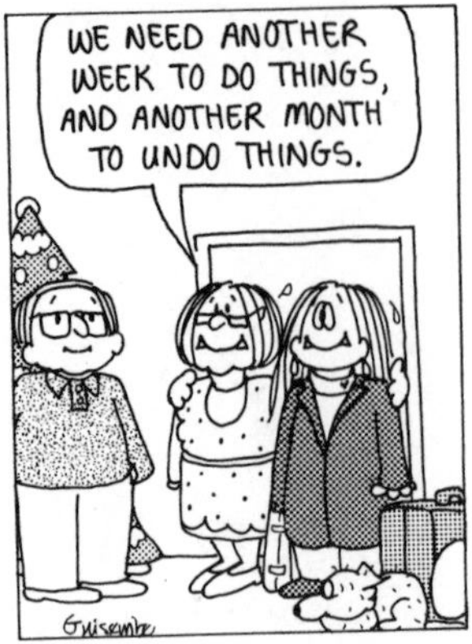
WE NEED ANOTHER WEEK TO DO THINGS, AND ANOTHER MONTH TO UNDO THINGS.

The Defender

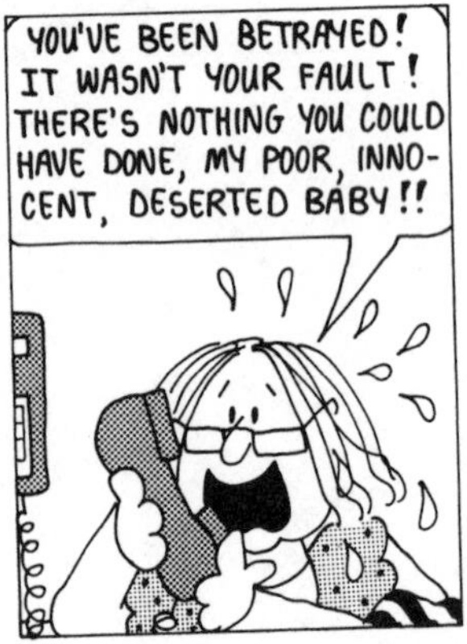
YOU'VE BEEN BETRAYED! IT WASN'T YOUR FAULT! THERE'S NOTHING YOU COULD HAVE DONE, MY POOR, INNO-CENT, DESERTED BABY!!

The Confidante

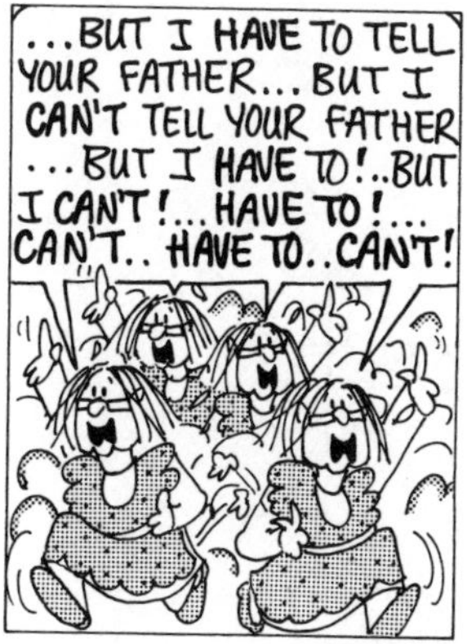
...BUT I HAVE TO TELL YOUR FATHER... BUT I CAN'T TELL YOUR FATHER ...BUT I HAVE TO!..BUT I CAN'T!...HAVE TO!... CAN'T.. HAVE TO..CAN'T!

The Saint

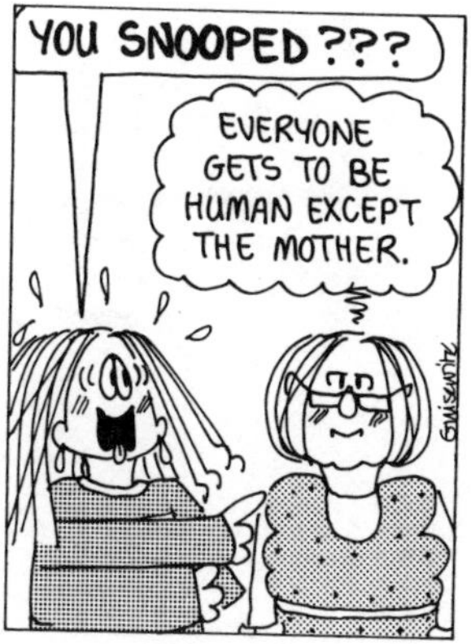
YOU SNOOPED???
EVERYONE GETS TO BE HUMAN EXCEPT THE MOTHER.

The Winner

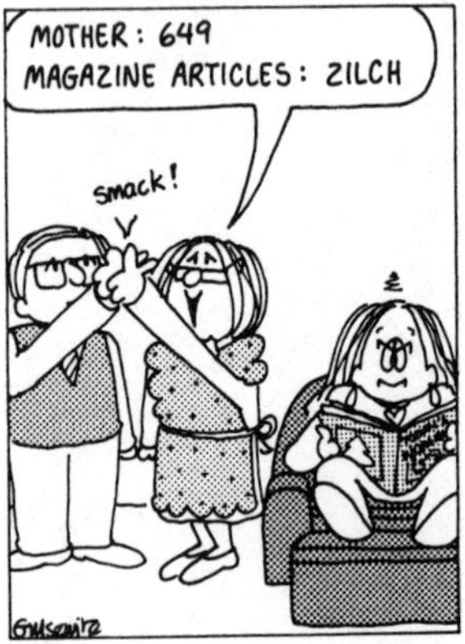
MOTHER: 649
MAGAZINE ARTICLES: ZILCH
smack!

The Clone

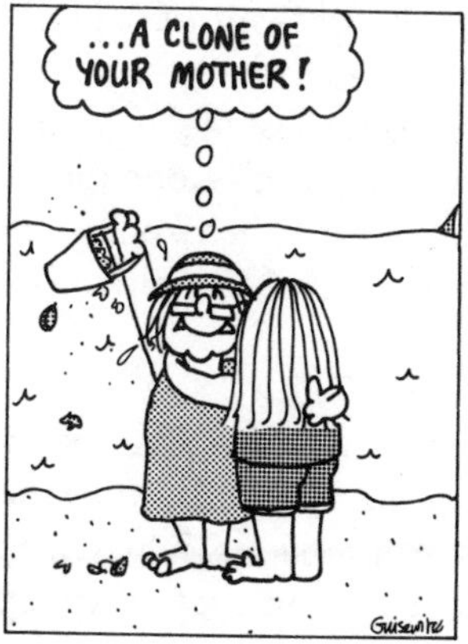
...A CLONE OF
YOUR MOTHER!
Guisewite

I watched my hand reach for the cold, charred piece of toast with the petrified blob of grape jelly squashed on the side that no one else would eat, and I realized it was all over for me.

Not only did it not bother me that I was doing something that made me crazy when my mother did it, I felt smug and sort of self-righteous about doing it.

I drank my room temperature coffee ("Oh, don't bother warming it up for just me") . . . in the icky, chipped cup ("I don't want to get a nice one all dirty") . . . leaned back in the wobbly chair ("I'll take this one; you might fall and hurt yourself") . . . and thought about how far I've come.

After 25 years of assertiveness training, self-help seminars, empowerment lectures, individuation workshops, Goddess retreats, affirmations, introspections, visualizations, therapy sessions, and support groups, I have become an exact clone of my mother.

Even more stunning, after all that, it seems that I'm way more like my mother than Mom was like her mother, and she never did an "actualization meditation" in her life.

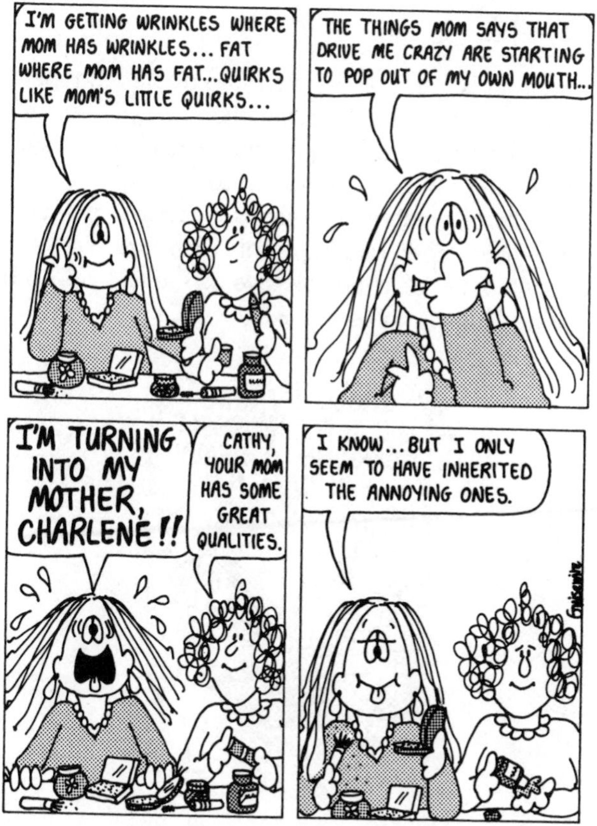
I'M GETTING WRINKLES WHERE MOM HAS WRINKLES... FAT WHERE MOM HAS FAT...QUIRKS LIKE MOM'S LITTLE QUIRKS...
THE THINGS MOM SAYS THAT DRIVE ME CRAZY ARE STARTING TO POP OUT OF MY OWN MOUTH...
I'M TURNING INTO MY MOTHER, CHARLENE!!
CATHY, YOUR MOM HAS SOME GREAT QUALITIES.
I KNOW... BUT I ONLY SEEM TO HAVE INHERITED THE ANNOYING ONES.

The truth is, after all the worrying about it happening, it's been a relief to finally become her.

First, there's someone to blame, which is always a beautiful thing. But mostly, it's just so freeing.

Now that I see that I'm truly as indecisive as Mom is, I can view it as "open minded," not "wishy-washy."

Now that I'm as overprotective as she is, I view it as "nurturing," not "smothering".

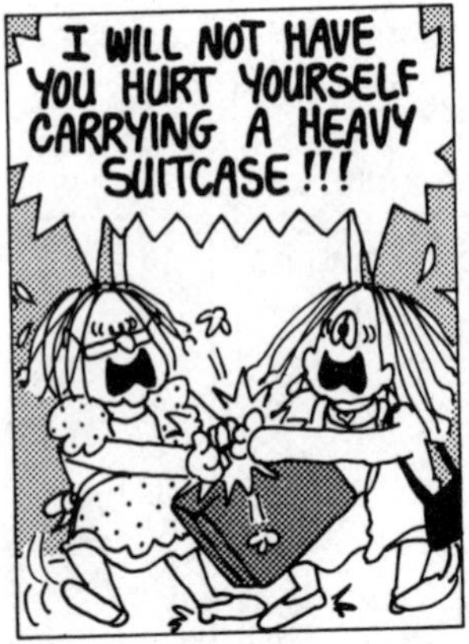
I WILL NOT HAVE YOU HURT YOURSELF CARRYING A HEAVY SUITCASE !!!

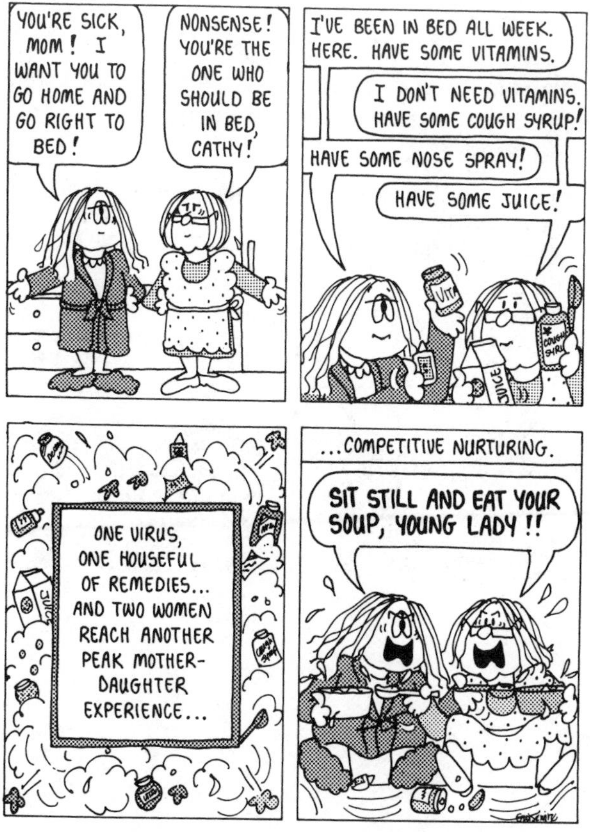
YOU'RE SICK, MOM! I WANT YOU TO GO HOME AND GO RIGHT TO BED!
NONSENSE! YOU'RE THE ONE WHO SHOULD BE IN BED, CATHY!
I'VE BEEN IN BED ALL WEEK. HERE. HAVE SOME VITAMINS.
I DON'T NEED VITAMINS. HAVE SOME COUGH SYRUP!
HAVE SOME NOSE SPRAY!
HAVE SOME JUICE!
JUICE
ONE VIRUS, ONE HOUSEFUL OF REMEDIES... AND TWO WOMEN REACH ANOTHER PEAK MOTHER-DAUGHTER EXPERIENCE...
...COMPETITIVE NURTURING.
SIT STILL AND EAT YOUR SOUP, YOUNG LADY!!

Now that I see that I procrastinate exactly as much as Mom, I can experience it not as an annoyance, but as a bonding event.

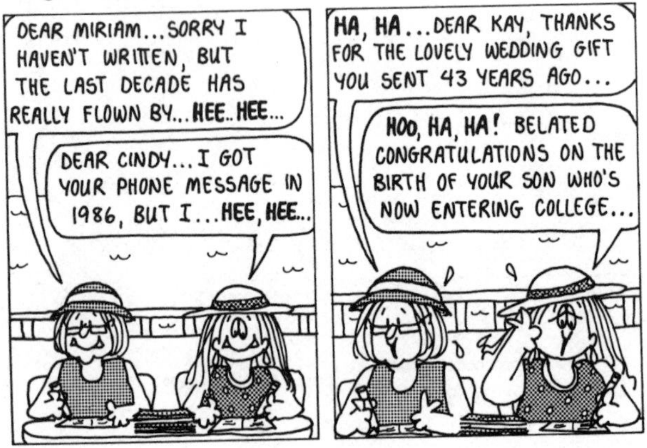
DEAR MIRIAM... SORRY I HAVEN'T WRITTEN, BUT THE LAST DECADE HAS REALLY FLOWN BY... HEE.. HEE...
DEAR CINDY... I GOT YOUR PHONE MESSAGE IN 1986, BUT I... HEE, HEE...
HA, HA... DEAR KAY, THANKS FOR THE LOVELY WEDDING GIFT YOU SENT 43 YEARS AGO...
HOO, HA, HA! BELATED CONGRATULATIONS ON THE BIRTH OF YOUR SON WHO'S NOW ENTERING COLLEGE...

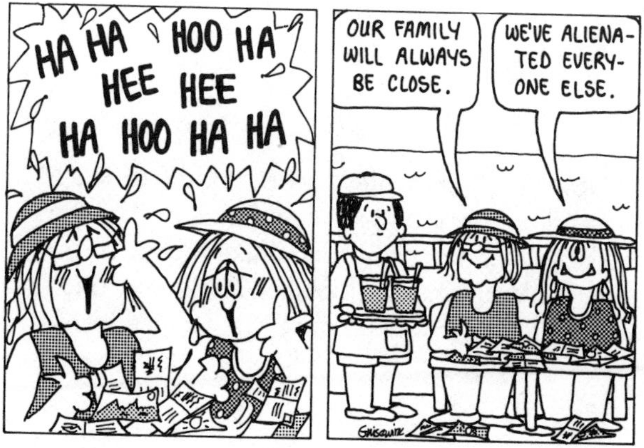
HA HA HOO HA
HEE HEE
HA HOO HA HA
OUR FAMILY WILL ALWAYS BE CLOSE.
WE'VE ALIENATED EVERYONE ELSE.
GUISEWITE

Now that, in real life, I have a husband like Mom, children like Mom, and my own home and all the responsibilities that come with it like Mom . . . now I can go to Mom's house, look her in the eye, and feel I'm finally standing solidly on my own two little feet.

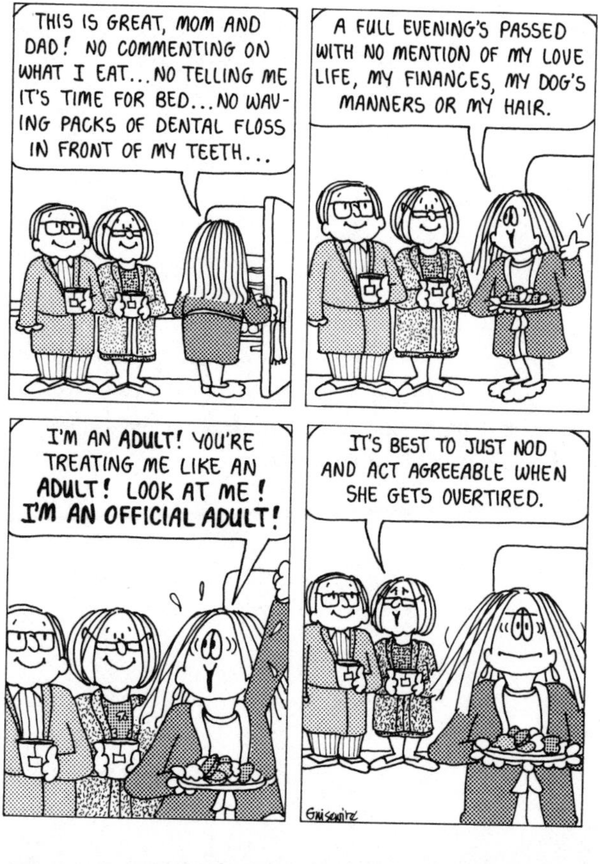
THIS IS GREAT, MOM AND DAD! NO COMMENTING ON WHAT I EAT... NO TELLING ME IT'S TIME FOR BED... NO WAVING PACKS OF DENTAL FLOSS IN FRONT OF MY TEETH...
A FULL EVENING'S PASSED WITH NO MENTION OF MY LOVE LIFE, MY FINANCES, MY DOG'S MANNERS OR MY HAIR.
I'M AN ADULT! YOU'RE TREATING ME LIKE AN ADULT! LOOK AT ME! I'M AN OFFICIAL ADULT!
IT'S BEST TO JUST NOD AND ACT AGREEABLE WHEN SHE GETS OVERTIRED.
Guisewite

I got to grow up with Mom in an amazing time for women. We experienced the women's movement together—alternately dragging each other forward, and hauling each other back.

1978

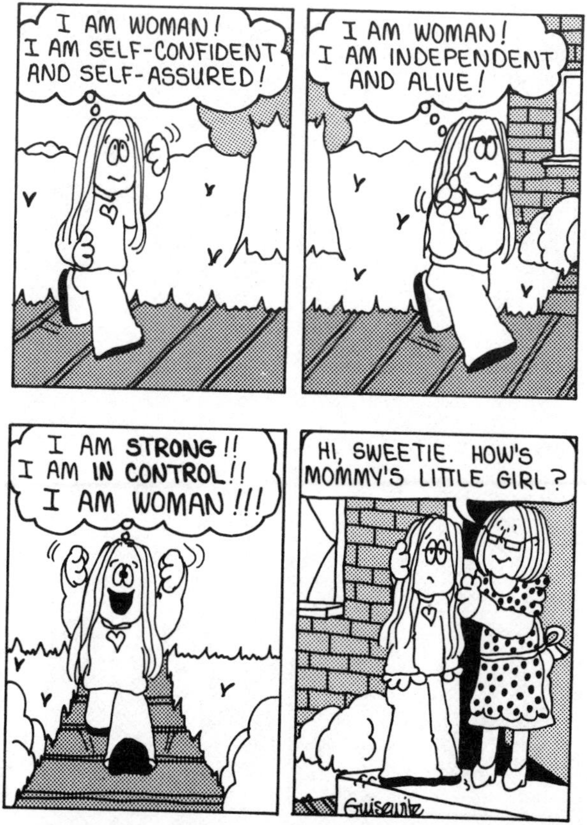
I AM WOMAN! I AM SELF-CONFIDENT AND SELF-ASSURED!
I AM WOMAN! I AM INDEPENDENT AND ALIVE!
I AM STRONG!! I AM IN CONTROL!! I AM WOMAN!!!
HI, SWEETIE. HOW'S MOMMY'S LITTLE GIRL?
Guisewite

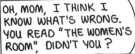

OH, MOM, I THINK I KNOW WHAT'S WRONG. YOU READ "THE WOMEN'S ROOM", DIDN'T YOU?

IT CAME IN MY BOOK CLUB.

I THOUGHT IT WAS GOING TO BE A CUTE LITTLE ROMANCE... AND WHAT DO I FIND OUT??

I'M A VICTIM IN A MAN'S WORLD! AN **UNPAID SLAVE!** MY LIFE IS A WASTE!!

MOM.. MOM... LET'S TALK ABOUT THIS!

NOT NOW, DEAR. I HAVE TO FIX DINNER BEFORE YOUR FATHER GETS HOME.

1982

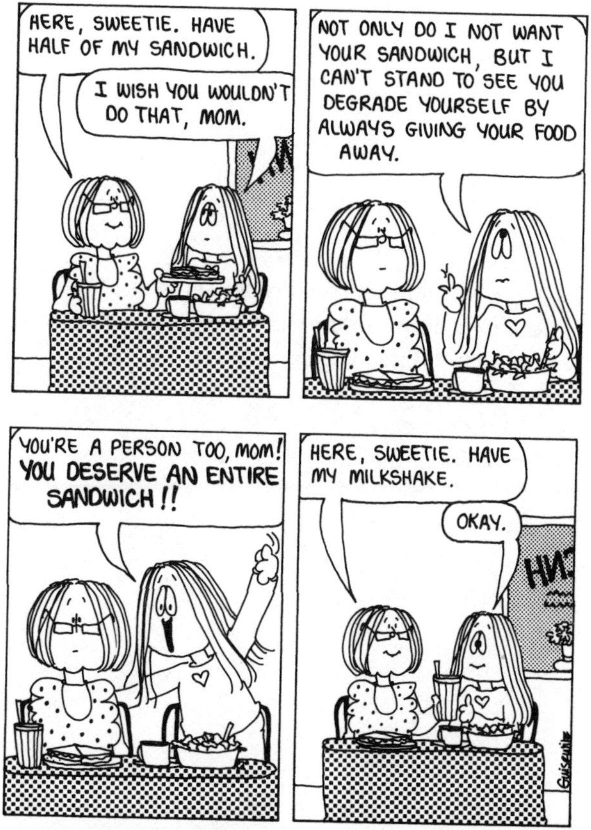
HERE, SWEETIE. HAVE HALF OF MY SANDWICH.
I WISH YOU WOULDN'T DO THAT, MOM.
NOT ONLY DO I NOT WANT YOUR SANDWICH, BUT I CAN'T STAND TO SEE YOU DEGRADE YOURSELF BY ALWAYS GIVING YOUR FOOD AWAY.
YOU'RE A PERSON TOO, MOM! YOU DESERVE AN ENTIRE SANDWICH!!
HERE, SWEETIE. HAVE MY MILKSHAKE.
OKAY.
Guisewite

All the ancient mother-daughter separation stuff got played out in a new world where women's rights were the lead feature on the evening news . . .

Where learning to stand up for yourself was a college course, not disrespect . . .

Where "blaming Mom" was a best-seller.

1979

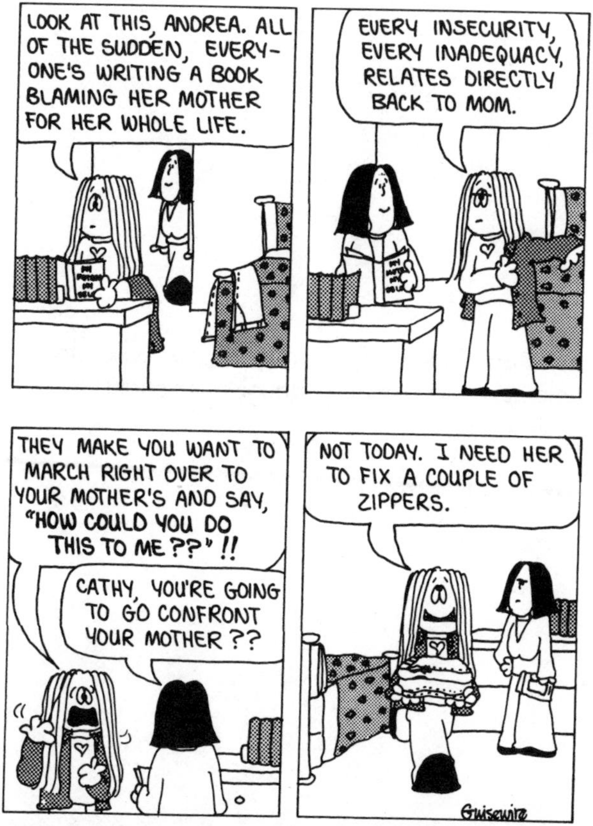
LOOK AT THIS, ANDREA. ALL OF THE SUDDEN, EVERYONE'S WRITING A BOOK BLAMING HER MOTHER FOR HER WHOLE LIFE.
EVERY INSECURITY, EVERY INADEQUACY, RELATES DIRECTLY BACK TO MOM.
THEY MAKE YOU WANT TO MARCH RIGHT OVER TO YOUR MOTHER'S AND SAY, "HOW COULD YOU DO THIS TO ME??" !!
CATHY, YOU'RE GOING TO GO CONFRONT YOUR MOTHER??
NOT TODAY. I NEED HER TO FIX A COUPLE OF ZIPPERS.
Guisewite

Because of the times, Mom and I got to be pioneers in a whole new sort of mother-daughter relationship.

1980

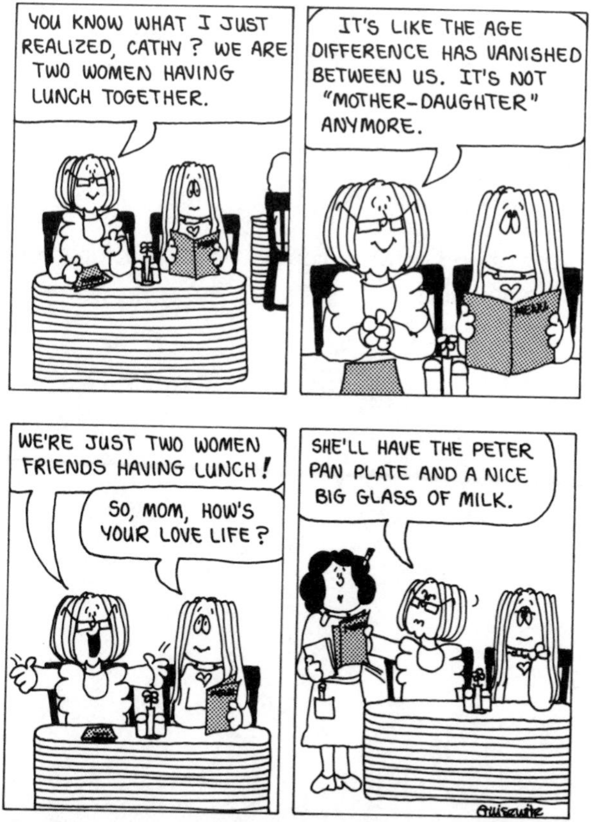
YOU KNOW WHAT I JUST REALIZED, CATHY? WE ARE TWO WOMEN HAVING LUNCH TOGETHER.
IT'S LIKE THE AGE DIFFERENCE HAS VANISHED BETWEEN US. IT'S NOT "MOTHER-DAUGHTER" ANYMORE.
WE'RE JUST TWO WOMEN FRIENDS HAVING LUNCH!
SO, MOM, HOW'S YOUR LOVE LIFE?
SHE'LL HAVE THE PETER PAN PLATE AND A NICE BIG GLASS OF MILK.
MENU
©Guisewite

We had conversations Grandma couldn't have dreamed of.

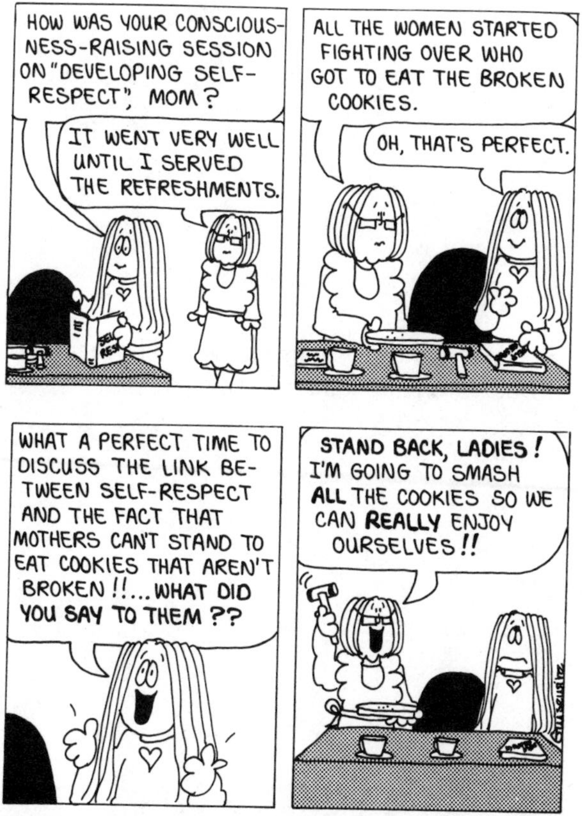
HOW WAS YOUR CONSCIOUSNESS-RAISING SESSION ON "DEVELOPING SELF-RESPECT", MOM?
IT WENT VERY WELL UNTIL I SERVED THE REFRESHMENTS.
ALL THE WOMEN STARTED FIGHTING OVER WHO GOT TO EAT THE BROKEN COOKIES.
OH, THAT'S PERFECT.
WHAT A PERFECT TIME TO DISCUSS THE LINK BETWEEN SELF-RESPECT AND THE FACT THAT MOTHERS CAN'T STAND TO EAT COOKIES THAT AREN'T BROKEN!!... WHAT DID YOU SAY TO THEM??
STAND BACK, LADIES! I'M GOING TO SMASH ALL THE COOKIES SO WE CAN REALLY ENJOY OURSELVES!!

We had discussions that would have made
Great-Grandma faint.

1982

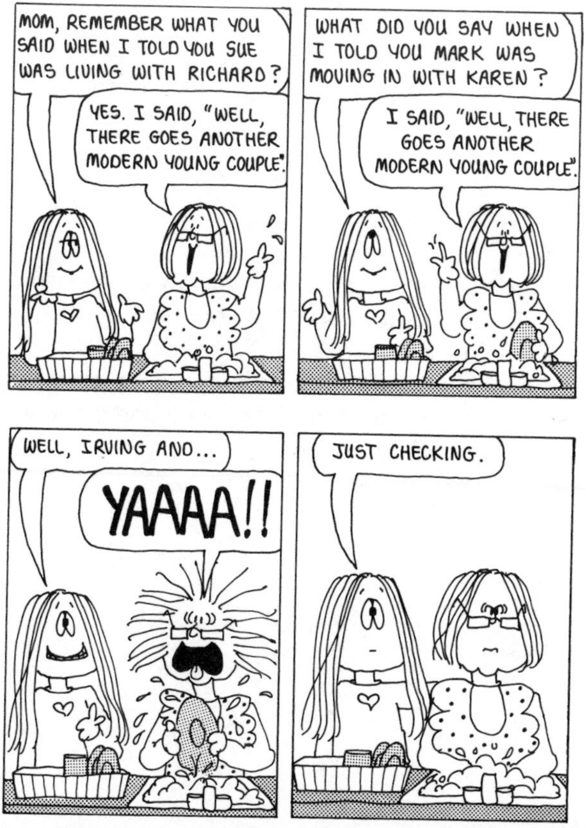

MOM, REMEMBER WHAT YOU SAID WHEN I TOLD YOU SUE WAS LIVING WITH RICHARD?
YES. I SAID, "WELL, THERE GOES ANOTHER MODERN YOUNG COUPLE".
WHAT DID YOU SAY WHEN I TOLD YOU MARK WAS MOVING IN WITH KAREN?
I SAID, "WELL, THERE GOES ANOTHER MODERN YOUNG COUPLE".
WELL, IRVING AND...
YAAAA!!
JUST CHECKING.

I look at my daughter and the new universe she's growing up in and wonder how our mother-daughter relationship will play out.

I have a pretty good idea that, in spite of my highly advanced communication skills, I'll be one more link in the "ignored advice" chain.

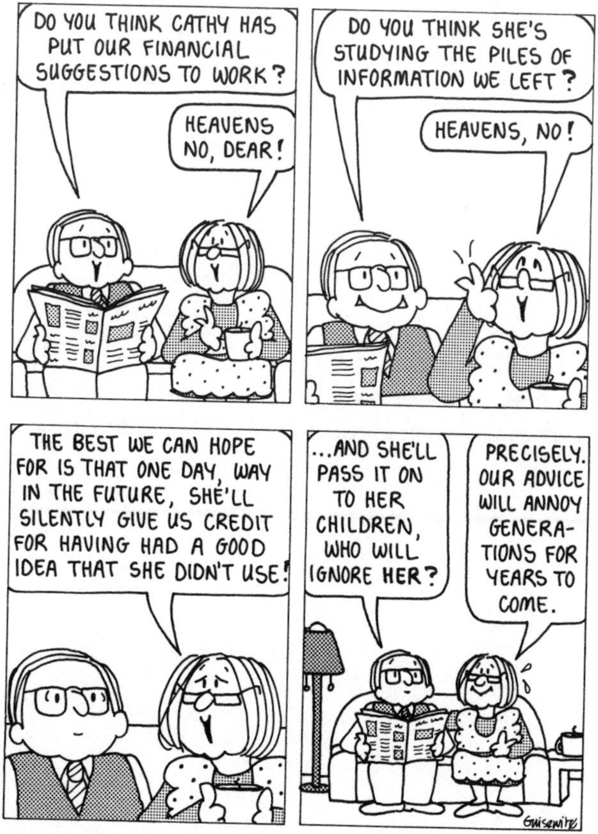
DO YOU THINK CATHY HAS PUT OUR FINANCIAL SUGGESTIONS TO WORK?
HEAVENS NO, DEAR!
DO YOU THINK SHE'S STUDYING THE PILES OF INFORMATION WE LEFT?
HEAVENS, NO!
THE BEST WE CAN HOPE FOR IS THAT ONE DAY, WAY IN THE FUTURE, SHE'LL SILENTLY GIVE US CREDIT FOR HAVING HAD A GOOD IDEA THAT SHE DIDN'T USE!
...AND SHE'LL PASS IT ON TO HER CHILDREN, WHO WILL IGNORE HER?
PRECISELY. OUR ADVICE WILL ANNOY GENERATIONS FOR YEARS TO COME.
Guisewite

I suspect that all my years of campaigning for women's independence will not make one speck of difference when my daughter's packing to leave.

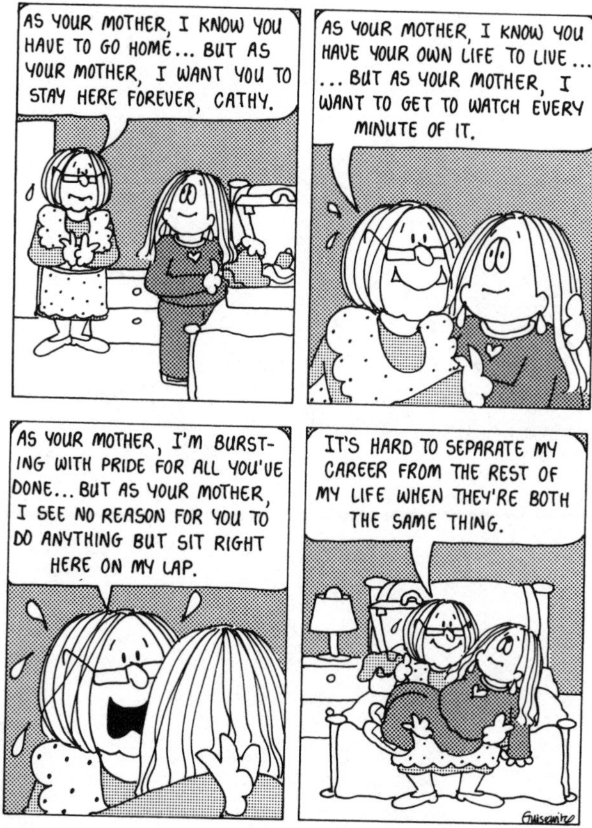
AS YOUR MOTHER, I KNOW YOU HAVE TO GO HOME... BUT AS YOUR MOTHER, I WANT YOU TO STAY HERE FOREVER, CATHY.
AS YOUR MOTHER, I KNOW YOU HAVE YOUR OWN LIFE TO LIVE... ...BUT AS YOUR MOTHER, I WANT TO GET TO WATCH EVERY MINUTE OF IT.
AS YOUR MOTHER, I'M BURSTING WITH PRIDE FOR ALL YOU'VE DONE... BUT AS YOUR MOTHER, I SEE NO REASON FOR YOU TO DO ANYTHING BUT SIT RIGHT HERE ON MY LAP.
IT'S HARD TO SEPARATE MY CAREER FROM THE REST OF MY LIFE WHEN THEY'RE BOTH THE SAME THING.
Guisewite

I'm guessing that, even though I wrote all this, my daughter will read it one day, roll her eyes, and still believe I don't understand her.

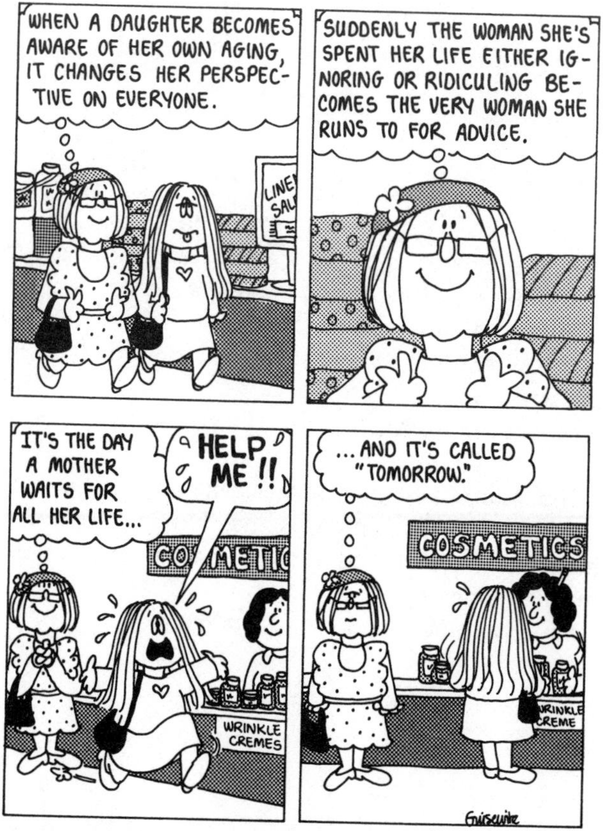
WHEN A DAUGHTER BECOMES AWARE OF HER OWN AGING, IT CHANGES HER PERSPEC-TIVE ON EVERYONE.
SUDDENLY THE WOMAN SHE'S SPENT HER LIFE EITHER IG-NORING OR RIDICULING BE-COMES THE VERY WOMAN SHE RUNS TO FOR ADVICE.
IT'S THE DAY A MOTHER WAITS FOR ALL HER LIFE...
HELP ME !!
WRINKLE CREMES
...AND IT'S CALLED "TOMORROW."
COSMETICS
Guisewite

For now, I just know that after 25 years of rebelling, I buy more sensible shoes than my mother does.

After a lifetime of accusing her of nagging, I call Mom up to make sure she's getting enough exercise.

And when my husband looked at me one day and said, "You're just like your mother," I didn't run from the room screaming.

I said, "Thank you."

The truth is, when I'm overwhelmed by all the roles I have to fill and all the projects I need to finish and all the dreams I only just started, I look in the mirror and notice something amazing:

It's very comforting to see Mom there.

CALL ME WHEN YOU GET HOME... CALL ME IF YOU NEED HELP UNPACKING... CALL ME WHEN YOU GET THE PICTURES BACK...
CALL ME IF THE SPOT DOESN'T COME OUT OF YOUR SKIRT... CALL ME IF YOU HAVE A BAD REACTION TO THAT AVOCADO... CALL ME IF YOU WANT THE ADDRESS FOR THOSE PEOPLE WE MET... CALL ME IF YOU NEED HELP WITH ELECTRA...
WHY DON'T YOU AND DAD JUST MOVE IN WITH ME AND THEN WE COULD SIT AND TALK ALL DAY EVERY DAY, MOM?
OH, HA, HA! SORRY! I GOT A LITTLE CARRIED AWAY, CATHY!
CALL ME IF YOU WEREN'T JOKING.
Guisewite

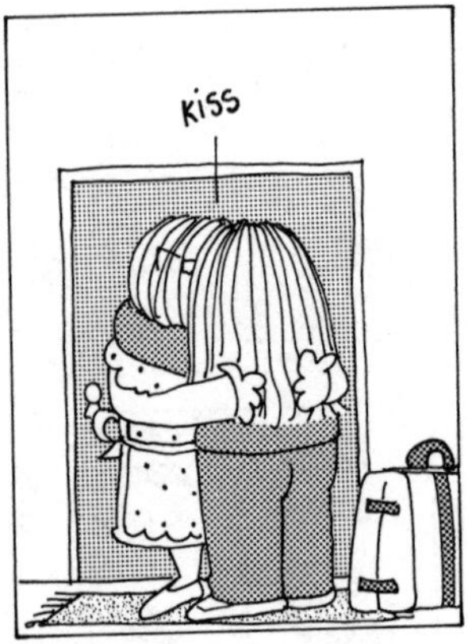
KISS